T0291204

Health Technology Assessment

Using Biostatistics to Break the Barriers of Adopting New Medicines

Health Technology Assessment

Using Biostatistics to Break the Barriers of Adopting New Medicines

Robert B. Hopkins, MA, MBA, PhD

*PATH Research Institute, St. Joseph's Healthcare Hamilton,
Department of Clinical Epidemiology & Biostatistics,
Faculty of Health Sciences, McMaster University*

Ron Goeree, MA

*PATH Research Institute, St. Joseph's Healthcare Hamilton,
Department of Clinical Epidemiology & Biostatistics,
Faculty of Health Sciences, McMaster University*

CRC Press
Taylor & Francis Group
Boca Raton   London   New York

CRC Press is an imprint of the
Taylor & Francis Group, an **informa** business

A PRODUCTIVITY PRESS BOOK

CRC Press
Taylor & Francis Group
6000 Broken Sound Parkway NW, Suite 300
Boca Raton, FL 33487-2742

© 2015 by Taylor & Francis Group, LLC
CRC Press is an imprint of Taylor & Francis Group, an Informa business

No claim to original U.S. Government works

Printed on acid-free paper
Version Date: 20150217

International Standard Book Number-13: 978-1-4822-4452-6 (Hardback)

Visit the Taylor & Francis Web site at
http://www.taylorandfrancis.com

and the CRC Press Web site at
http://www.crcpress.com

Contents

Authors xi

Preface xiii

1 **Regulation, Reimbursement and Health Technology
   Assessment** 1
   Introduction 1
       Regulatory Approval 2
           Regulatory Approval for Prescription Drugs 3
           Regulatory Approval for Devices 10
           Regulatory Approval for Public Health and Other
           Non-Drug, Non-Device Approvals 12
       Reimbursement Approval for Drugs 13
           Initiation of Drug Review for Reimbursement 14
           Further Clinical Evidence for Drug Reimbursement 14
           Consideration of Cost in Drug Reimbursement Decisions 15
           Drug Price Negotiations 15
       Reimbursement Approval for Devices 16
       Health Technology Assessment 17
           Step 1: Identify the Topic for Assessment 20
           Step 2: Clear Specification of the Problem 22
           Step 3: Gathering the Evidence 24
           Step 4: Aggregation and Appraisal of the Evidence 25
           Step 5: Synthesize and Consolidate Evidence 27
           Step 6: Collection of Primary Data (Field Evaluation) 28
           Step 7: Economic Evaluation, Budget and Health Systems
           Impact Analysis 29
           Step 8: Assessment of Social, Ethical and Legal
           Considerations 30

Step 9: Formulation of Findings and Recommendations 30
Step 10: Dissemination of Findings and Recommendations 32
Step 11: Monitoring the Impact of Assessment Reports 32
Summary 33
References 33

2 Requirements and Sources of Data to Complete an HTA 37
Data Requirements to Complete an HTA...37
Cost-Effectiveness..37
Introduction to Health-Related Quality of Life 41
Introduction to Resource Utilization and Costs 44
Need for Modelling..46
    Decision Analytic Model 47
    Markov Model...48
Start with the Trials: Safety and Efficacy..49
Secondary Data Requirements 50
    Rare Diseases 52
    Effectiveness versus Efficacy...53
    Long-Term Outcomes 54
    Health-Related Quality of Life 55
    Resource Utilization and Costs 56
    Epidemiology...59
Summary 60
References 60

3 Meta-Analysis...65
Overview of Meta-Analysis..65
Initial Steps before a Meta-Analysis 67
A Comment on Frequentist and Bayesian Approaches 68
Steps in a Meta-Analysis 69
Step 1: Identify the Type of Data for Each Outcome 70
Step 2: Select an Appropriate Outcome Measure 72
    Outcomes for Continuous Data 74
Step 3: Conduct the Preliminary Analysis with an Assessment
of Heterogeneity..75
    Weighting of Each Study...75
    Random or Fixed Effects...76
    Testing for Heterogeneity...77
Step 4: Adjustment for Heterogeneity...78
Step 5: Assess Publication Bias...80

Step 6: Assess the Overall Strength of Evidence 81
An Example of Meta-Analysis...82
    Outliers 86
    Risk-Adjusted or Unadjusted Analysis 87
    Publication Bias...89
Meta-Analysis of Diagnostic Accuracy Studies......................90
Example of Meta-Analysis for Diagnostic Accuracy 95
    Hierarchical Summary Receiver Operator Curve 99
Summary 101
References 101
Appendix I: Diagnostic Accuracy Measures 103
Appendix II: Estimation of Cohen's Kappa Score................104

4 Network Meta-Analysis 105
Introduction..105
    Head-to-Head and Placebo-Controlled Trials..............105
Step 1: Establish Potential Network Diagram of Linking Studies..........110
Step 2: Check for Consistency in Outcomes for Common
Linking Arms..112
Step 3: Conduct Meta-Analysis and Assess Heterogeneity within
Common Comparators...114
Step 4: Conduct Indirect Meta-Analysis across the Comparators..........116
    Network Meta-Analysis Software....................................116
Step 5: Conduct Subgroup and Sensitivity Analyses............120
Step 6: Report Network Meta-Analysis Results 121
Bayesian Mixed Treatment Comparisons.............................122
Network Meta-Analysis Example..122
    Assessing Robustness: Homogeneity and Consistency
    of Evidence 123
    Adjustment for Difference in Baseline Characteristics....123
Network Meta-Analysis of Diagnostic Accuracy 124
References 125

5 Bayesian Methods 127
Introduction..127
    Study Power for Trials of Rare Diseases.........................128
    Interpretation of Bayesian Results 129
Bayesian Theorem 130
Step 1: Specify the Model..131
Step 2: Assign the Prior(s)...134

Step 3: Conduct the Simulation 135
Step 4: Assess Convergence 137
Step 5: Report the Findings 142
Advanced Bayesian Models 143
    Advanced Example 1: Combining RCTs and Observational Data ... 144
    Advanced Example 2: Covariate Adjustment 144
    Advanced Example 3: Hierarchical Outcomes 145
Summary 146
References 147

6 Survival Analysis 149
Introduction 149
Kaplan–Meier Analysis 150
Exponential, Gompertz and Weibull Models 156
Establishing and Using Risk Equations 162
    Diabetes Modelling 168
Acceptability of Surrogates 169
Survival Adjustment for Crossover Bias 170
Building a Life Table from Cross-Sectional Data 173
Summary 175
References 175

7 Costs and Cost of Illness Studies 179
From Clinical Events to Resource Utilization to Costs 180
    Measurement of Resource Utilization 181
Attribution and Adjustment for Comorbidities 182
    Strategies to Isolate the Cost of an Event 184
    Regression Methods 186
    Other Strategies to Estimate Costs 186
    Unit Costs Valuation for Resources 188
Perspective and Types of Costs 189
Burden of Illness Study 191
Budget Impact Analysis 193
    Statistical Issues with Cost Data 194
Summary 195
References 196

8 Health-Related Quality of Life 199
Why QOL? 200
Good Properties of Scales 202

Guidelines for Using QOL in HTA 204
From Utility to QALY 204
Assessing Change in QOL Scales 205
   Change in Level of HRQOL and Domains over Time 205
   Minimal Clinically Important Difference for HRQOL 207
Obtaining QOL Estimates from Trials and Literature 209
Independent QOL Study..210
Mapping between QOL Scales 211
Summary 212
References 213

9 Missing Data Methods **215**
Common Trial Gaps..216
   Missed Visits and Loss to Follow-Up 217
   Explainable or Unexplainable Patterns of Missing Data...............218
   Intention-to-Treat or Per-Protocol Analysis.................................219
   Multiple Imputation for Trial Data 221
      Beautiful Bootstrap...223
Meta-Analysis Gaps...223
   Missing Measures of Central Tendency 224
   Missing Measures of Variance...224
   Missing Data for Diagnostic Accuracy Studies 227
Unknown Lifetime Variances for Costs 228
Summary 230
References 230

10 Concluding Remarks.. **231**
Concluding Remarks 231
Academic Writing from a Biostatistician's Point of View......................232
   Introduction 233
   Discussion and Conclusion 234
   Sentences and Paragraphs...235
   Time Management for Writing 236
Future Research...236
Improving Reimbursement Submissions 239
Summary 241
References 242

Index **243**

Authors

Robert B. Hopkins, PhD, has been the biostatistician at the Programs for the Assessment of Technology in Health (PATH) Research Institute at McMaster University for the past 10 years and has more than 25 years of experience in health care. His role as the lead biostatistician includes: educational support at the graduate level and for other professionals at workshops and seminars or by consultation; designing, analyzing and reporting of systematic reviews, clinical studies (field evaluations), economic studies such as trial-based and model-based economic evaluations, cost and burden of illness studies, quality of life studies, and health technology assessments; and providing peer review for more than 20 academic journals and government agencies.

Rob was the lead biostatistician for more than 75 funded research projects worth over $15 million, which generated over 100 peer-reviewed publications and abstracts and 40 technical reports for the government, as well over 200 conference, academic or government presentations. Recent methodological issues explored include handling of missing data in meta-analysis, trials and economic evaluations; network meta-analysis; trial-based economic analysis and cost/burden of illness studies.

Rob has presented his research at the following conferences: Society of Medical Decision Making, International Society for Pharmacoeconomics and Outcomes Research, Drug Information Association, Canadian Association for Population Therapeutics, Canadian Agency for Drugs and Technologies in Health (CADTH), Canadian Association for Health Services and Policy Research, Society for Clinical Trials, Health Technology Assessment International, Canadian Statistical Society, American Statistical Society, Canadian Health Economics Association and International Health Economics Association.

Ron Goeree, MA, is currently a professor in the Department of Clinical Epidemiology & Biostatistics, Faculty of Health Sciences, at McMaster University in Hamilton, Ontario, Canada, where he is the founding field leader for graduate studies of health technology assessment (HTA) at McMaster University.

Ron has established workshops on HTA all over the world, from Singapore to Oslo, and has published extensively (over 400 books, chapters, articles and abstracts). He has reviewed over 120 journal submissions and 80 national or provincial drug submissions or reports. Ron has served on nearly 50 industry advisory boards and more than 60 government and decision-maker committees and boards.

Ron's research is conducted at the Programs for Assessment of Health Technology Research Institute at St. Joseph's Healthcare Hamilton, where he has been the director since 2006. 'As director of PATH, he has demonstrated the essential role health technology assessment can and should play in meeting the needs of health of health decision-makers. As an innovator, he helped pioneer the methodological framework for the field evaluation of non-drug technologies. As a dedicated professor and mentor, he has trained literally thousands of students, researchers, and decision-makers, making an immense contribution to the capacity in Canada to produce and use health technology assessment', said O'Rourke, President and CEO of CADTH. O'Rourke further said that 'Professor Goeree is one of the pre-eminent HTA researchers and educators in the world' (CADTH News Release 2012). Ron was the 2012 recipient of the CADTH HTA Excellence Award for lifetime and sustained achievement. He is co-editor of *Value in Health* and sits on the editorial boards of *Medical Decision Making* and the *Journal of Medical Economics*.

Preface

Bringing a new drug to market and into the hands of a patient is a long, long process, and time is not always the patient's best friend. Patients who have a medical need are left to wonder why there isn't a cure and why does it take so long to be made available to everyone. The news that a promising cure has been discovered in the lab but that a treatment for patients is still 5 to 10 years away adds to their frustrations.

Doctors, who know that the current standard of care isn't perfect, continue to read their medical journals and attend medical conferences looking for better ways of treating their patients. Is this a new cure? Is it better than what is already out there? What are the side effects?

Governments, who receive requests to fund everything under the sun, are looking for that health technology that can make patients healthier, and, who knows, maybe even reduce costs. How much does it cost? How many patients will use it? Will the new drug save lives? How does it affect our budget? Is it worth the extra cost? Which treatment should we choose to fund?

Advocacy groups, who fight for the needs of patients, want their patient's collective voices heard and their patients to be served with dignity. Ethics and fairness must be addressed. Why are they withholding this particular drug? Why can't we have the best care for our patients? Are we being marginalized?

Even worse for patients is when a drug finally makes it through the long journey of research and has been proven effective, and makes it to the drug store, the insurance plan or government public plans won't cover it. They may say, 'The drug does not have good value for money' or 'The drug costs too much'. The focus of this book is whether the final value-for-money decision was made correctly or not, and after working through the chapters we provide examples where value for money could have been presented differently. But the value-for-money decision is just one of the questions that are asked by one of the users of a health technology assessment: the patients, the clinical users, the government, the patient advocacy groups and the insurance plan. A health technology assessment seeks to answer all of their questions and more.

Long Life of a Drug

Before any new drug can be tested in humans, regulatory authorities throughout the world require some non-human testing. These tests can be on tissue, lab animals or data gathered in previous studies for the same drug used in a different way. If the drug passes this early stage without safety concerns and shows promise of providing benefit, then testing can begin in humans and proceed through the four phases (U.S. Food and Drug Administration 2014).

In Phase I, the new drug is given to a small group of people for the first time to evaluate its safety, determine a safe dosage range and identify side effects. In Phase II, the drug is given to a larger group of patients to see if it works well, to find the optimum dose that provides maximum benefit and to further evaluate its safety. In Phase III, the drug is given to a large group of patients to confirm how well it works compared to commonly used treatments, further monitoring of side effects and collection of detailed information so that the drug can be prescribed and marketed safely. And finally in Phase IV, further studies are conducted after the drug has been approved for the market to gather information on the drug's effect in various populations and any side effects associated with long-term use. Drugs can be offered to the market based on successful Phase III trials, sometimes Phase II trials, but sometimes requiring ongoing Phase IV trials.

Whether a new drug makes it through the four phases and into the market is really a lottery. Only 1 in 5,000 compounds that enter preclinical testing proceeds to human testing. The process is exceedingly long, taking 10–15 years for a new drug to go from preclinical trials to the pharmacy. However, many drugs drop out during the trial phases. The success rate for new drugs that pass Phase I making it to market is less than 1 in 10, and in recent years has been falling (BioMedTracker 2012). The rate of success is only half of what it was 10 years ago. In addition, the cost to a drug developer is very high; if a drug fails, the cost may be passed on to the cost of the next successful drug. The cost to bring a prescription drug from development to market costs, on average, is about $500 million but has been known to be as high as US$1.7 billion. In addition, the 10–15 years it takes to bring the drug to the market hurts the drug company that holds exclusive patents, which last only 20 years. For every day lost in gaining approval from the U.S. Food and Drug Administration, the manufacturer loses US$1.3 million.

Competition for Health Dollars

As drugs struggle to enter the market, other types of health technologies are also being introduced at a high rate and compete for scarce health care dollars. The many drugs, devices and programs that can improve and extend quality of life are called health technologies. For example, competing with health care dollars are education programs that lead to the reduction in progression of a disease, such as for kidney disease. Having a patient with kidney disease meet with a nurse educator every three months can reduce costs by 20% (Hopkins et al. 2011); meanwhile, the patients showed improvements, and not harm, in lab values such as cholesterol and blood sugar (Barrett et al. 2011). About 7% of the American population have kidney failure, or looking at it another way, about 25% of Americans aged 60 and older will develop renal failure. In the United States, the cost of treating kidney failure in 2009 was $40 billion (Smith et al. 2004), and finding a 20% reduction in costs without risking the health of anyone would be helpful. An even longer list of health technologies that are competing with health care dollars would include biotechnology, diagnostic imaging, molecular diagnostics, organ and tissue replacement, surgical techniques, wound care, computer technology, education programs and public health programs.

With the ageing of society, increase in use of medical technology and advances in drugs the strain on the health care budget has never been greater. Many have said that the health care system is in crisis, but most public health care systems have always been in a crisis to find new levels of financing. Even now, the development of biologics, which are genetically engineered proteins derived from human genes, has flourished and will continue to escalate with the ongoing mapping of the human genome. Do we have a gene that gives us cancer or do we lack the gene that prevents cancer? If so, once we know the gene we could create the biologic to fill in for our own missing DNA. Adding to the demand for health dollars are the increased computer resolution with ultra-high definition imaging; the increased need for more home-based nursing care from more people being discharged from the hospital quicker; increases in the number of people with obesity, diabetes, kidney failure and so on. Decision-makers, on the other hand, are looking for ways to reduce costs while still maintaining or even improving health. This is where a health technology assessment comes in, to provide evidence to help make these choices, and is the focus of this book. We also thought it would be beneficial to level the playing field. By providing a set of statistical procedures, that public health plans or insurance companies now implement to ration care, that drug companies should know, that advocacy groups should be aware of, we can try to ensure that the chance of the success of a beneficial drug reaching market ends up in the hands of patients is not limited by shortcomings of the analysis.

Need for This Book

The best way to present the material comes from our experience of what we know works for submissions for reimbursement. Both of the authors have considerable experience in generating evidence for submissions and reviewing submissions to decision-makers for funding. One of us has received a nationally recognized lifetime achievement award in this area. Often we note that the drug submission seems like a one-sided courtroom battle where one lawyer didn't do their homework. Worse yet, decision-makers almost never allow a second try, with the chances of a submission being successful on the second attempt being less than 20%.

Other than relying on our inside knowledge of the decision-making processes, we rely on the outside view looking in from research that we were involved in and the research of others (Drummond and Sculpher 2005). We note cases where the drug submissions were not successful, even though the drug may have potential health benefits. For example, Canada has among the lowest rates of reimbursement approval, ranking 23rd out of 29 OECD countries. Canada's list rate (50%) and Australia's (54%) are both well below that for the same drugs in the United Kingdom (87%) (Clement et al. 2009). A closer look at the reason for lack of reimbursement approval in Canada indicates a potential for a change in statistical methods to improve the chances of success (Rocchi et al. 2012). We pointed out that the reasons for rejection for reimbursement appear to be similar across countries, with Canada and Australia being extreme.

Why Reimbursement Submissions Fail?

After reviewing the posted web documents for the reasons for rejection of reimbursement in addition to viewing the successful submissions, a number of obvious factors emerge. When a comment appears that there was an inappropriate comparator, the rejection rate was 72%. This suggests that a meta-analysis that lists all of the comparators was not done. It would be nice if all of the studies were randomized controlled trials but often the data are placebo-controlled trials or observational data. Methods of indirect comparisons for pooling studies with uncommon comparators or Bayesian methods for pooling observational data are available but may not have been used.

A similar problem occurs when there is evidence but the evidence was deemed inappropriate. A reason that triggers a 92% rejection is when there is a statement where the outcome was not acceptable. This is similar to the rejection problem when there was mention of a scale or surrogate (intermediate endpoint) as the primary outcome of the trials. Using a scale as the primary endpoint of a trial leads to a rejection rate of 75%. The main problem with using scales or unacceptable outcomes is that the scale or outcome has not been validated as a surrogate for the main outcome for the particular disease. Developing long-term risk equations have increased the validity of using surrogate outcomes and have provided statistical support for the acceptability of surrogate endpoints as being able to predict final endpoints for some disease but not others. Current acceptable surrogate outcomes include Haemoglobin A1c for Type II diabetes, bone mineral density for osteoporosis fractures and viral load for HIV.

Interestingly, all surrogates including those deemed acceptable are not perfect. Bone mineral density measures the amount of mineral in the internal mesh of the bones but fracture risk also depends on the overall structure of bones, which is partially explained by family history of fracture, rates of smoking and alcohol consumption and other medical histories such as rheumatoid arthritis (Leslie et al. 2010). Thus, even acceptable surrogates are not perfect, but when the decision-makers are well aware they are not perfect, the surrogate may be considered acceptable. The problems of surrogates, scales or lack of appropriate comparators can all lead to a mention of overall clinical uncertainty, which leads to a 84% rejection rate.

Other common problems for rejection for reimbursement are economic uncertainty around costs, quality of life and overall incremental cost-effectiveness ratios. In submissions where the economic evidence was not reliable, the rejection rate was 92%. Improved costs and quality of life analysis could reduce the existing rejection rates for analgesia 88%, diabetes 83%, which was mostly Type I or neurology 76%. In our textbook, we describe how to generate robust cost and quality of life estimates from trial data, if they were not collected as part of the trial, and how to use other secondary data.

While Canada might be considered on the extreme end for drug reimbursement rejection, Australia, which acts independently, has similar rates of rejection for the same reasons: lack of clinical significance, poor cost effectiveness, high cost to the government and lack of severity of disease (Harris et al. 2008). In Australia, the main reason again was clinical uncertainty from inadequate study design, inappropriate comparators or non-validated surrogate endpoints.

By establishing clinical benefit with meta-analysis, by creating risk rejections to increase the validity of surrogates and by conducting more robust cost-effectiveness analysis, the potential for cost-effectiveness or even cost savings can be more fairly evaluated. Having a fair process that is not limited by the availability of the important evidence could change the chances of approval. The long list of other agencies that follow the same procedures for reimbursement or listing drugs on public plans includes 57 government agencies in 32 countries listed by the International Network of Agencies for Health Technology Assessment (www.inahta.org) as well as private agencies such as Health Managed Organizations (HMOs) and insurance companies.

Focus of the Book

The purpose on this book is to focus only at a small component of the health technology assessment, the statistics part. This includes evaluating health improvements with its associated economic consequences. We do not focus on the other important issues of equity, ethics, implementation, policy impact or disruption. The textbook outline follows many of the shortcomings of submissions for drug or device reimbursement.

In Chapter 1, we begin by contrasting the differences between regulatory approval, i.e. the right to market the drug, and reimbursement approval, i.e. the decision that the public payer such as health plans will cover some or all of the cost of the drug. We introduce health technology assessment, including the potentially large scope that the health technology assessment (HTA) may have. We review the principles and outline the steps of conducting an

HTA, including why different agencies will have a different focus for their scope in the HTA. After providing the overview, we restrict our focus on HTA to reimbursement and whether a public payer or private insurance plan or HMO should provide funding for a drug. We only briefly introduce regulatory approval because most of the data to conduct an HTA is generated for regulatory approval, and this will fit in our discussion of data sources. The process of regulatory approval follows closely the overall process of an HTA, with less emphasis on costs and economics. However, the focus of this book is on reimbursement approval, although some of the statistical issues overlap. The rest of the textbook describes in detail how to implement and correct the shortcomings of many reimbursement submissions. For every subsequent chapter, we provide a simple introduction to each statistical topic, provide the most common methods that are implemented, provide some leading edge methods and then provide some worked examples to demonstrate how to implement the various statistical techniques.

In Chapter 2, we discuss the data requirements to complete a reimbursement decision. For regulatory approval for devices and drugs, there are a series of different types of studies that need to be completed. For reimbursement approval, there is a broader scope of evidence required and there is an additional need to show economic impact either as a budget impact analysis or as an economic evaluation. In order to conduct an economic evaluation, secondary data sources are required that may not have been captured by a successful clinical trial. These include among others, long-term safety, quality of life, unit cost data, comparisons of the relative safety profiles, efficacy or cost effectiveness to all available comparators and epidemiology to determine how many patients could benefit from the new drug.

In Chapter 3, we focus on the world what Dr. Gord Guyatt referred to as *evidence-based medicine* with the purpose of analyzing all available data for all of the comparators for all of the relevant outcomes (Guyatt, Cairns, and Churchill 1992). We begin by explaining the purpose of a meta-analysis and how to conduct and interpret a meta-analysis for clinical trials and diagnostic accuracy studies. In Chapters 4 and 5, we take this analysis further and enter the recent hot topics of network meta-analysis, the ability to pool across studies that have different drugs and the Bayesian world, to make even greater inference from available data for meta-analysis and to deal with pooling of data that is not similar.

In Chapter 6, we introduce the concepts of survival analysis and demonstrate how to take results from the shorter duration of a clinical trial and extrapolate to lifetime profiles and estimate the long-term benefit of a new drug or therapy. Along this line of logic, we also look at how to generate risk equations that predict the long-term outcome of changes from a short-term clinical trial. We finish with a discussion of surrogates, which are intermediate endpoints between the therapy and the final outcomes of survival or other patient-relevant 'hard' outcomes such as heart attacks and stroke.

In Chapter 7, we focus on estimating the cost of clinical events and the cost of an illness. We focus on different methods to obtain cost estimates and separate disease-related costs from non-disease-related costs. We justify the effort to estimate the cost of illness because this type of study will provide most of the data needed for a reimbursement decision. In Chapter 8, we focus on the quality of life that comes from clinical improvements, how to measure changes in quality of life and how to estimate improvements in quality of life if the changes were not directly measured in a clinical trial. Measuring improvements in quality of life is one of the most often missed components of a landmark clinical trial, and this is problematic since it is overall health-related quality of life which is the current metric that most, but not all, decision-makers currently use to make reimbursement decisions.

After you have collected clinical, cost and quality of life data and are ready to conduct a meta-analysis and conduct your HTA, you will discover that you are missing some important parameters. Chapter 9 demonstrates the different types of missing data and the straightforward techniques to fill in these annoying data parameter gaps. Finally, in Chapter 10, we provide a statistician's and peer reviewer's guide to presenting the results with clarity, so that future reviewers and decision-makers will consider your work to have been conducted with high standards. It would be shocking for some authors to discover that every paper will eventually be reviewed for quality reporting and their paper will receive a low score because they have missed a few important items. We finish with a brief discussion of the frontiers of medical research, the human genome and individualized medicine.

The book is written with both an expert and a novice in mind. We highlight many of the methodological advances that have occurred since HTA research began, to provide researchers and decision-makers a common framework that is the current state of the art. But we also provide the logical bases for the methods and very simple instructions on how to conduct the various techniques. Our risk is that we often make everything look too simple, just like we have done for our past industry workshops and for our previous graduate students. We expect that this material will eventually lead into undergraduate courses for degrees and diplomas. Looking for value for money for shrinking health care dollars will continue for a long while, ensuring the demand to understand this content. We hope you enjoy reading this book and find it useful.

Robert B. Hopkins
McMaster University

Ron Goeree
McMaster University

References

Barrett B.J., Garg A.X., Goeree R., Levin A., Molzahn A., Rigatto C., Singer J., Soltys G., Soroka S., Ayers D., and Parfrey P.S. 2011. A nurse-coordinated model of care versus usual care for stage 3/4 chronic kidney disease in the community: A randomized controlled trial. *Clinical Journal of the American Society of Nephrology* 6 (6): 1241–1247.

BioMedTracker. 2012. Clinical development success rates for investigational drugs. *Pharma Competitive Intelligence Conference 2012*. New Jersey, September 11.

CADTH. 2012. *CADTH Annual Symposium*. News release, Ottawa, Ontario: CADTH. April 17. http://www.cadth.ca/en/media-centre/2012/ron-goeree-receives-2012-award-of-excellence-from-cadth.

Clement F.M., Harris A., Li J., Yong K., Lee K.M., and Manns B.J. 2009. Using effectiveness and cost-effectiveness to make drug coverage decisions: A comparison of Britain, Australia, and Canada. *Journal of the American Medical Association* 302 (13): 1437–1443.

Drummond M., and Sculpher M. 2005. Common methodological flaws in economic evaluations. *Medical Care* 43 (7 Suppl): 5–14.

Guyatt G., Cairns J., and Churchill D. 1992. Evidence-based medicine: A new approach to teaching the practice of medicine. *Journal of the American Medical Association* 268 (17): 2420–2425.

Harris A.H., Hill S.R., Chin G., Li J.J., and Walkom E. 2008. The role of value for money in public insurance coverage decisions for drugs in Australia: A retrospective analysis 1994–2004. *Medical Decision Making* 28 (5): 713–722.

Hopkins R.B., Garg A.X., Levin A., Molzahn A., Rigatto C., Singer J., Soltys G., Soroka S., Parfrey P.S., Barrett B.J., and Goeree R. 2011. Cost-effectiveness analysis of a randomized trial comparing care models for chronic kidney disease. *Clinical Journal of the American Society of Nephrology* 6 (6): 1248–1257.

Leslie W.D., Lix L.M., Johansson H., Oden A., McCloskey E., and Kanis J.A. 2010.
Independent clinical validation of a Canadian FRAX tool: Fracture prediction and model calibration. *Journal of Bone and Mineral Research* 25 (11):
2350–2358.

Rocchi A., Miller E., Hopkins R.B., and Goeree R. 2012. Common drug review
recommendations an evidence base for expectations. *PharmacoEconomics*
30 (3): 229–246.

Smith D.H., Gullion C.M., Nichols G., Keith D.S., and Brown J.B. 2004. Cost of
medical care for chronic kidney disease and comorbidity among enrollees in a
large HMO population. *Journal of the American Society of Nephrology* 15 (5):
1300–1306.

U.S Food and Drug Administration. 2014. 'The FDA's drug review process: Ensuring
drugs are safe and effective'. Available from www.pharmacoconference.com/
files/Clinical_Development_Success_Rates_for_Investigational_Drugs.pdf.
Accessed on December 2, 2014.

Chapter 1

Regulation, Reimbursement and Health Technology Assessment

Introduction

There are two main decision-making processes for drugs and devices before they are made available for patient use, regulatory approval and reimbursement approval. Regulatory approval by Food and Drug Administration (FDA), European Medicines Agency (EMEA) or Health Canada allows a health care professional to prescribe a drug or to use a device for patients. Reimbursement approval by a government or an insurance plan creates a list of eligible services (coverage) and the level of reimbursement for the services that are covered. The decision-making process of the different bodies is well known, with regulatory approval being conditional upon the trade-off of safety and efficacy. Reimbursement, on the other hand, adds in budget impact and, lately for most countries and agencies, a further consideration for value for money. The reimbursement approval relies on the evidence for regulatory approval and may include additional evidence, which is generated after regulatory approval. The demonstration of value for money or budget impact is our primary focus, but we first need to describe the evidence that is generated through the regulatory approval process.

Regulatory Approval

The regulatory approval process includes the initial approval, ongoing assessment and monitoring of the safety and efficacy of drugs. Before any physician can prescribe a medication, before a pharmacy can sell a drug or before a hospital can administer a drug, there is a lengthy process with clinical studies to ensure that the drug is safe to use and provides a health benefit. The regulatory authority also has pre-specified regulatory activities to evaluate and monitor the safety, efficacy and quality of drugs after they are marketed. Drugs that are intended to be sold over the counter without a prescription may be approved based on lower quality evidence than prescription drugs, but there is still ongoing review to ensure that the drug's benefits outweigh its risks. The over-the-counter drugs are approved for self-purchase if the active ingredients are generally recognized as safe and effective. However, when a new active ingredient is being brought to the market, a lengthy process for drug approval through the various phases of trials must occur.

Along with a new active ingredient, a new device must also pass regulatory approval. The criterion for approval for devices has a greater emphasis on safety. If the device is simply a modification of an earlier device, no approval is necessary. When the new device is substantially different from an existing device, safety must be established.

One major difference between drug and device approval is the regulatory requirement to demonstrate efficacy. For drugs, efficacy must be proven in adequately powered randomized clinical trials, while for devices efficacy must be demonstrated for invasive or active devices that are considered as high risk to the patient. The factors leading to a high-risk designation include duration of contact to the patient, clinical effects on the body, effect on diagnostic decision making or incorporation of a medicinal product.

Besides drugs and devices, programs that we can call non-drug non-device technologies also require some approval before they are implemented. These could include, for example, education programs, changes in staff competency to perform a therapy, home aids, addition of electronic databases or computer software. Because the safety risk is small, these types of programs do not require a safety study and can be implemented by local regulatory approval such as a hospital or regional medical authority. The local authority is then assumed to continually monitor the programs for safety risk.

Regulatory Approval for Prescription Drugs

The regulatory approval process for a drug is common across most countries being built on the processes established by the FDA. The FDA was founded in 1930, although the regulatory functions began with the passage of the Pure Food and Drugs Act in 1906 which produced laws that restricted marketing of adulterated and misbranded food and drugs (U.S. Food and Drug Adminstration [USFDA] 2014b). By 1938, the FDA provided laws that required that drugs be safe, and by 1962, it ensured that new drugs must be *efficacious* prior to marketing. In 1963, the process to demonstrate efficacy included the current *phases* of clinical trials.

Similar timelines in other countries such as Canada followed the development of drug laws in the United States. However, with the rise in drug tragedies such as thalidomide in the 1960s, countries began to increase their regulatory vigilance. With the creation of the European Union (EU) and the Single European Act in 1987 to encourage the free flow of goods (EU 1987), there was a strong need to standardize the regulatory process. In April 1990, the International Conference on Harmonisation (ICH) was initiated to consolidate the regulations for the FDA, Health Canada and all countries of the EU represented by the EMEA (ICH 2014). The harmonization is ongoing but most of the standards of conducting and reporting of clinical trials are now common across these countries. Now drugs must pass through preclinical development and then as experimental drugs in clinical trials.

Preclinical Development

Before any drug can be tested in humans, a lengthy and costly research process is conducted to generate evidence from studies involving tissue samples or lab animals, with a lot of failures and few successes. Occasionally, the preclinical development has already been completed from a by-product of earlier clinical research. This can occur when, for example, a common available drug produces a favourable side effect. A classic example would be the common aspirin, acetylsalicylic acid, which was first used as an analgesic to reduce pain. Patients who took the medication had higher rates of bleeding, but at lower doses aspirin was demonstrated to be manageably effective as an antiplatelet to prevent clots. The antiplatelet activity is especially helpful for preventing first or subsequent heart attacks and strokes (Nemerovski et al. 2012) and may have other clinical benefits such as cancer prevention. The full pharmaceutical profile from the preclinical studies including other safety effects was previously reviewed and included, for example, that children with a viral illness who take aspirin have increased risk of Reye's syndrome, a potentially lethal swelling of the liver or brain (Nemerovski et al. 2012). The regulatory bodies err on the side of caution and provide a pre-emptive warning about using aspirin in children.

Clinical Trials: Classification of Drug Studies by Phase or Objective

The information from preclinical development is packaged for the regulators, and clinical testing can begin to establish safety and efficacy. The package will include a drug sample, the manufacturer's global clinical development plan (including the drug's regulatory status in other countries), the rationale for the proposed clinical trials, clinical trial protocols and a summary of the drug's chemistry and manufacturing data (USFDA 2014a). The study protocols for phases I–IV must be submitted to the FDA before any trial begins and include details of recruitment, trial managers, data collection procedures and pre-approved ethics review. The information is submitted and if there are no concerns, studies can begin or alternatively deficiencies must be addressed. The processes through the four phases are similar in the United States and Canada, but EU adds some complexity for final approval.

There are four main types of clinical trials, each with its own purpose. The four phases of clinical trial are as follows: Phase I, designed to gather information on the drug's human safety and clinical pharmacology; Phase II, designed to gather information on the drug's clinical safety, efficacy versus placebo and optimal dosage and Phase III, designed to confirm or expand the safety profile and to establish if efficacy outweigh the safety risks (Table 1.1). In addition, Phase IV trials are conducted after a drug has been approved for sale to monitor safety and efficacy in a broader set of patients (Figure 1.1). The drug manufacturer is required to report all serious drug reactions or adverse events and other side effects, but this is not always published. Clinical trial data are mostly transferable, with trials conducted in one country being accepted in other countries.

Specific outcomes are generated from the different phases. Phase I studies seek to answer questions of tolerability; drug's absorption, distribution, metabolism and excretion; time the drug remains in the body; the safety profile and the risk of side effects of different doses. There are a small number of subjects, often 20–100, that are either from healthy volunteers if the drug does not have potential serious side effects or from a smaller sample of exacerbated patients who have advanced disease with no other options.

Table 1.1   Summary of Trial Phases for Drugs

Trial	Objectives of Trial
Phase I	Safety, tolerability, bioactivity, explore drug–drug interaction in exacerbated patients or healthy volunteers Maximum treatment dose
Phase IIa	Short-term side effects Observation for possible efficacy Dose range exploration
Phase IIb	Efficacy dose finding studies with efficacy as primary endpoint
Phase IIIa	Safety Statistically significant efficacy
Phase IIIb	Studies intended to support publication and claims or to prepare launch, which start before approval but are not intended for regulatory submissions
Phase IV	Post-marketing surveillance studies New patient subgroups

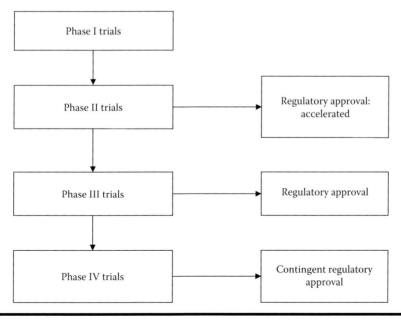

Figure 1.1   Drug regulatory approval by trial phases.

The latter set of patients in theory will ethically risk having unknown side effects in the hopes of having clinical benefit that is not possible elsewhere.

Phase II studies that are defined to establish safety and show some proof of benefit are often split into two categories. Phase IIa studies include a proof of concept, pilot or feasibility study with healthy volunteers, while Phase IIb studies include a well-controlled target population. Sometimes if a pilot study includes randomization of treatment, the study is classified as an early Phase III study (Thabane et al. 2010). Phase III studies provide the stronger evidence for safety and efficacy, because they include a randomized control design with an active comparator, often the current standard of care. Phase IIIa trials are the main phase of clinical trial to support approval for drugs, but Phase IIIb studies are initiated to look for additional indications.

Sometimes studies are published and listed by objectives of the study and do not mention the specific phase number. This makes it difficult to search the published literature and classify the available trials. The clinical studies would include, for example, a *proof of concept* or equivalently a proof of principle. At this stage, you really don't know if the intervention works at all. In these studies, you have patients with a definitive disease that have a potential to improve in health. It is often a small trial, with the duration long enough to observe the effects of the disease. The purpose is to gather exploratory statistics on safety and efficacy outcomes, without statistical power. At the end of the study, you are asking: Did it work? How well did it work? What side effects were observed? Does the risk/benefit ratio seem appropriate for the disease being studied?

A study that is labelled as a *feasibility* study is often a Phase IIa study. If you find that a treatment works and has some benefits and acceptable risk/benefit ratio, you can move to a feasibility study. The objective of a feasibility study is to evaluate the feasibility of administration of a small clinical study and from this you can predict whether a larger study is feasible, that is, the feasibility study will also tell you whether to proceed or not. The endpoint is not safety or efficacy measures, and instead the endpoints are feasibility factors that affect successful trial conduct: the ease of recruitment, availability of capable clinicians, completeness of data or establishment of key outcomes and costs.

A third class of Phase II, or sometimes called an early Phase III study can be a *pilot study*. Once the feasibility study has identified that a trial can be achieved, a pilot study can be established to look at safety and sometimes efficacy. The purpose of the pilot study is to obtain an estimate of a critical piece of information under the same conditions (procedures, eligibility criteria and outcomes) as a large clinical study. Often, a pilot study will give an estimate of the mean and standard deviation of the primary efficacy outcome to allow the estimation of sample size for a well-powered study (Thabane et al. 2010).

The key difference in the types of studies is the primary outcome of each type of study which affects sample size calculation and power. A proof-of-concept study looks for any benefit as a secondary outcome and can be a comparison study between the new intervention versus placebo, standard care or historical controls. For feasibility studies, the sample size is based on a feasibility issue, such as the percentage of patients that provide signed consent of those that are eligible. The sample size for a pilot study might be based on safety or efficacy versus placebo (or standard care). The pilot study is often weakly powered and the real purpose is to gather information to power a larger study.

Statistical Issues with Using Early Phase Studies for Clinical Efficacy

A major difference between Phase II, Phase III and Phase IV trials is the perceived hierarchy of quality, and the degree to which the trial results are generalizability to the intended population (Table 1.2).

Phase II trials are weakly powered, which means that the sample size used to establish power would be small, if powered at all. In addition, studies in Phase II are typically conducted in a group of patients who are selected by relatively narrow criteria, leading to a relatively homogeneous population. From a weakly powered study, there is an increased chance that the patients were not equally randomized between the two treatment groups, and this imbalance could have created a biased estimate of treatment effect. In addition, the low power could also create a spurious (arbitrary) non-reproducible finding. However, if the Phase II results and the Phase III results are consistent, this is less of a concern.

Phase III trials are adequately powered with a defined dosage established after Phase II results. Thus, the results are more believable but the intended population may still not have been fully presented in the trial. There may be a lack of generalizability of the results, which relies on the assumption that the characteristics of the patients in the trial are similar to the characteristics of the patients for which the drug is intended. A clinician can easily tell you if the subjects in a drug trial have the same characteristics that they typically

Table 1.2   Level of the Quality of Evidence by Type of Study

Level	Description
I	Meta-analysis or a systematic review of Level II studies
II	Randomized controlled trial or a Phase III/IV clinical trial
III-1	Pseudo-randomized controlled trial or a meta-analysis/systematic review of Level III-1 studies

III-2	Comparative study with concurrent controls
	    Phase II clinical trial
	    Non-randomized, experimental trial
	    Controlled pre-/post-test study
	    Adjusted indirect comparisons
	    Interrupted time series with a control group
	    Cohort study
	    Case-control study or a meta-analysis/systematic review of Level III-2 studies

III-3	A comparative study without concurrent controls
	    Phase I clinical trial
	    Historical control study
	    Two or more single-arm study
	    Unadjusted indirect comparisons
	    Interrupted time series without a parallel control group
	    A meta-analysis/systematic review of Level III-3 studies

IV	Case series with either post-test or pre-/post-test outcomes or a meta-analysis/systematic review of Level IV studies

Source: National Health and Medical Research Council (NHMRC), *Levels of Evidence and Grades for Recommendations for Developers of Guidelines*, Australian Government, Canberra, Australia, 2009.

see in their practice. In addition, the Phase III trials often include the standard of care as the comparative group. However, there may be more than one standard of care, the standard of care may have changed over time or there may be an absence of a standard of care.

Phase IV studies usually occur after drug approval and often are required to continue regulatory approval (e.g. long term safety) or reimbursement approval (e.g. long-term utilization, response, or event rates). The Phase IV studies usually include a boarder set of patients and different comparators to confirm safety and efficacy in the broader intended population. In addition, Phase IV is larger and well powered, quantifies rare outcomes and establishes long-term safety.

Because of the different purposes, interpretation and issues of the different phases, there is a need to state the hierarchy of evidence by study phase (Table 1.2). The common level of hierarchy lists that the highest Level I evidence comes from a pooling of multiple Phase III or Phase IV studies (National Health and Medical Research Council [NHMRC] 2009). Level II evidence includes a single Phase III/IV study. Level III-1 evidence includes pseudo-randomized trials (e.g. a trial that assigns participants to a treatment group by alternating between groups as they present or by date of admission). These are essentially lower quality randomized controlled trials (RCTs). Level III-2 evidence includes Phase II trials, and Phase I trials are considered as Level III-3 evidence. The ultimate question for us is how to pool the available evidence to allow comparisons between treatments, which we will save for discussion for Chapters 3 through 5.

Other Issues with Regulatory Approval

Following successful completion of clinical trials, the manufacturer files a new drug submission (NDS) or equivalently elsewhere a new drug application (NDA), the purpose of which is to provide sufficient information that will allow the new drug to be marketed. In the EU, there is a split between a centralized and a decentralized process (EMEA 2014). The centralized procedure is designed for drugs derived from biotechnology and innovative medical products. A marketing approval obtained via the centralized authority is valid for all EU Member States. The decentralized procedure is designed for new indications, new manufacturing processes and/or new active substances not previously approved for human use in the EU. In the decentralized procedure, one Member State may act on another Member State's approval of a marketing application with or without formal application by the pharmaceutical manufacturer.

Although there are many similarities in the regulatory approval process, there are important differences in the duration for regulatory approval. For 2012 in the United States, the median time for approval of new active substances was 304 days, while in the EU with a median 489 days the centralized procedure was 10–15 months and the decentralized procedure was 10–22 months (Kumar and McAuslane 2014). In Canada, the 2012 benchmark for screening and review is one year, and this has not yet been achieved.

Table 1.3   Medical Device Classification System in Canada, Europe and the United States

Canada	Europe	The United States	Risk	Examples	License Requirements
I	I	I	Lowest	Elastic bandages, examination gloves and hand-held surgical instruments	Not required
II	IIa	II	Low	Contact lenses, acupuncture needles, powered wheelchairs, infusion pumps	License with annual renewal required
III	IIb	III	Moderate	Haemodialysis machines, corneal implants, coronary stents, PSA tests	
IV	III	III	High	Cardiac pacemakers, breast implants, prosthetic heart valves, HIV test kits	

The NDA contents are similar for the United States and the EU, while Canada's NDS also includes an economic focus, requiring pricing and supply information, and a pharmacoeconomic evaluation. Thus, Canada's drug approval time is significantly longer than that of the United States.

Regulatory Approval for Devices

The regulatory approval for devices is simpler than for new drugs, relying primarily on safety studies. Even when the device is intended to have a therapeutic benefit, regulatory approval may be based on a lower phase clinical study that might be for regulatory approval of a drug (e.g. Phase III/IV clinical trial). The requirement for a clinical study for a device depends on the class of the device (Table 1.3). In Canada, Europe and the United States, there are different classes of devices based on the following four main factors:

1. The degree of invasiveness, the length of invasiveness and the body system exposed to the device.
2. Whether the device relies on a source of energy.

3. Whether the device diagnoses or is therapeutic.
4. Whether or not the device delivers energy to the patient (e.g. the device emits radiation).

The classification of medical devices is unique across Canada, the United States and the EU (Table 1.4). Canada classifies devices as I–IV; United States uses the classes I–III and the EU uses I, IIa, IIb and III system. To standardize the classification systems, the Global Harmonization Task Force (GHTF) was conceived in 1992 in an effort to respond to the growing need for international harmonization in the regulation of medical devices (Gagliardi 2009). In the future, the devices will be classified by risk as A to D, with special regulatory approval existing for class C and D (Table 1.5). From the GHTF in 2006, there was the initiation of the scheme to guide the classification process, published in the document *Principles of Medical Devices Classification*. In 2012, the GHTF issued an update of the classification scheme that included 17

Table 1.4   Definitions of Devices Leading to Differential Regulatory Approval

Invasive device	A device that, in whole or in part, penetrates inside the body, either through a body orifice or through the surface of the body.
Active medical device	Any medical device, operation of which depends on a source of electrical energy or any source of power other than that directly generated by the human body or gravity and which acts by converting this energy. Medical devices intended to transmit energy, substances or other elements between an active medical device and the patient, without any significant change, are not considered to be active medical devices.

Table 1.5   Suggested Harmonization of Classification System for Devices

Class	Risk Level	Device Examples
A	Low	Surgical retractors/tongue depressors
B	Low–moderate	Hypodermic needles/suction equipment
C	Moderate–high	Lung ventilator/bone fixation plate
D	High	Heart valves/implantable defibrillator

Source: Global Harmonization Task Force (GHTF), *Principles of Medical Devices Classification*, 2012 (GHTF/SG1/N77:2012, Study Group 1—Pre-Market Evaluation). Global Harmonization Task Force.

rules and algorithms to establish classes A–D for non-invasive devices, invasive devices and active devices (GHTF 2012). Because these have not been fully implemented, we follow the descriptions of the individual regions.

Both the United States and Canada have similar definitions for different classes. Class I devices are not intended to help support or sustain life or be substantially important in preventing impairment to human health and may not present an unreasonable risk of illness or injury. Class II devices further require that they are designed to perform as indicated without causing injury or harm to patient or user. Class III devices are usually those that support or sustain human life, are of substantial importance in preventing impairment of human health, or present a potential, unreasonable risk of illness or injury.

In the United States, the device classification is listed by general control, special control and further addition of pre-market approval. Class I devices require general control which include evidence of good manufacturing practices, registration and reports of malfunction. Class II devices additionally require special control which include special labelling, mandatory performance standards and post-market surveillance. Class III devices additionally require pre-market approval, a scientific review to ensure the device's safety and effectiveness, in addition to the general and special controls. Devices therefore can be approved with safety and effectiveness evidence but more invasive active devices require clinical studies. Similar levels of evidence are important for devices as well as drugs. When the device produces an intervention and is invasive, the same level of clinical evidence is required for the device as for drugs. When the device is not invasive, a lower level of evidence is required for regulatory approval. This is important because researchers who wish to conduct health technology assessments (HTAs) for a device may not find a Phase III or Phase IV trial for most devices. For approval of most devices, Phase II or even Phase I studies will be considered sufficient for regulatory purposes.

Regulatory Approval for Public Health and Other Non-Drug, Non-Device Approvals

Another problem facing the researcher who wishes to conduct an HTA is the availability of evidence to evaluate a non-drug non-device medical program such as an education program or a public health initiative. For public health initiatives we know that the main causes of loss of health in most modern countries are preventable and modifiable risk factors of smoking, lack of physical activity, obesity and alcohol misuse (World Health Organization [WHO] 2014). However, the design and evaluation of a public health program would not follow the classic four phases. Instead a small trial with a historical control is the most common level of evidence, and based on the established hierarchy, this would only be classified as III-3. The policy makers, on the other hand, may not wish to invest in a lengthy RCTs to make funding decisions. We will discuss this in Chapter 2, but suffice to say here that the evidence created for regulatory approval is different for the device world and is generally not recognizable for the non-drug, non-device world. However, the reimbursement process is quite similar and that is where we move to next.

Reimbursement Approval for Drugs

The reimbursement approval process involves a decision whether the payer such as a government or insurance plan or employer will provide coverage, the decision to put on a reimbursement list, the level of reimbursement, and the percentage of the cost covered by the plan. This has been adopted by many formulary systems throughout the world as one means to control growth in drug expenditure. The public's cost for health care is, on average in the OECD countries, three times more than the cost of private health care. In addition, the expenditures of drugs in the public plans are 1.5 times more than for private expenditures, including expensive countries such as Greece (2.4 times higher), the United States (2.1 times higher), Canada (1.9 times higher), and less expensive countries like the United Kingdom (1.0 times higher) or Luxembourg and Norway (0.6 times higher) (OECD 2011).

In Canada, in 2003, the Common Drug Review (CDR) was created to provide a single national process to review the comparative clinical evidence and cost-effectiveness of new outpatient drugs and to make formulary listing recommendations to Canadian publicly funded federal, provincial and territorial drug benefit plans (excluding Quebec) (Canadian Agency for Drugs and Technologies in Health [CADTH] 2014). The chart shows that coincident with the introduction of the CDR process, the annual growth in drug costs was lower than the annual growth in public health care budget (Figure 1.2). The annualized growth rate is still higher than the average for OECD countries over the period 2000–2009 (Canadian Institute for Health Information [CIHI] 2012).

There are important differences across countries in reimbursement approval leading to different cost and approval consequences. A recent review of 34 countries or agencies including Canada, the United Kingdom, the United States Veteran Affairs and the United States Medicare highlighted these differences (Barnieh et al. 2014). In the next section, we highlight the

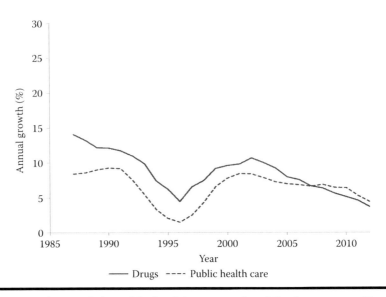

Figure 1.2   Annual growth in pubic health care and public drug expenditures in Canada, 1985–2012. *Note:* Canada's common drug review was started in 2003. (Data from Canadian Institute for Health Information [CIHI], *National Health Expenditure Trends, 1985 to 2012*, CIHI, Ottawa, ON, Canada, 2012.)

major differences between countries and agencies in their processes for reimbursement approval.

Initiation of Drug Review for Reimbursement

The initiation of the reimbursement review is not always automatic except in England, Ireland, Spain and the United States Veterans Affairs. More often than not, it is the drug company who initiates the process for a drug to be evaluated for reimbursement approval in the public plans. Sometimes patients can make the request, which is allowed in Israel, Scotland and Estonia. For the Medicare plan in the United States, because all drugs approved by the FDA are covered, there is no special initiation of the process.

Further Clinical Evidence for Drug Reimbursement

The clinical evidence that is required for reimbursement decision making is often beyond the evidence required for regulatory approval. This would include comparative evidence to the current standard of care or comparisons to all available comparators. This is true with almost all countries with the exception of Japan, Luxembourg and the United States Medicare. Japan reimburses nearly all drugs based on regulatory evidence while Luxembourg does not require clinical evidence for listing on the formulary. For the United States Medicare, most of the drugs are reimbursed following regulatory approval without further consideration of additional clinical evidence, even if the evidence is the benefit relative to placebo. The source of evidence can be from the manufacturer for confidential data or from only published literature. The review for reimbursement approval can be conducted by an independent decision-making agency, from internal government review or from multiple assessment processes. A review can be targeted for one drug only, or as in England or Canada, to serve as a cue to assess the evidence for all of the comparators of the drug.

Consideration of Cost in Drug Reimbursement Decisions

Most countries consider cost within the drug reimbursement decision-making process (Barnieh et al. 2014), with the exceptions being Greece, Japan, Luxembourg and the United States Medicare. About two-thirds of the countries require both the cost of the drug and budget impact analysis and suggest cost-effectiveness information. The level of information for the cost-effectiveness varies widely across countries. Most of the countries post their own jurisdiction-specific guidelines on how to prepare the economic evaluations. For decision-making, the cost-effectiveness analysis is one piece of the evidence and is not a binding determinant except in England, Ireland and the Slovak Republic.

Drug Price Negotiations

A further and more recent trend is the inclusion of price negotiation as part of the reimbursement decision-making process. Where the cost-effectiveness analysis for adopting a new technology was not favourable, the price that makes the drug cost effective is currently negotiated in 12 countries including Australia, Austria, Belgium, Canada, England, Estonia, Israel, Italy, New Zealand, Norway, Poland and United States Veterans Affairs. In United States, Medicare, price negotiation may be undertaken by one of the prescription drug plans that administer Part D Medicare for drugs in classes in which not all drugs are required to be covered. In Canada, a price ceiling is set by an independent process, the Patent Medicine Price Review Board which sets drug prices as the median of at least five comparator countries: France, Italy, Germany, Sweden, Switzerland, the United Kingdom and United States (Figure 1.3). Even further, Canadian public drug coverage is provincially based and some provinces regulate generic

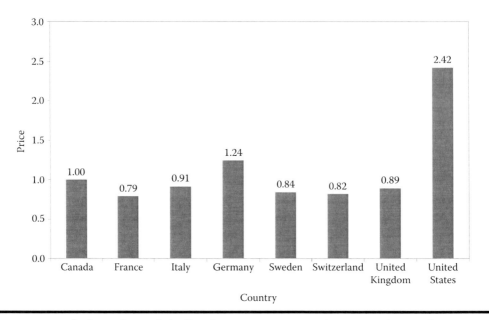

Figure 1.3   Relative prices of similar drugs across countries, at market exchange rates, 2012. Prices are relative to Canadian dollar (value = 1.00). (Data from Patented Medicine Prices Review Board [PMPRB], Canada.)

prices. Most of the provinces have moved to limit the price of generic drugs to be no more than 25% of the price of the brand name drug. Also, in Canada we have the pan-Canadian Pharmaceutical Alliance (pCPA) to enhance collective provincial purchasing power.

In summary, there are large variations across countries for reimbursement decisions. However, there has been an evolution to the addition of cost-effectiveness evidence to be included in the reimbursement decisions. Currently, some countries require additional clinical information, some require value for money analysis and most require budget impact analysis.

Reimbursement Approval for Devices

The reimbursement of devices is different than the reimbursement of drugs. Drugs are reimbursed to provide the manufacturer a fee for every pill used. Once a device has received regulatory approval, the decision to purchase and use the device may be made by the end-user (i.e. hospital, clinic, and physician). However, some devices will require formal reimbursement approval such as from public health plans.

The most common types of reimbursement for devices are adding a billing fee for the each time the device is used or as an agreement to make a capital purchase. For example, reimbursement in Ontario, Canada, for the use of a new green-light laser in a procedure for prostate surgery was provided through a new billing fee code to encourage the use of new device. The fee covered part of the cost of the disposable fibres used for each procedure and a portion of the fee was intended to cover the capital cost portion of the equipment and system. The decision to make a capital purchase can be at the central government level, but often the decision to purchase a device is made by a clinic or within a hospital. The increasing justification for value for money for purchases of capital equipment at hospitals has resulted in the creation of the institution's own HTA research units. One way that drug and device reimbursement decisions are similar is that both drug and devices can be delisted, and reimbursement be withdrawn if the drug or device has been proven to be ineffective or cost ineffective.

Health Technology Assessment

We now move to a discussion of HTA, a multidisciplinary field of policy analysis. HTA 'studies the medical, social, ethical, and economic implications of development, diffusion, and use of health technology' (International Network of Agencies for Health Technology Assessment [INAHTA] 2014). HTA has a broader perspective than regulatory or reimbursement approval, but the methods that have been formalized for approval are common. A full HTA goes beyond the assessment of safety and efficacy, cost-effectiveness and budget impact analysis and includes the implementation strategy, social impact, legal issues, ethical issues and policy impact (Table 1.6).

Formally, the objectives of an HTA are as follows (INAHTA 2014):

■ Identify evidence, or lack of evidence, on the benefits and costs of health interventions
■ Synthesize health research findings about the effectiveness of different health interventions
■ Evaluate the economic implications and analyse cost and cost-effectiveness
■ Appraise social and ethical implications of the diffusion and use of health technologies as well as their organizational implications
■ Identify best practices in health care

Just one of many examples of agencies which evaluates devices and procedures from an HTA perspective is Ontario Health Technology Advisory Committee in the province of Ontario in Canada. OHTAC is a standing

Table 1.6   Summary of Regulation, Reimbursement, Cost-Effectiveness, Budget Impact Analysis and Health Technology Assessment

	Regulation	Reimbursement	Cost-Effectiveness Analysis	Budget Impact Analysis	Health Technology Assessment
Technical properties	√	√			√
Safety	√	√			√
Efficacy	√	√			√
Effectiveness		√	√		√
Affordability		√		√	√
Good value for money		√	√		√
Comparing all alternatives			√		√
Cost per unit health outcome			√		√
Total expenditures		√		√	√
Short time horizon		√	√	√	√
Long time horizon			√		√
Implementation strategy					√
Social impact					√
Legal issues					√
Ethical issues					√
Policy impact					√

advisory subcommittee for the Ontario Ministry of Health and Long Term Care which makes recommendations about the uptake, diffusion, distribution or removal of health interventions in Ontario (Health Quality Ontario [HQO] 2014). Their mandate includes systematic reviews of existing literature, commissioning evidence development from new trials, economic evaluations and economic simulation models, and assessing ethics and impact of their decisions. The process began in 2004 for assessing non-drug technologies such as devices and programs.

One example of the process was the decision to approve for funding the endovascular repair of abdominal aortic aneurysms in 2006. Historically, the first intervention to repair an aneurysm involved an open surgical repair where a section of the aorta was replaced. A newer intervention that proved to be cost effective was endovascular repair where a synthetic graft was inserted like a patch inside the section of the aneurysm. Instead of opening the full chest cavity, the graft could be inserted with a catheter into a blood vessel in the leg. The endovascular repair was estimated from the Ontario commissioned clinical study to reduce mortality, eliminate the need for an intensive care suite and reduce the number of hospital days, and patients still in the work force were allowed to return to work months earlier. Overall, the new technology improved health and saved money (Tarride et al. 2011).

However, at the time of reimbursement approval very few surgeons in the whole country knew how to perform the procedure. Thus, the implementation strategy was required to establish a training program, determine the minimum number of assisted surgeries required before the surgeon would be comfortable on their own and decide where the surgeons would be trained. When assessed for ethics, patients preferred the endovascular repair. However, the long run policy impact includes a small risk of cancer of repeated CT scans to ensure than the synthetic graft did not slip or twist. Another policy impact was the potential for technology creep, where the use of endovascular repair could be used in similar vessels such as cranial or renal vessels even though cheaper alternatives such as stenting may be cost effective.

This is just of hundreds of technologies reviewed by OHTAC, which is considered a world leader in the coverage for evidence development. While the OHTAC process is intended to be comprehensive in their analysis because of the direct policy recommendations to the province's health care system, there are many institutions and situations where a full HTA is not required.

To get an understanding of the full comprehensiveness of an HTA (Table 1.7), we introduce the steps of a full HTA, with a focus on the

Table 1.7   Steps in a Health Technology Assessment

1	Identify the topic for assessment
2	Clear specification of the problem
3	Research evidence for health technology assessment/systematic literature review
4	Aggregation and appraisal of the evidence
5	Synthesize and consolidate evidence
6	Collection of primary data (field evaluation)
7	Economic evaluation, budget and health systems impact analysis
8	Assessment of social, ethical and legal considerations
9	Formulation of findings and recommendations
10	Dissemination of findings and recommendations
11	Monitoring the impact of assessment reports

primary role of biostatistics at each step (Table 1.8), and then provide examples where only a part of the HTA will be sufficient to address the user's questions (Table 1.9).

Step 1: Identify the Topic for Assessment

There is an upfront decision to conduct an HTA on a topic from among many possible choices. In some agencies, the prioritization to conduct an HTA is transparent. For example in Ontario, the published criteria include an unmet clinical need, clinical benefit (safety and effectiveness), value for money and budget impact, feasibility of adoption (economic and organizational feasibility) and consistency with expected societal and ethical values (The Queensland Policy and Advisory Committee on New Technology [QPACT] 2014). The clinical need and clinical benefit could include the nature of the health problem or disease, epidemiology and burden of disease and treatment alternatives for the disease. A pre-existing value for money analysis is often rare, but for a regulatory submission for a new technology, at a minimum, it would include the direct costs of the technology and an assessment of potential cost savings. The feasibility of adoption is defined as a measure with which the health technology can be adopted into the health care system.

Many organizations have moved to establishing transparent multi-decision criteria to select the next technology for assessment, while sometimes the

Table 1.8 Biostatistics Primary and Secondary Roles in Steps of Health Technology Assessment

	Step in Health Technology Assessment	*Biostatistics Primary Role*	*Biostatistics Secondary Role*
1	Identify the topic for assessment		
2	Clear specification of the problem		√
3	Research evidence for health technology assessment/systematic literature review		√
4	Aggregation and appraisal of the evidence	√	
5	Synthesize and consolidate evidence	√	
6	Collection of primary data (field evaluation)	√	
7	Economic evaluation, budget and health systems impact analysis	√	
8	Assessment of social, ethical and legal considerations		
9	Formulation of findings and recommendations		√
10	Dissemination of findings and recommendations		
11	Monitoring the impact of assessment reports		

Note: The biostatistician may have a minor role in steps 1,8,10,11.

Table 1.9 Health Technology Assessment Scope by Potential Users

User	*Scope*
Regulatory agencies	Whether to permit the commercial use
Health care payers, providers and employers	About whether technologies should be included in health benefits plans or disease management programs, addressing coverage (whether or not to pay) and reimbursement (how much to pay)
Clinicians and patients	Appropriate use of health care interventions for a particular patient's clinical needs and circumstances
Hospitals, health care networks, group purchasing organizations	Regarding technology acquisition and management

(Continued)

Table 1.9 (*Continued*)   Health Technology Assessment Scope by Potential Users

User	Scope
Standards-setting organizations	Manufacture, use, quality of care and other aspects of health care technologies
Health care product companies	About product development and marketing decisions
Investors and companies	Venture capital funding, acquisitions and divestitures and other transactions concerning health care product and service companies

prioritization is a non-structured judgement. Even in these latter cases, the review process often includes disease burden, clinical impact, alternatives, budget impact, economic impact and available evidence (Husereau, Boucher, and Noorani 2010).

The specific details of an HTA depend on who conducts the HTA and their target audience. HTAs conducted for a hospital may focus on hospital costs and only discuss other potential factors. Managed care organizations, government and private sector payers may focus on overall cost, safety and efficacy. Other agencies may have a specific focus on safety such as regulatory body or biomedical groups, or on other factors such as usability and provider preferences for clinical groups. Patients and advocacy groups may focus on access, ethics and equity. Other agencies such as health product companies or investor groups may consider product evolution.

A further decision to undertake the full HTA process depends on the stage of diffusion, whether investigational or established. New products will have little evidence and the HTA might serve to control diffusion, while a review of established drugs will create an evidence-based decision among multiple comparators. This in turn leads to the need to clearly specify the problem.

Step 2: Clear Specification of the Problem

The specification defines the scope and the target audience of the HTA. The specification follows the PICO format (*p*atient, *i*ndication, *c*omparator and *o*utcome) or sometimes PICO(S), S for setting, or PICO(T), T for time (Table 1.10). The identification of patients can sometimes seem obvious. The patients could be identified by sex (women or men), disease type (diabetes juvenile type I or adult type II), new or existing cases (incident or prevalent),

Table 1.10 Literature Scope Classification According to Patient, Indication, Comparator and Outcome

P	Patient
I	Indication
C	Comparator
O	Outcomes
(S)	Setting
(T)	Time horizon

or with a pre-specified history (uncontrolled or controlled blood glucose levels). The context helps to specify the population, such as a hospital conducting an HTA would focus on uncontrolled patients with diabetes who often seek emergency or admission care.

The definition of the target *I*ntervention is the simplest specification to identify and refine the scope. It is often one single intervention that is being considered for funding, either being new or ongoing, or being reviewed for discontinuation of funding. The difficult part is to identify the *comparator(s)*.

For some organizations such as at NICE in the United Kingdom, when one drug is considered for assessment, this is the cue to assess all available drugs. A further extreme that occurs is, for example, when there is an apparent gap in the care for patients with a disease such as osteoporosis. Sometimes, the HTA organization will consider all interventions that impact the quality of life of all patients with osteoporosis. This process, sometimes called a mega-analysis, would assess all drugs and include devices, such as hip protectors, and physical education programs. Other examples of mega-analysis have included diabetes which insulin, other drugs, diet and exercise programs; educational programs and other lifestyle modifications. Most often the HTA focuses a new drug versus the evidence from all of its comparators. In this typical case, the HTA's objective is to assess whether the new drug adds benefit to the current list of available drugs.

The definition of the *Outcomes* helps to define the search strategy for the clinical studies and could include therapies designed to improve health, prevent events and diagnosis disease; aetiology to assess risk factors that lead to a disease; or prognosis to predict the success of treating the disease. Each of the different types of outcomes is generated by different types of clinical studies. For therapy to improve health, RCT are the gold standard and highest level of evidence. For aetiology, case control studies are preferred to isolate risk factors, while the outcome of prognosis is best achieved from a long-term cohort study. The highest level of evidence for diagnostic accuracy occurs when each patient is diagnosed with the new technology and simultaneously with a gold standard technology, and not by randomization.

The final two factors, i.e. setting and timing, affect the focus of the search strategy and the analysis. For setting, is it a hospital wishing to choose between new equipment, a region wishing to choose between programs or a government wishing to evaluate all possible alternatives trying to guide evidence-based practice? The timing refers to the time frame for the focus of the data collection and analysis. This timing would include events that occur within a hospital, or within 6 weeks or within 12 months after discharge.

Step 3: Gathering the Evidence

In an HTA, the goal is to synthesize the highest level of evidence that is available from the literature. The next step after identifying the PICO is to develop a search strategy to gather this evidence, and this is often the point that third-party research organizations submit research proposals for established and possibly negotiate PICO. For example, an osteoporosis society or a drug company may request a review to establish the benefit of a new drug versus standard of care to prevent second fractures. The review of the clinical evidence might include patients with osteoporosis who have had one fracture (P) and who receive a bisphosphonate (I) compared to all other drugs (C), to prevent the second fracture (O), in nurse-based residential care (S) using five years as a time frame (T).

Once the PICO is established, the evidence is gathered from a pre-designed literature search of multiple databases. Databases can include National Library of Medicine which is packaged as Medline to gather clinical literature and some economic studies, with Medline being a subset of PubMed. Another commonly used database with partial overlaps to Medline is EMBASE (Excerpta Medica). Medline focuses on biomedicine and health and includes about 5600 journals, while EMBASE has a broad biomedical scope with in-depth coverage of drugs and pharmacology in 8000 journals (Higgins and Green 2011a). In addition to searching for clinical literature, a search of economic studies can be done in economic literature databases, such as Health Economic Evaluations Database (HEED). HEED consolidates studies of cost-effectiveness and other forms of economic evaluation of medicines and other treatments and medical interventions from over 5000 journals. One important additional search is from the Cochrane Library to see if a literature review has already been conducted. In addition, to maintain high standards for literature reviews, the Cochrane Collaboration holds many international workshops.

The clinical search involves keyword search as well as using the medical subject headings (MeSHs). MeSHs are available for disease type as well as for types of studies. The search strategy should be developed and tested by an experienced medical/library information specialist. The search strategy is defined by ideal seed articles to see if the strategy is inclusive. This also helps to define the scope of the project, and the search strategy and number of possible articles required for third-party project budgets. The use of a medical/library information specialist is important because the language is not always straightforward. For example, a search for cancer will lead to many articles where cancer is mentioned but cancer studies have been categorized under the MeSH as neoplasm. In addition, the medical/library information specialist also has knowledge of methodological filters, which are a series of terms that the databases use to categorize studies, to limit the number of articles retrieved by type of study. For example, RCTs can be found under the MeSH 'controlled clinical trial'. In addition to retrieving published literature, the grey (or fugitive) literature should be searched. These include important websites such as producers of HTA reports should be reviewed, such as United Kingdom's NHS, Canada's CADTH and the United States' AHRQ.

Step 4: Aggregation and Appraisal of the Evidence

After defining the PICO, developing and executing the search strategy, a review and selection of articles that are relevant must be made (Table 1.11). For a formal search of the literature, the current standard is the preferred reporting items for systematic reviews and meta-analyses (PRISMA) checklist for reporting how the literature search and selection process was done. PRISMA is an evidence-based minimum set of items for reporting in systematic reviews and meta-analyses (Liberati et al. 2009). For an HTA organization, the study protocol including search strategy for the literature review should be peer reviewed and registered with Cochrane Library. This is important because many journals will not accept systematic review publications unless the study protocol (i.e. the systematic review question) has been previously registered. Items 5–16 in the PRISMA checklist describe the methods that are currently expected for academic publication including HTA reports.

Table 1.11   Preferred Reporting Items for Systematic Reviews and Meta-Analyses Checklist for Conducting a Systematic Review

Methods		
Section/Topic	*#*	*Checklist Item*
Protocol and registration	5	Indicate if a review protocol exists, if and where it can be accessed (e.g. web address) and, if available, provide registration information including registration number.
Eligibility criteria	6	Specify study characteristics (e.g. PICOS, length of follow-up) and report characteristics (e.g. years considered, language, publication status) used as criteria for eligibility, giving rationale.
Information sources	7	Describe all information sources (e.g. databases with dates of coverage, contact with study authors to identify additional studies) in the search and date last searched.
Search	8	Present full electronic search strategy for at least one database, including any limits used, such that it could be repeated.
Study selection	9	State the process for selecting studies (i.e. screening, eligibility, included in systematic review and, if applicable, included in the meta-analysis).
Data collection process	10	Describe method of data extraction from reports (e.g. piloted forms, independently, in duplicate) and any processes for obtaining and confirming data from investigators.
Data items	11	List and define all variables for which data were sought (e.g. PICOS, funding sources) and any assumptions and simplifications made.
Risk of bias in individual studies	12	Describe methods used for assessing risk of bias of individual studies (including specification of whether this was done at the study or outcome level) and how this information is to be used in any data synthesis.
Summary measures	13	State the principal summary measures (e.g. risk ratio, difference in means).
Synthesis of results	14	Describe the methods of handling data and combining results of studies, if done, including measures of consistency (e.g. I^2) for each meta-analysis.

(Continued)

Table 1.11 (*Continued*)   Preferred Reporting Items for Systematic Reviews and Meta-Analyses Checklist for Conducting a Systematic Review

Methods		
Section/Topic	*#*	*Checklist Item*
Risk of bias across studies	15	Specify any assessment of risk of bias that may affect the cumulative evidence (e.g. publication bias, selective reporting within studies).
Additional analyses	16	Describe methods of additional analyses (e.g. sensitivity or subgroup analyses, meta-regression), if done, indicating which were pre-specified.

PICOS, patient, indication, comparator, outcome and setting.

The current standard for aggregating the evidence is that there are two independent reviewers of the titles and abstract, who review based on pre-defined inclusion criteria. This is referred to as Level 1 screening and usually occurs within the software database that contains the title and abstracts such as Reference Manager. After two independent reviews, the differences of inclusion of the articles are resolved by consensus, and the Cohen's kappa statistic is usually reported. After finalizing the Level 1 list of included studies, Level 2 begins by reviewing the full text of articles, also based on predefined criteria. Similarly, consensus and kappa can be estimated for the two reviewers for Level 2 screening. From these final articles, data abstraction onto printed data abstraction sheets, excel or access worksheets can begin, and data abstraction should also be double checked. After all of the evidence is gathered, we can begin the meta-analysis. Typically, 10% of articles pass Level 1 and 10%–20% pass Level 2, but this can be highly variable for novel topics.

Step 5: Synthesize and Consolidate Evidence

After the studies have been identified and abstracted, there are two essential steps. One step is to appraise the evidence based on quality checklists or other criteria for each study. Available checklists have been used such as assessing appropriate randomization or risk of bias, but more recently there has been an emphasis to assess the overall body of evidence. This is discussed in step 9, the formulation of the findings. The second step is to conduct a formal meta-analysis given that there is sufficient similar evidence that allows for pooling to estimate a common effect. The objective of a meta-analysis is to estimate a summary effect, which is a weighted mean of individual effects, as well as an estimate the uncertainty of the summary effect. Since meta-analysis is the focus of Chapters 3 and 4, we will only briefly discuss meta-analysis.

The Cochrane Handbook for Systematic Reviews of Interventions (Higgins and Green 2011b) is the current standard for conducting reviews in health care and pharmaceutical industries.

The Cochrane Handbook provides a general framework for synthesis by considering four questions:

1. What is the direction of effect?
2. What is the size of effect?
3. Is the effect consistent across studies?
4. What is the strength of evidence for the effect?

Step 6: Collection of Primary Data (Field Evaluation)

Three possible scenarios may occur for the strength and consistency of clinical evidence after the systematic review and meta-analysis. The first scenario is that the clinical evidence is overwhelmingly positive, and the new health technology improves health above current standards by reducing safety risk, improving efficacy or both. In this case, the review of budget impact and cost-effectiveness will proceed.

A second scenario is that the clinical evidence is overwhelmingly negative that the new health technology does not improve or even worsens health when compared to current standards after increasing safety risk and decreasing efficacy. The correct decision is to stop the review and make a recommendation for not listing or delist the service, regardless of economics.

The third scenario is that in many situations, the evidence is not overwhelmingly positive or negative and further evidence is required. Common evidence gaps include data on effectiveness, feasibility and costs from a relevant real-world setting.

One possibility to address these gaps is to conduct a local clinical study. The balance between time and expense must be outweighed by expected benefits. In Ontario, there may be a temporary provision of funding that is conditional on collecting clinical and economic data to make a future decision. These field evaluations often take one year to design and begin, one year to recruit and treat patients, with subsequent analysis and decision-making. For health technologies where trials are not expected to occur, or where local real-world setting evidence is preferred, the field evaluations have been verified as useful investments. A second possibility to address gaps in the data is to make assumptions and use modelling techniques, which is covered in Chapter 2.

Step 7: Economic Evaluation, Budget and Health Systems Impact Analysis

Economic evaluation is a general term used when a value for money analysis was conducted and includes most often cost-effectiveness and cost–utility analysis (Table 1.12). The purpose of an economic evaluation is to compare the incremental costs versus incremental benefits of the health technology under review versus other health technologies. The incremental costs include the cost of the treatment plus the cost to treat the events or disease progression for the patients during the study period. The incremental benefit can be a clinical measure such as heart attacks avoided or relative reductions in blood pressure, which, for example, creates a cost per heart attack avoided. The incremental benefit is often health-related quality of life, which is a scale that is affected by disease severity and safety or efficacy events. Rarely, there is an attempt to monetize all the effects on quality of life to derive a dollar value for the benefit, but this is not currently recommended.

Economic evaluations are derived from two sources: a landmark trial or more commonly modelling-based analysis based on literature review. In either case, there is a need to build the economic evaluation by collecting

Table 1.12   Type of Economic Evaluation Studies by Clinical Outcome

Type	Outcomes
Cost minimization analysis	No outcome, only differences in cost matter
Cost-effectiveness analysis	Biologic measure Blood pressure, heart attacks and deaths

Cost–utility analysis	Quality-of-life measure
	    Life year
	    Quality-adjusted life year
	    Health years equivalent

Cost–benefit analysis	Cost: all clinical benefits are monetized by willingness to pay value

Note: All types of economic evaluation studies will estimate differences in cost, but differ by the choice of clinical impact outcome (none, biological, quality of life or cost).

data outside the trial or to supplement the evidence from the literature review. This is discussed in detail in Chapter 2.

Along with or instead of the economic evaluation, a budget impact analysis is typically required, which provides an estimate of the potential financial impact of introducing a new health care intervention into a health care system. Comprehensive budget impact analyses incorporate not only the cost of the new intervention and the reduction in use of the interventions' direct comparators, but also changes to any other health care resources that could be affected by the new interventions' introduction. Budget impact analysis is discussed in Chapter 7.

Step 8: Assessment of Social, Ethical and Legal Considerations

This step is unique to an HTA and questions whether the technology is consistent with social and ethical values. The values include the impact on access and equity, basic human rights, any potential psychological harm and third-party benefits. Access refers to being able to obtain health care that depends on financial, organizational and social or cultural barriers. Access can be limited by affordability, physical accessibility and acceptability of services. Equity refers to the fairness of utilization based on need and not on past allocations. Social considerations would include society's preference for health care. For example, palliative care is rarely cost effective, does not save money or extend life, but would be considered essential for a society that values dignity. Legal considerations reflect the balance between legislation and health care need and would include the use of medical marijuana for pain or the establishment of safe injection sites for drug users.

Ethical considerations were apparent after a review of the diagnosis of epilepsy in children. The current standard of care included inserting 100 invasive electrodes into the child's brain after drilling through the skull versus the new technology of non-invasive external surface recording of magnetic fields with magnetoencephalography. The prioritization to review the non-invasive procedure would be high and may later affect decision-making regardless of cost-effectiveness.

Step 9: Formulation of Findings and Recommendations

HTA should link explicitly the quality of the evidence to the strength of their findings and recommendations as well as draw attention to any limitations. The strength of clinical evidence can be, for example, assessed with

Table 1.13 Grades of Recommendation, Assessment, Development and Evaluation Strength of Evidence

Strength	Description
High	High confidence that the evidence reflects the true effect. Further research is very unlikely to change our confidence in the estimate of effect.
Moderate	Moderate confidence that the evidence reflects the true effect. Further research may change our confidence in the estimate of effect and may change the estimate.
Low	Low confidence that the evidence reflects the true effect. Further research is likely to change the confidence in the estimate of effect and is likely to change the estimate.
Insufficient	Evidence either is unavailable or does not permit a conclusion.

the *Grades of Recommendation, Assessment, Development and Evaluation* (GRADE) approach (Brozek et al. 2009) (Table 1.13). The GRADE approach defines the quality of a body of evidence as the extent to which one can be confident that an estimate of effect or association is close to the quantity of specific interest. The quality of a body of evidence involves consideration of within-study risk of bias (methodological quality), directness of evidence, heterogeneity, precision of effect estimates and risk of publication bias.

The GRADE approach for each study assigns the highest quality rating to RCT evidence. Review authors can, however, downgrade randomized trial evidence to moderate-, low- or even very low-quality evidence, depending on the presence of the following five factors:

1. Limitations in the design and implementation of available studies suggesting high likelihood of bias
2. Indirectness of evidence (indirect population, intervention, control, outcomes)
3. Unexplained heterogeneity or inconsistency of results (including problems with subgroup analyses)
4. Imprecision of results (wide confidence intervals)
5. High probability of publication bias

Usually, quality rating will fall by one level for each factor, up to a maximum of three levels for all factors. If there are very severe problems for any one factor (e.g. when assessing limitations in design and implementation, all studies were unconcealed, unblinded and lost over 50% of their patients to follow-up), randomized trial evidence may fall by two levels due to that factor alone. Alternatively, the GRADE approach can categorize the overall quality of all evidence as high, moderate, low or very low.

Step 10: Dissemination of Findings and Recommendations

Findings must be translated into relevant and understandable information, including lay summary and recommendations. The information is often disseminated through published literature, conferences, collegial communication and various other public forums (e.g. Internet). The attempt is to increase the transparency of evidence which leads to the decision and the decision-making process. Ideally, any clinical and economic evidence should be peer reviewed for quality and relevance or posted to provide a window of opportunity to solicit feedback.

Knowledge transfer, which is the process of moving information and knowledge from one point to another, is important for HTA reports. The goals of knowledge transfer are to reduce the gap between knowledge and practice and to avoid the need to duplicate the research findings.

The framework for knowledge transfer consists of five questions as follows:

1. What should be transferred to decision-makers (the message)?
2. To whom should research knowledge be transferred (the target audience)?
3. By whom should research knowledge be transferred (the messenger)?
4. How should research knowledge be transferred (the knowledge-transfer processes and supporting communications infrastructure)?
5. With what effect should research knowledge be transferred (evaluation)?

Step 11: Monitoring the Impact of Assessment Reports

A rarely completed step is to maximize the intended effects and prevent harmful consequences of misinterpretation or misapplication. Some recommendations are translated into policies with clear and quantifiable impacts (adoption of new technology, change in third-party payment). Others go unheeded and are not readily adopted into general practice.

Summary

Overall, the ability to conduct an HTA as a complex multidisciplinary process requires the expertise of several areas of research: clinical opinion, patient preferences, information specialists, biostatistical analysis, economical evaluation expertise, ethics and policy impact analysis, among many others. By providing a comprehensive review with a systematic and transparent process, the recommendations that are created from the review may have lower risk of a bias. Many times we have seen a limited review of the evidence that does not fully probe all of the facets of a health technology, which guided recommendations in one direction. We also acknowledge that the extent of the evidence is a limiting factor of the scope of an HTA, with Rapid Reviews, Horizon Scanning or Top Ten lists becoming more common to highlight the early evidence for recent advances in technologies which are still early in the technology diffusion cycle. These types of reviews often provide some information on the potential benefit and do not provide evidence-based guidance on optimal treatment selection.

Our primary focus in this book is on the technologies that have been established, with clinical studies completed, and there is an ability to use this information along with other secondary data sources to make recommendations. In Chapter 2, we focus on the types of available data, including primary and secondary data sources for clinical, economic, quality and epidemiological parameters.

References

Barnieh L., Manns B., Harris A., Blom M., Donaldson C., Klarenbach S., Husereau D., Lorenzetti D., and Clement F. 2014. A synthesis of drug reimbursement decision-making processes in organisation for economic co-operation and development countries. *Value in Health: The Journal of the International Society for Pharmacoeconomics and Outcomes Research* 17 (1): 98–108.

Brozek J.L., Akl E.A., Alonso-Coello P., Lang D., Jaeschke R., Williams J.W., Phillips B., Lelgemann M., Lethaby A., Bousquet J., Guyatt G.H., and Schunemann H.J. 2009. Grading quality of evidence and strength of recommendations in clinical practice guidelines. Part 1 of 3. An overview of the GRADE approach and grading quality of evidence about interventions. *Allergy* 64 (5): 669–677.

Canadian Agency for Drugs and Technologies in Health (CADTH). 2014. *Common Drug Review*. Ottawa, ON, Canada: CADTH.

Canadian Institute for Health Information (CIHI). 2012. *National Health Expenditure Trends, 1985 to 2012*. Ottawa, ON, Canada: CIHI.

European Medicines Agency (EMEA). 2014. 'European medicines agency.' Available from http://www.ema.europa.eu/ema/. Accessed on December 2, 2014.

European Union (EU). 1987. *Single European Act Amending Treaty Establishing the European Economic Community.* Vol. I. Luxembourg: Office for Official Publications of the European Communities. http:europa.eu/eu-law/decision-making/treaties/pdf/treaties_establishing_the_european_communities_single_european_act/treaties_establishing_the_european_communities_single_european_act_en.pdf. Accessed on December 2, 2014.

Gagliardi J. 2009. The global harmonization task force: What you need to know. *Biomedical Instrumentation and Technology* 43 (5): 403–405.

Global Harmonization Task Force (GHTF). 2012. *Principles of Medical Devices Classification.* GHTF/SG1/N77:2012, Study Group 1—Pre-Market Evaluation. Global Harmonization Task Force. http://www.imdrf.org/docs/ghtf/final/sg1/technical-docs/ghtf-sg1-n77-2012-principles-medical-devices-classification-121102.docx. Accessed on December 2, 2014.

Health Quality Ontario (HQO). 2014. 'Ontario health technology advisory committee.' Available from http://www.hqontario.ca/evidence/evidence-process/about-the-ontario-health-technology-advisory-committee. Accessed on December 2, 2014.

Higgins J.P.T., and Green S. (eds.) 2011a. *Cochrane Handbook for Systematic Reviews of Interventions Version 5.1.0.* [updated March 2011]. Chapter 6.2.1 Bibliographic databases, Section 6.2.1.3 MEDLINE and EMBASE. The Cochrane Collaboration. Available from www.cochrane-handbook.org. Accessed on December 2, 2014.

Higgins J.P.T., and Green S. (eds.) 2011b. *Cochrane Handbook for Systematic Reviews of Interventions Version 5.1.0.* [updated March 2011]. The Cochrane Collaboration. Available from www.cochrane-handbook.org. Accessed on December 2, 2014.

Husereau D., Boucher M., and Noorani H. 2010. Priority setting for health technology assessment at CADTH. *International Journal of Technology Assessment in Health Care* 26 (03): 341–347.

International Conference on Harmonisation of Technical Requirements for Registration of Pharmaceuticals for Human Use (ICH). 1998. ICH Harmonised Tripartite Guideline. 'Statistical principles for clinical trials E9.' Available from http://www.ich.org/fileadmin/Public_Web_Site/ICH_Products/Guidelines/Efficacy/E9/Step4/E9_Guideline.pdf. Accessed on December 2, 2014.

International Network of Agencies for Health Technology Assessment (INAHTA). 2014. HTA Tools & Resources. Available from http://www.inahta.org/hta-tools-resources/. Accessed on December 2, 2014.

Kumar H. and McAuslane N. 2014. *New Drug Approvals in ICH Countries 2003 to 2012.* Focus on 2012. R&D Briefing 52. United Kingdom: Centre for Innovation in Regulatory Science (CIRS). Accessed from http://cirsci.org/sites/default/files/CIRS_R&D_Briefing_52_May_2013.pdf. Accessed on December 2, 2014.

Liberati A., Altman D.G., Tetzlaff J., Mulrow C., Gøtzsche P.C., Ioannidis J.P.A., Clarke M., Devereaux P.J., Kleijnen J., and Moher D. 2009. The PRISMA statement for reporting systematic reviews and meta-analyses of studies that evaluate health care interventions: Explanation and elaboration. *Annals of Internal Medicine* 151 (4): W-65.

National Health and Medical Research Council (NHMRC). 2009. *Levels of Evidence and Grades for Recommendations for Developers of Guidelines.* Canberra, Australia: Australian Government.

Nemerovski C.W., Salinitri F.D., Morbitzer K.A., and Moser L.R. 2012. Aspirin for primary prevention of cardiovascular disease events. *Pharmacotherapy: The Journal of Human Pharmacology and Drug Therapy* 32 (11): 1020–1035.

Organisation for Economic Co-Operation and Development (OECD). 2011. *Health at a Glance : OECD Indicators.* Paris, France: OECD Publishing. Accessed from http://dx.doi.org/10.1787/health_glance-2011-en. Accessed on December 2, 2014.

The Queensland Policy and Advisory Committee on New Technology (QPACT). 2014. *Decision-Making Framework for Health Technology Investment in Queensland Health: A Guidance Document.* Queensland, Australia: The State of Queensland (Queensland Health). Accessed from http://www.health.qld. gov.au/newtech/docs/qpactdecguid.pdf. Accessed on December 2, 2014.

Tarride J.E., Blackhouse G., De R.G., Bowen J.M., Nakhai-Pour H.R., O'Reilly D., Xie F., Novick T., Hopkins R., and Goeree R. 2011. Should endovascular repair be reimbursed for low risk abdominal aortic aneurysm patients? Evidence from ontario, Canada. *International Journal of Vascular Medicine* 2011: 308685.

Thabane L., Ma J., Chu R., Cheng J., Ismaila A., Rios L., Robson R., Thabane M., Giangregorio L., and Goldsmith C. 2010. A tutorial on pilot studies: The what, why and how. *BMC Medical Research Methodology* 10 (1): 1.

U.S. Food and Drug Administration (USFDA). 2014a. 'The FDA's drug review process: Ensuring drugs are safe and effective.' Available from http://www. fda.gov/Drugs/ResourcesForYou/Consumers/ucm143534.htm. Accessed on December 2, 2014.

U.S Food and Drug Adminstration (USFDA). 2014b. 'History of the FDA.' Available from http://www.fda.gov/aboutfda/whatwedo/history/default.htm. Accessed on December 2, 2014.

World Health Organization (WHO). 2011. *Global Status Report on Noncommunicable Diseases 2011.* Geneva, Switzerland. Accessed from http://www.who.int/gho/ncd/en/. Accessed on December 2, 2014.

Chapter 2

Requirements and Sources of Data to Complete an HTA

Data Requirements to Complete an HTA

Health technology assessment (HTA) is an assessment of the clinical outcomes of safety, efficacy, effectiveness and economic outcomes of cost-effectiveness and budget impact. Strictly speaking, we require the probabilities and timing of every safety or efficacy event (outcome) and the value of those events. The value of an event is twofold, one is the impact on the individual and the second is the impact on the health care payer. For the individual, the most widely accepted standard for effect is the impact on health-related quality of life (HRQOL) that includes survival, while for the payer the relevant impact is cost (Caro et al. 2012; Drummond et al. 2003). Other important measures of effect for the patient or payer are wait times, patient treatment volume, efficiency or equity which can be thought of as inputs into either the quality of life or the cost. For example, a change in wait times impacts patient's quality of life, while treatment volume or efficiency has an impact on average cost. Before we can describe the sources of data, we need to introduce why we need all of this data.

Cost-Effectiveness

The metric used for value for money decision is the incremental cost-effectiveness ratio (ICER), which is used in cost-effectiveness and cost–utility analyses. The ICER is the ratio of the incremental costs divided by the incremental benefits of a therapeutic intervention or treatment versus a comparator (Willan and Briggs 2006). The equation is ICER = $(C1 - C2)/(E1 - E2)$, where C is the cost and E is the effect such as the number of events in a cost-effectiveness analysis or can be the overall quality of life in a cost-utility analysis. We will use the term *cost-effectiveness* to refer to both cost-effectiveness analysis and cost–utility analysis, similar to convention. When the effect is quality of life, the summation of the values of the HRQOL scale over a time period is referred to quality-adjusted life years (QALYs) (Luyten et al. 2011). Built into the assumption of a QALY is that quality of life or *utility*, valued at 0 to represent death and 1 to represent perfect health, is that 1 year of perfect health is equivalent to 2 years of life with a quality of life of only 0.5 (if we ignore discounting future events). The ICER analysis is preferably reported in this standard format (Table 2.1). Consider two drugs A and B with costs and QALYs for a one-year trial. In this case, the incremental costs for patients that received Drug A is $100 more than the costs associated with patients that received Drug B, and patients taking Drug A had 0.20 higher QALYs than patients taking Drug B. This creates the ICER of $500/QALY, which when stated formally is, Drug A may be more cost effective than Drug B if society is willing to pay more than $500 per gain in 1 QALY.

The ICER allows comparisons between drugs, devices and programs across similar disease states and treatments, however comparing across diseases is not recommended and is not the focus of incremental analysis. By using this ratio, comparisons can be made between treatment modalities

Table 2.1 Calculation of an Incremental Cost-Effectiveness Ratio

	Costs ($)	Quality-Adjusted Life Years	Incremental Cost-Effectiveness Ratio
Drug A	1500	0.95	
Drug B	1400	0.75	
Incremental	100	0.20	$500/QALY

Note: C1 = all costs that occurred for patients that received Drug A.

C2 = all costs that occurred for patients that received Drug B.

E1 = sum of QALYs for Drug A.

E2 = sum of QALYs for Drug B.

ICER = $(C1 - C2)/(E1 - E2)$ = ($1500 - $1000)/(0.95 - 0.75) = $100/0.20 = $500/QALY.

ICER, incremental cost-effectiveness ratio; QALY, quality-adjusted life year.

within a disease to determine which treatment provides a more cost-effective therapy, and where to allocate limited resources (Drummond et al. 2008). Built into this incremental framework is the economic theory that continual incremental optimization of resources will lead to an overall Pareto optimal solution, that is, where no more incremental allocations provide benefit to allocative efficiency, and the health care dollars have been optimized to maximize the value of health.

One important step before estimating the ICER is to evaluate each of the incremental costs and incremental effects separately. If there is costs savings with Drug A and there are higher QALYs with Drug A, Drug A is considered *dominant* to Drug B and the ICER is not reported (Table 2.2). Statistically, this creates a negative ICER (−$100/0.20 = −$500/QALY), which if reported would add to the confusion since the negative ICER can occur either when costs are reduced and health is improved or, conversely, when costs are increased and health has been reduced. Since a negative ICER can be either option, either Drug A dominates Drug B or Drug B dominates Drug A, a negative ICER is usually not reported and a statement of dominance is made.

One often asked additional statistic for ICERs is the 95% confidence intervals around the ICER. This is not a common measure that is reported because of a few irregular properties. First, to generate a confidence interval for a ratio, the analyst must apply Fieller's theorem or use a simulation technique such as bootstrapping. Fieller's theorem is not simple and the correlation between cost and effects must be considered (Willan and O'Brien 1996).

The lower confidence interval can be approximated by

$$L1 = (X - [X2 - YZ]1/2)/Y$$

Table 2.2 Example of Dominance

	Costs ($)	Quality-Adjusted Life Year	Incremental Cost-Effectiveness Ratio
Drug A	1400	0.95	
Drug B	1500	0.75	
Incremental	−100	0.20	Dominance

Note: Dominance – On average, patients who received Drug A have lower costs and higher health than patients who received Drug B.

Table 2.3 The One Reason Why 95% Confidence Intervals for Incremental Cost-Effectiveness Ratio Are Usually Not Reported

	Lower 95% Confidence Interval	Mean Effect	Upper 95% Confidence Interval
Incremental costs	$1,000	$1,000	$1,000
Incremental QALYs	−0.010	0.001	0.010
ICER	−$100,000/QALY	$1,000,000/QALY	+$10,000/QALY

Note: Mean ICER = $1,000,000/QALYS (95% CI = −$100,000/QALY, +$10,000/QALY).

The mean value is outside the 95% confidence interval.

ICER, incremental cost-effectiveness ratio; QALY, quality-adjusted life year.

The upper confidence interval can be approximated by

$$L2 = (X + [X2 − YZ]1/2)/Y$$

where:

$$X = \Delta E \Delta C − f_{v,1-\alpha} r s \Delta E \, s \Delta C$$

$$Y = \Delta E^2 f_{v,1-\alpha} r s_{\Delta E}^2$$

$$Z = \Delta C^2 f_{v,1-\alpha} r s_{\Delta C}^2$$

where:
  ΔE and ΔC are the mean difference in effect and cost
  $s_{\Delta E}^2$ and $s_{\Delta C}^2$ are estimated variances
  r is the estimated Pearson correlation coefficient between costs and effects
    $f_{v,1-\alpha}$ is the upper percentage point of the F-distribution with 1
  v is the number of degrees of freedom upon which the estimated variance $\Delta E − \Delta C$ is based

As you can see, this is not a transparent calculation and requires means and standard deviation for cost and effects and the correlation between cost and effects. Even if you could estimate the 95% confidence intervals, two important failures exist which are presented as examples. Suppose the ICER was the same as mentioned earlier at $500/QALY, the 95% CI could be −$300/QALY to $1300/QALY. Here we have a negative limit in the confidence interval, which is awkward to interpret as mentioned earlier, and most researchers in this field have commented that this decreases transparency. Logically, if society is willing to reduce costs by $300 in exchange for improved QALY, Drug A is cost effective. In reality, any reduction in cost with an increase in QALYs is preferred and is called dominance, and the magnitude of the cost savings is not important. Thus, how far the confidence interval becomes negative is not important.

Another statistical failure of the confidence interval is the case when the denominator approaches zero within the confidence interval. Consider a difference in QALYs of 0.001 as the mean difference in incremental QALYs, with 95% confidence intervals of −0.010 and 0.010. Further, consider for simplicity that costs do not vary with a mean difference in costs of $1000.

The mean and 95% confidence intervals of the ICER would be mean = $1,000,000/QALYs (95% CI = −$100,000/QALY, +$10,000/QALY) (Table 2.3). That is, the upper bound of the ICER is lower than the estimate of the mean. Sometimes though, the confidence interval for ICER is reported when both the lower and upper bound are positive. Perhaps because of the complexity of Fiellers' theorem or the irregular properties of the confidence intervals, bootstrapping is now performed more often to represent uncertainty, but bootstrapping has an important role in reducing sampling uncertainty (Briggs, Goeree et al. 2002), and briefly discussed in Chapter 9. Next, we need to discuss some of the statistical properties of QALYs and costs, and how they are generated.

Introduction to Health-Related Quality of Life

Although mortality and morbidity are the outcomes of greatest concern to patients, clinicians and decision-makers, they may sometimes be difficult to pool to provide an overall sense of difference in benefit between two treatments. HRQOL scales, also called indexes or measures, are increasingly used along with more traditional outcome measures to assess health care technologies, providing a more complete picture of the ways in which health care affects patients (Drummond 2001). The advantage of using HRQOL as an outcome measure is that there is one scale that represents the health state of patients who have multiple events or comorbidities. Ideally, the value of HRQOL can be captured in a pragmatic trial (where cost, HRQOL and clinical parameters are prospectively gathered) and can be reported to be comprehensive of all events.

For example, consider patients in a trial that have stroke as the major efficacy event and pain as secondary outcome. Strokes can be *minor* such as temporary loss of functionality (e.g. numbness or temporary slurring of speech). Alternatively, the strokes can be severe and result in major losses in long-term functionality. The secondary outcome, namely, pain could be minor or severe, with many variations in between. Putting this together, the possibility of stroke with different severity and different amounts of pain would create a question of which treatment is better.

In Example 1, the patients in Treatment group 1 experienced more strokes than Treatment group 2 (10% vs. 5%) but reported less pain (5% vs. 10%), and had higher quality of life, then we can conclude that the strokes may be minor. In Example 2, the rates of the events are the same, but patients in Treatment group 1 had HRQOL of 0.5 and Treatment group 2 had HRQOL of 0.7, which would indicate that strokes were more detrimental to quality of life (Table 2.4).

HRQOL scales can be either generic, widely applicable in many diseases, or disease-specific scales, designed for one specific disease. Disease-specific scales are usually more responsive to detect changes in the state of health of patients with that disease. However, the disease-specific scales have not been validated to reflect the general populations' values for different health states and are not reflective of the general population's willingness to pay for care for that disease. Examples of disease-specific scales include cancer (Karnofsky Performance Index), psychiatric (Hopkins Symptom Checklist), respiratory (Breathing Problems Questionnaire), neurologic (National Institute of Health Stroke Scale), rheumatoid arthritis (Western Ontario and McMaster Universities Arthritis Index), cardiovascular (New York Heart Association Functional Classification Scale) or diabetes (Quality of Life, Status and Change), which are a few of the many possibilities (Bowling 1997).

Table 2.4 Two Examples of Similar Rates of Events with Different Impact on Patients

Outcomes	Example 1		Example 2	
	Treatment 1	*Treatment 2*	*Treatment 1*	*Treatment 2*
Stroke (%)	10	5	10	5
Pain (%)	5	10	5	10
Health-related quality of life	0.70	0.50	0.50	0.70

Note: Example 1: Pain is severe and strokes are minor.

Example 2: Strokes are major and pain is not severe.

The generic scales have been validated by large cross-sectional studies to measure how members of the general population value different health states and to verify that the scales possess the desirable statistical properties of reliability and validity. The most common generic HRQOL scales are the Short Form (SF-36), the Euroquol 5 Dimension (EQ-5D) and the McMaster Health Utility Index (HUI-3). For all of these scales, there are subcategories that we will call *domains*, but others have called dimensions, factors, subscales or attributes. The effect that each of the domains has on overall HRQOL has been validated with tens or hundreds of thousands of subjects. The process for establishing the scale and validating the scale is covered nicely elsewhere (Streiner and Norman 2008).

The SF-36 is scored with eight domains including physical functioning, physical role limitations, bodily pain, general health, vitality, social functioning, emotional role limitations and mental health. Because the SF-36 does not provide an overall preference score based on all these domains, we can use the SF-6D that selects six questions to derive an overall utility score from the SF-36 scale (Brazier et al. 2004, 2005). The EQ-5D measures patient health status according to the five domains: mobility, self-care, usual activities, pain/discomfort and anxiety/depression (Dolan 1997). The HUI-3 has eight domains: vision, hearing, speech, ambulation, dexterity, emotional, cognitive and pain (Table 2.5) (Feeny et al. 2002).

As you can see in the table, the scales have some similarities, with pain, physical effects, emotional and mental health being incorporated. The major differences are that HUI-3 has more physical measures that are objective (vision, hearing, speech, cognition), while the SF-36 has a separate measure on overall health. For analysis, the scales are first converted to a unit measure referred to as HRQOL or utility (ranging from 0 representing death to 1 for perfect health) according to well-validated algorithms. Strictly speaking, the HRQOL represents the health state and utility represents the value of the health state (from 0 to 1), but HRQOL is commonly used to represent both. Occasionally, the health state, which refers to the characteristics of the health condition, produces a negative HRQOL. For example, for EQ-5D with five possible levels for each domain, if there are problems with three domains, self-care (unable to wash or dress themselves), severe pain (extreme pain or discomfort) and high levels of anxiety (extremely anxious or depressed), but lack of problems with two domains, where the patient can perform usual activities and does not have problems with walking, the estimated HRQOL according to scoring by the cross-sectional validation study in the United Kingdom is negative (-0.186). This is considered by the scale to be worse

Table 2.5 Domains of the Generic Health-Related Quality of Life

Concept Assessed by Domains	EQ-5D (5 domains)[a]	SF-36 (8 domains)	HUI-3 (8 domains)
Pain	Pain/discomfort	Bodily pain	Pain
Physical nature	Mobility Usual activities Self-care	Physical functioning Physical role limitations	Ambulatory Dexterity
Social nature/ mental	Anxiety/depression	Social functioning Vitality Emotional role limitations Mental health	Emotion
Other physical measures			Vision Hearing Speech Cognition
Overall health		General health domain	

Note: [a] EQ-5D is often conducted with a visual analogue scale in addition to the responses to the domain questions.

than death. Finally, we mention that the time that is spent in each state is added up to create a QALY. More detail is provided in Chapter 8 on quality of life, while our focus on this Chapter 8 is the source of this data.

Introduction to Resource Utilization and Costs

Costs are evaluated in two steps: first, identifying the resource utilization that is associated with events or disease condition, and second, applying a unit cost to each resource utilized. The most common resources are doctor visits, hospital stays and drugs prescribed. The unit costs included in the ICER calculation should be current prices in the local currency to reflect decisions today (Canadian Agency for Drugs and Technologies in Health [CADTH] 2006). The items included in the cost calculation depend on the following perspectives: hospital, payer or societal (Garrison et al. 2010; Mullins et al. 2010; Mycka et al. 2010).

The hospital perspective would only include the cost that the hospital will pay and includes hospital salaries and employment benefits and capital costs with associated overhead and maintenance costs. Many hospitals or groups of hospitals have developed case costing to fairly distribute the shared capital purchases and overhead to the cost of a single procedure or hospital stay. For example, the salary and benefits for an admission to a hospital for a hip fracture would include the time for the attending physician, surgeon, radiologist, nurses, porter, administrative clerks and managers, and shared time for security, cleaning and maintenance staff. The capital purchases would include the building; special equipments, such as X-ray machines and general equipments, such as beds and wheel chairs with annual or activity-based depreciation and maintenance costs. As you can tell, the effort required to estimate the cost for one type of admission would be enormous, but the decision to provide the cost for all services is done for private institutions to generate bills for service, or within public health care systems to allocate resources.

A broader perspective is the payer, which is applied for private insurance companies and for public health care systems. The costs would include services that were performed in hospital as well as outside of a single institution and relate to the experience of the broader health care system. This would include hospitalizations, emergency room visits, outpatient physician visits, tests, physical therapy, home-based nursing care, prescription drugs and devices such as a cane or a walker. The payer perspective includes the agency's costs and excludes any cost that the patient or family members will incur. These latter costs paid directly by the patient fall into the perspective of the society or societal costs.

Societal costs could include payer's cost plus out-of-pocket costs such as parking, co-payments and deductibles; payments to a caregiver who helps with daily living or patient's time loss from work. In addition, the cost for unpaid time loss for the patient and the caregiver can be included. The wages that are included for unpaid time have been reported as zero, minimum wage, nursing assistant wage to reflect level of care, average national wage and average wage of similar patients or caregivers that are employed. A final consideration is the duration of the wage loss, which is estimated either using a friction period method, which is the time it takes to replace a worker who becomes sick, or using the human capital method, which is the potential loss to the aggregate economy for the full duration of the illness. The duration of friction period can be approximated with the average duration of an unemployment spell (Hopkins, Goeree, and Longo 2010). An extreme example would be a young patient who has a spinal injury and never enters the work force. The friction period would include 20 weeks of wage loss under normal economic conditions, and the human capital approach would value the wage loss as forgone lifetime earnings.

After the perspective has been defined, the cost for safety and efficacy events can be identified and unit costs applied. The scope can include all safety and efficacy events or simply the events that are statistically different between two groups, especially if the analysis is literature based. There is no formal guidance on this, although United Kingdom favours being more inclusive. In addition, there are background disease-related non-event costs that may be included. The costs of having a disease may include daily medications and annual assessments, which would not necessarily be included in a cost-effectiveness analysis between two treatments of the disease because they would cancel each other out, while the background cost would be included in the cost of a disease for an intervention that attempted to prevent a new case of the disease or prevented increased severity of the disease.

A further refinement is the selection or attribution of costs to the disease or events (Goeree et al. 2010; Hopkins et al. 2013). When the cost-effectiveness analytic is trial based between two comparators, the typical analytic strategy is to estimate the cost for all of the resource utilization that occurred within the trial period (Hopkins et al. 2011). However, the costs may be limited to only disease-related costs, which can be either straight forward or if questionable should be included. For example, in a one-year trial between two drugs to prevent heart attacks, the exclusion of the non-disease cost of one patient who had mental illness which required $1 million in institutional care for mental health would be prudent. We discuss more about refining cost analysis in Chapter 7.

Need for Modelling

When the cost-effectiveness analysis is for a short duration, there are only two treatment comparators, where the choice of treatment occurs only at the start of the trial, when events occur over just one time period, a simple cost-effectiveness analysis of the trial is fairly straight forward. However, when the trial becomes longer with different phases, for example, hospital discharge and long-term follow-up, there are more than two comparators, where treatment can change during trial, or when literature values are necessary to supplement the trial data, an economic model that pools different data sources including their means and their distributions is preferable to increase transparency (Caro et al. 2012; Akehurst et al. 2000; Philips et al. 2004; Roberts et al. 2012). Each of the model inputs lists such as trial data, literature clinical events, natural history of the disease, resource utilization, unit costs and quality of life can be highlighted and described in detail. Quite often there are preliminary estimations that must occur in order to populate the economic model with the required parameters.

First, the trial may not include all of the comparators that are available for that treatment. The analysis must be supplemented by literature values, either from a meta-analysis or from a network meta-analysis. Second, the trial may be short and the safety and efficacy may need to be projected to a longer time period and verified by cohort studies. If the disease is chronic, a *lifetime model* that simulates the patient's heath states until death is preferred (Dias et al. 2013). Lifetime models include the time period until all the patients have died, which is often limited to 100 years of age and validated with half of the control patients having died at the normal life expectancy of approximately 80 years. In addition, some of the evidence such as cost estimates or quality of life may not be available and assumptions may be required. The economic model conducted as a simulation model then builds on all of the above-mentioned parameters and estimations. Two types of simulation models are commonly used, decision analytic modelling and Markov modelling, which are both becoming increasingly advanced with associated checklists for quality of conduct and reporting.

Decision Analytic Model

Decision analytic modelling is presented as a decision tree to increase transparency and represents the sequence of clinical decisions and its health and economic impacts (Figure 2.1) (Akehurst et al. 2000).

The basic steps of building the decision analytic model are as follows:

1. Develop a model (the decision tree) that demonstrates the decisions and relevant outcomes (health states) of these choices.
2. Assign estimates of the probabilities of each outcome (branch).

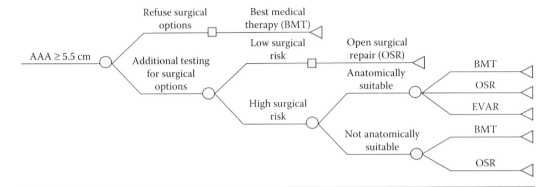

Figure 2.1   Decision analytic model. *Note:* **The decision analytic model describes the selection of three treatment options: best medical therapy, open surgical repair and endovascular repair. A circle represents a choice node, such as the choice to refuse surgical options versus additional testing for surgical options. For each choice node, the probability of each choice must be estimated for trial or observational data sources. Triangles represent end nodes, which indicate the end of the decision tree branch. Squares represent outcomes, which sometimes may be branched with known probabilities. Abdominal aortic aneurysm (AAA) ≥ 5.5 cm. The characteristics of the patients to be included in this model have an AAA greater than 5.5 cm in diameter.**

3. Assign estimates of the value of each outcome: costs and HRQOL.
4. Calculate the expected value of the outcomes associated with each decision leading to those outcomes. This is done by multiplying the probabilities by the value of each outcome to generate sum of the costs and the effects.
5. Finally, estimate the ICER with the current standard of care as the reference treatment (Treatment group 2) to estimate the cost-effectiveness.
6. Conduct sensitivity analysis on the parameters and model structure to test the robustness of the model (Briggs, Claxton, and Sculpher 2006).

Markov Model

A Markov model represents and quantifies changes from one health state to another and allows returning to a previously existed state (Figure 2.2a and b) (Spiegelhalter and Best 2003). This type of state-transition model is useful when patients frequently return to a common health state, for which the costs and quality of life are known. Examples would include gastroesophageal reflux disease where the reflux can be severe, mild or in remission (Briggs et al. 2002). During the severe period, the patient will start on higher doses of medication and have lower quality of life, and when the symptoms subside, the medication costs and quality of life will change. Similar

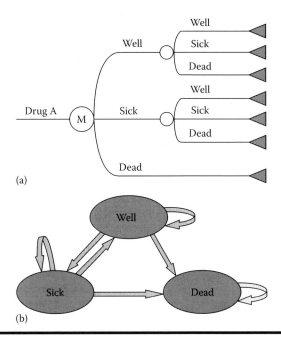

Figure 2.2 **(a) Markov model. (b) Simplified version of Markov model.** *Note:* **There are three distinct health states: well, sick and dead. In each subsequent cycle, patients can move unidirectionally (single arrows) from well to dead or sick to dead, bidirectionally (double arrows) between well and sick, or do not transition between states (curved loops) remaining sick, well or dead. The probabilities for every arrow are known and may be constant for all cycles.**

diseases that have episodes of higher costs and lower quality of life would include the management of pain for rheumatoid arthritis or the management of exacerbations for COPD. Like in decision analytic modelling, the lifetime of the patient cohort is generally followed for chronic diseases. The Markov model breaks down the lifetime into recurring cycles (periods or length of episodes) such as three months, six months or one year being the most common. For each cycle, we require the probability of moving to each of the different health states from the current state at each time point, and the costs and quality of life in each health state for the duration of the health state.

Start with the Trials: Safety and Efficacy

Once the model has been structured to follow the clinical decision pathways and expected events, the model is populated with parameters. The major source of data to generate cost-effectiveness analysis is from the trial data that were created for regulatory approval. Data from a Phase I trial are always underpowered to provide comparative estimates of relative rates of safety events and are not often published. If they were published, the types of events that occur are more important than the rates of events. For example, if a Phase I trial reported nausea and rashes, this directs our focus to look at the other trials, registries or databases to quantify those events. Most of the data for an HTA will come from Phase II or Phase III trials. Phase II trials may be placebo controlled, while Phase III trials will often include only one active comparator to the new drug. To provide comparisons to all available treatments including standards of care, network meta-analysis is possible (discussed in Chapter 4).

From the trial data, the rates of safety and efficacy events if reported can be used for the HTA. Statistically speaking, the probabilities and variances of the probabilities of the events are needed. For every outcome that can possibly occur, the impact on cost and quality of life should also be estimated. In an ideal setting such as a pragmatic trial, detailed records of health care resource utilization for every event should capture, and quality of life should be measured periodically to assess the benefit of the therapy from bad events or preferably improvement in health from new therapy. However, these data are not always collected, and even if they were collected, further data outside the trial are often required to complete the economic evaluation. For these, we focus on the additional data that are required and their potential sources.

Secondary Data Requirements

While randomized controlled trials (RCTs) are the *gold standard* of internal validity for causal relationships, they are not necessarily the best method for answering all questions of relevance to an HTA. Other types of studies may be preferred to RCTs for different questions. For example, a good way to describe the prognosis for a given disease or condition may be a set of follow-up studies of patient cohorts at uniform time points in the clinical course of a disease (Table 2.6). Case-control studies are often used to identify risk factors for diseases, disorders and adverse events. The table highlights some of the preferable sources of data to complete an HTA. The major types of data are trials, observational studies, administrative

Table 2.6   Sources and Uses of Data to Conduct an HTA

Data Source	Safety Efficacy	Long-Term Safety Efficacy, Effectiveness	Quality of Life	Resource Utilization and Costs	Epidemiology
Randomized controlled trials	√		(√)[a]	(√)[a]	
Observational studies Prospective cohort studies Case-control studies Case series		√	√	√	
Linked administrative data Case/disease registries Retrospective cohort study Regional/ community-based studies	(√)	√	(√)	√	√
Single-source administrative data Utilization databases Hospital-based studies Medical/patient records National mortality/life tables		(√)		(√)	(√)

(*Continued*)

Table 2.6 (*Continued*)   Sources and Uses of Data to Conduct an HTA

Data Source	Safety Efficacy	Long-Term Safety Efficacy, Effectiveness	Quality of Life	Resource Utilization and Costs	Epidemiology
Primary data collection (non-RCT) Quality-of-life surveys Cost/burden of illness studies Epidemiological studies Micro-costing studies			√	(√)	(√)
Expert opinion Consensus opinions (Delphi) Single opinion				(√)	

Note: √, high-quality source of information; (√), possible source of information.

[a] Collected prospectively during the trial (i.e. pragmatic trial).

data (linked or single source), primary data collection or opinions. Most data sources will fall into these categories; however, they are not exclusive.

Rare Diseases

One gap that often creates a dilemma for those who conduct HTAs is when the focus of the HTA is on a rare disease, rarely used technology or a disease with rare events. In these situations, a well-powered RCT may not be feasible for one jurisdiction or country. Consider a disease that has fewer than 1000 cases every year and the probability of the primary outcome was 10%. To conduct an RCT where the new drug, device or program can reduce the bad primary outcome to 5%, the estimated sample size would be 1242 patients. Given that the typical voluntary recruitment for a trial can be less than 10% of the population, then the recruitment for this trial would take 12.42 years. Thus, a local trial that is sufficiently powered would not be feasible, and even further, the trial would be meaningless given that the technology would likely change in less than 12 years. This situation is typical for certain types of cancers, epilepsy and many other diseases of the heart, lung, skin and so on. The main point is that even if there are no well-powered trials, conducting an HTA on the highest quality of data would provide decision-makers with at least some information for funding decisions. It is possible that a definitive trial may never be conducted.

The perceived quality of data for an HTA has been a focus of some research, but no consensus has been reached on the best source of information for each parameter. Some factors that increase the perceived quality of data would include that the data are current, local, representative of similar patients with the disease, verified or cross-validated, previously peer-reviewed for similar work and from a large sample. With the increase in quality of the data, there is a reduced chance of a biased estimate. We now focus in detail on how each data source can provide some meaningful parameters.

Effectiveness versus Efficacy

There is no debate that a well-designed, well-powered, well-executed, well-reported RCT may provide an unbiased estimate of the relative efficacy for the clinical primary outcome. Any true difference between two groups is the result of the treatment effect, and any differences in baseline or prognostic factors are assumed to be well balanced between the groups because of randomization. However, a number of important caveats must be noted. The RCT is designed to detect a difference in the primary outcome, for the duration of the study, and for the enrolled population. For an RCT, only the primary outcome has been evaluated with adequate power, and all secondary safety and efficacy outcomes may not be adequately powered (Berger et al. 2012; Philips et al. 2004). A meta-analysis of available trials increases the statistical power for the analysis of the secondary outcomes.

Most trials are short in duration and do not predict the long-term outcomes of the patients. As an example, the early trials for drug-eluting stents to prevent myocardial infarction in patients with stenosis (lesions) were 1–2 years. In the earliest versions of the devices, long-term cohort studies indicated a high rate of restenosis after two years, and later versions of the drug-eluting stents improved on the later outcome.

Another major issue with the early drug-eluting stent studies, which was also remedied with later evidence, was that the patient population who met the inclusion criteria for the early RCTs. The early studies included patients with a short single lesion. The lack of generalizability to the cardiac population was that most patients, who report to the cardiologist for chest pain, will at the time of diagnosis already have more than one lesion before symptoms are reported, and the lesion length is often longer. Thus, the evidence lacked generalizability to the average characteristics of the target population. Subsequent RCTs and long-term registry analysis that included a broader set of patients were mandated at the time of regulatory approval and later strengthened the generalizability to the broader population.

Long-Term Outcomes

Trials are often one year or shorter and occasionally have extensions out to five years. A few gaps exist when comparing a new treatment to the current standard of care or placebo-controlled outcomes. The important piece of information to build a lifetime model is the patient's *natural history* including lifetime profile of the disease. This lifetime model relies on very long-term administrative data to capture the experience of the patient in each decade of life (Dias et al. 2013). Data that can be used would include, for example, the probability of death for each year of life or probability of an event for each year of life. For example, the lifetime risk of a hip fracture is built on cross-sectional for each decade of life, which is summarized for a life table using the Sullivan method (Hopkins et al. 2012). It is unfeasible to track patients over a long period, especially in the presence of declining fracture risk over time.

The long-term outcomes can be derived from a comprehensive linked database that could be used to create a retrospective cohort study, which would include linkage of hospital admissions, emergency room visits, clinics, drug utilization, and physician billings. Linkage by way of using a unique patient identification number would ensure that the different databases can recognize the unique individual and are not double counting the number of patients and underreporting the average cost per patient. A set of linkable databases is preferable to a single database such as hospital admissions which would capture only severe cases or to a physician database that would exclude hospital admissions.

Once a lifetime profile for a disease has been built, then the effect of a new treatment option can be applied to predict how the life trajectory changes. Since the trial has limited duration, the effect over time from new treatment must be estimated using regression methods. The regression methods for each of the outcomes can be taken from the trial and verified with administrative data, or taken directly from administrative data. This is especially true with risk equations that estimate the probability of an event over a long time period.

Some of the events are captured in administrative databases if they lead to resource utilization such as an emergency room visit or admission, while other rare events may be obtained from single cohort studies or case series, or some events impact quality of life but not costs (Tarride et al. 2012). Ideally, data should be linked to capture complex multi-faceted care. For example, patients with heart attacks can be reported by doctors, emergency room or admissions, and linked data have been proven to be more sensitive (accepting true cases) and specific (rejecting non-cases) (Lix et al. 2008).

Administrative data can be used to capture cases to build a prospective cohort study, which captures pre-specified events, resource utilization, costs and quality of life, and are often more comprehensive being collected at regular intervals. Successful prospective cohort studies include the Canadian Multicentre Osteoporosis Study that began in the year 2000 (Kreiger et al. 1999), the United Kingdom Prospective Diabetes Study (Adler et al. 2000), the earlier prospective evidence from Rochester Epidemiology Project (Melton 1996) and the Framingham study of cardiovascular risk (Kagan et al. 1962).

Health-Related Quality of Life

While the comparative safety and efficacy can be updated with effectiveness evidence, a more common problem with RCTs is that not all of the evidence that is required to complete an HTA is gathered during the RCT. The common missing parameter is estimates of generic quality of life. Some RCTs include disease-specific measures of quality of life, but these scales need to be translated or *mapped* onto a generic quality of life scale that is acceptable to decision-makers (Grootendorst et al. 2007). The evidence for quality of life is often obtained from a systematic literature review to capture all relevant quality of life studies.

One required measure is the baseline quality of life for patients with a disease, for example, if the cost-effectiveness analysis was for patients with COPD. Luckily for the COPD analysis, there are published estimates of level of HRQOL for different stages of COPD (levels 1–4) (Stahl et al. 2005).

If there was no published data on baseline HRQOL, a few options are possible. One is to conduct a cross-sectional analysis as a survey of a sufficient sample to estimate HRQOL. The study should be large enough to allow estimates with small confidence intervals for subgroup analysis, based on level of the disease. Ideally, the study would also provide a predictive tool such as a regression model that allows prediction of quality of life based on covariates, such as age, sex, duration of disease, level of disease and important comorbidities.

Another necessary set of parameters is the impact of clinical events on HRQOL. To conduct the cost-effectiveness analysis, an estimate of the mean and variance of changes in HRQOL for every clinical event that occurs must be known. For most trials, this can include dozens of possible events. If the quality of life was not collected that allowed the compilation of the cumulative effects into one measure, the impact on quality of life for each of the clinical events must be quantified. For diabetes, the prevention or reduction in the consequences of the diseases would include quantifying the impact on seven known major disease-related reasons for hospitalization or emergency room visits from clinical events: cardiovascular heart disease, stroke, nephropathy, retinopathy, neuropathy, ketoacidosis and hypoglycaemia (Mount Hood 4 Modeling Group 2007). To produce even higher quality evidence, the impact on quality of life for patients with diabetes should be estimated. This may be different that the impact on quality of life for the general population, since multiple factors may have multiplicative effects. If a patient has myocardial infarction and stroke within a narrow time period, the effect on quality of life may be more than each event alone. Secondary data such as cross-sectional analysis as surveys or cohort studies are the most common source of these parameters. We are unaware of an institution or physician group that has become systematic requiring all visits to have an HRQOL assessment, which is unfortunate because the possibility of research and the opportunity to add to clinical knowledge would be great.

Resource Utilization and Costs

Once the probabilities of all events have been quantified, and the impact on quality of life has been estimated, a final parameter to estimate is the cost of events and the cost of disease state(s). For example, the cost of a myocardial infarction, or stroke, must be quantified. For many cases, the cost can be obtained from the published literature if the costs estimates are from the same country and are recent. However, it is well established that costs or even resource utilization for a clinical event will differ across countries and are not transferable because of differences in patterns of care for similar events. The lack of transferability requires that a local source of data be identified (Goeree et al. 2011). In most cases, researchers rely on administrative databases, such as local hospitals that conduct case costing, or managed care estimates or Medicaid/Medicare estimates.

Often, the data source is not complete providing only a portion of the total costs for an episode. For example, a hospital-based case costing system will provide the cost of an admission for an event such as a hip fracture, but the costs of rehabilitation, follow-up clinical visits or home care assistance are not captured. Either additional sources of data must be linked to the event, or clinical opinion of normally prescribed care is required, (Xie et al. 2014) or a time and motion study can be conducted (Xie et al. 2012).

An individual clinician or group of clinicians who have reached consensus with a Delphi panel may offer the opinion that a patient who has a hip fracture typically should have a six-week follow-up visit with X-ray, should undergo three weeks of physiotherapy, and should be given six months of assistance for daily living at home. The next step is quantifying the cost of follow-up visit, X-ray, physiotherapy and home care. The resource utilization that is associated with the clinical event is offered by the clinician, but the unit cost per each cost item must also be obtained, often from local billing fee schedules or case costing. One drawback of using the clinical opinion and fee schedules is the lack of variance for costs items. It is assumed that all patients who have the hip fracture have exactly one follow-up visit, one X-ray and so on. A community or clinical database, in this case, provides more information because it can offer an estimate of variability.

Another important resource utilization and cost estimate is the level of usual care for patient with a disease or health state. In a study on patients with COPD, the goal of the intervention such as an education program on smoking is to prevent a case or reduce the probability of reaching a higher stage of the disease. The trial may be short duration and use an intermediary marker such as lung function, and then a background estimate of resource utilization and costs of the higher levels of the disease is needed. The ideal source of information is a published Cost of Illness Study conducted for the target population.

A cost of illness study will incorporate all of the resource utilization and cost for a disease or health state (Akobundu et al. 2006). Many cost (or burden) of illness studies include all of the cost drivers such as admissions, tests, emergency room visits, clinic visits, rehabilitation, home assistance, nurse-based residential care, drugs, devices and appliances, employment loss and caregiver expense. In the absence of a cost of illness study, the individual cost items listed above must be estimated. Other outcomes derived from a cost of illness study are the rates of events, the cost of each events, the incidence and prevalence of the disease, and the national total cost/burden for the disease for new cases and existing cases. A further benefit of a cost of illness study is that the publication should provide descriptions of the highest quality of cost data that are available for that disease.

Within cost analysis, an important issue is that the cost of an event is different for patients with different diseases. For example, the average cost for an emergency room visit in the province of Ontario ranges for a small selection of diseases from $291 to $490 (Table 2.7). The cost of the visit varies because of the reasons for the visit, which implies that using an average cost of an emergency room visit without selecting the reasons and underlying comorbidities would be misleading. If the ICER was $100/QALY that was driven by differences in the rates of emergency room visits, selecting the appropriate unit cost for the emergency room visit would be important. Even further, the cost of an event such as a myocardial infarction may be different for patients with diseases such as diabetes than the cost for patients without diabetes (Goeree et al. 2009). One final note about costs is that sometimes there is a total cost and the itemized resource utilization is not needed. This would include patient's expenses for co-payments or for parking, when the perspective was the payer or the hospital.

Table 2.7 Cost of Emergency Room Visit by Type of Disease

Disease	Emergency Room Visit Average Cost ($)
Osteoporosis	490
Cancer	444
Diabetes Type 1	409
Diabetes Type 2	385
Rheumatoid arthritis	291

Source: Ontario Case Costing Initiative (2011). Ontario Ministry of Health and Long-Term Care.

http://www.occp.com/.

Epidemiology

Another important set of parameters that are required for reimbursement are the rates of incidence (new cases) and prevalence (existing cases). These numbers are essential to estimate the budget impact of introducing a new technology and the potential cost savings that may occur. Incidence and prevalence can come from new epidemiological studies that combine multiple sources of data, from new cost of illness studies, from published data, from access to administrative databases or from projections from community or clinical databases. In reality, no database is perfect and an awareness of missed patients should always be identified and explained.

A stand-alone database such as a hospital registry may exist, or in the case of Canada, hospital admissions, emergency room visits and hospital-based clinics are available at the national level. These data provided by Canadian Institute for Health Information are continually collected, reviewed and standardized and are the primary source of data for cost analysis and health care budgets in the country. Unfortunately, data is in isolation and only at each of the provinces can physician billing and drug utilization be linked. Only when there is linkage to all the main cost-driver databases, we can be more, confident, sure of the epidemiological estimates of incidence and prevalence. One reason is that low-risk cases may have not yet been to the emergency room or had an admission for their disease. Diseases such as hypertension or diabetes may be diagnosed by the clinician at their office with confirmation by an outpatient laboratory.

A further feature of physician databases is the need for repeated visits for the same disease, because the records may show one visit for a disease and it would be unclear if the visit is to treat the disease or to test for the presence of the disease. If a second visit does not occur for the same reason with a time period such as one year, the visit is often considered screening for the disease, and is not validated for the disease, such as diabetes.

In Canada, obtaining linked data at the national level is impossible, and obtaining linked provincial level is difficult. In most provinces, a direct request from industry is not allowed, and if allowed, requires an academic group to lead the project, and even then can take 1–2 years to initiate and conduct. If when approved, for example, in Quebec, only a 20% sample is available with similar reasoning to the 5% sample for Medicare in the United States.

Summary

To conduct an economic evaluation or a budget impact analysis requires the identification and synthesis of multiple data sources, with every data source having different amounts of statistical quality (Table 2.6). In most cases, the quality of the data varies by the jurisdiction and by the disease condition. Some countries such as Sweden have high-quality linkable data that are provided by a single source, while other countries have data that may be fractious such as in Canada, and other countries may have non-linked low-quality unstandardized data. For common diseases or diseases with long-standing treatment options, there may be high-quality robust data that may be comprehensive such as a RCT or a registry. For rare diseases, diseases with rare events or orphan diseases (without current therapy), data to conduct a comprehensive HTA would be sparse.

For most diseases, there are multiple data sources, and a systematic review of the available evidence is considered high quality in the eyes of the decision-makers. The use of a single source for the estimate of an HTA parameter would be seen as incomplete. If multiple data sources for an HTA parameter do exist, it is left to the judgement of the reviewer if the data source was the best choice and whether alternate estimates should be tested in sensitivity analysis. This in turn relies implicitly on the judgement of the reviewer to comment on appropriateness of the choice of data from several possible options, which we hope has been described in this chapter.

References

Adler A.I., Stratton I.M., Neil H.A., Yudkin J.S., Matthews D.R., Cull C.A., Wright A.D., Turner R.C., and Holman R.R. 2000. Association of systolic blood pressure with macrovascular and microvascular complications of type 2 diabetes (UKPDS 36): Prospective observational study. *British Medical Journal* 321 (7258): 412–419.

Akehurst R., Anderson P., Brazier J., Brennan A., Briggs A., Buxton M. et al. 2000. Decision analytic modelling in the economic evaluation of health technologies. A consensus statement. *PharmacoEconomics* 17 (5): 443–444.

Akobundu E., Ju J., Blatt L., and Mullins C.D. 2006. Cost-of-illness studies: A review of current methods. *PharmacoEconomics* 24 (9): 869–890.

Berger M.L., Dreyer N., Anderson F., Towse A., Sedrakyan A., and Normand S.L. 2012. Prospective observational studies to assess comparative effectiveness: The ISPOR good research practices task force report. *Value in Health: The Journal of the International Society for Pharmacoeconomics and Outcomes Research* 15 (2): 217–230.

Bowling A. 1997. *Measuring Health: A Review of Quality of Life Measurement Scales*, 2nd ed. Buckingham: Open University Press.

Brazier J., Akehurst R., Brennan A., Dolan P., Claxton K., McCabe C., Sculpher M., and Tsuchyia A. 2005. Should patients have a greater role in valuing health states? *Applied Health Economics and Health Policy* 4 (4): 201–208.

Brazier J., Roberts J., Tsuchiya A., and Busschbach J. 2004. A comparison of the EQ-5D and SF-6D across seven patient groups. *Health Economics* 13 (9): 873–884.

Briggs A.H., Claxton K., and Sculpher M. 2006. *Decision Modelling for Health Economic Evaluation*. Oxford: Oxford University Press.

Briggs A.H., Goeree R., Blackhouse G., and O'Brien B.J. 2002. Probabilistic analysis of cost-effectiveness models: Choosing between treatment strategies for gastroesophageal reflux disease. *Medical Decision Making* 22: 290–309.

Canadian Agency for Drugs and Technologies in Health (CADTH). 2006. *Guidelines for the Economic Evaluation of Health Technologies: Canada*, 3rd ed. CADTH, Ottawa, ON, Canada.

Caro J.J., Briggs A.H., Siebert U., and Kuntz K.M. 2012. Modeling good research practices – Overview: A report of the ISPOR-SMDM modeling good research practices task force – 1. *Value in Health: The Journal of the International Society for Pharmacoeconomics and Outcomes Research* 15 (6): 796–803.

Dias S., Welton N.J., Sutton A.J., and Ades A.E. 2013. Evidence synthesis for decision making 5: The baseline natural history model. *Medical Decision Making* 33 (5): 657–670.

Dolan P. 1997. Modeling valuations for EuroQol health states. *Medical Care* 35 (11): 1095–1108.

Drummond M. 2001. Introducing economic and quality of life measurements into clinical studies. *Annals of Medicine* 33 (5): 344–349.

Drummond M., Brown R., Fendrick A.M., Fullerton P., Neumann P., Taylor R., and Barbieri M. 2003. Use of pharmacoeconomics information – Report of the ISPOR task force on use of pharmacoeconomic/health economic information in health-care decision making. *Value in Health: The Journal of the International Society for Pharmacoeconomics and Outcomes Research* 6 (4): 407–416.

Drummond M.F., Schwartz J.S., Jonsson B., Luce B.R., Neumann P.J., Siebert U., and Sullivan S.D. 2008. Key principles for the improved conduct of health technology assessments for resource allocation decisions. *International Journal of Technology Assessment in Health Care* 24 (3): 244–258.

Feeny D., Furlong W., Torrance G.W., Goldsmith C.H., Zhu Z., DePauw S., Denton M., and Boyle M. 2002. Multiattribute and single-attribute utility functions for the health utilities index mark 3 system. *Medical Care* 40 (2): 113–128.

Garrison L.P., Jr., Mansley E.C., Abbott T.A., III, Bresnahan B.W., Hay J.W., and Smeeding J. 2010. Good research practices for measuring drug costs in cost-effectiveness analyses: A societal perspective: The ISPOR drug cost task force report – Part II. *Value in Health: The Journal of the International Society for Pharmacoeconomics and Outcomes Research* 13 (1): 8–13.

Goeree R., He J., O'Reilly D., Tarride J.E., Xie F., Lim M., and Burke N. 2011. Transferability of health technology assessments and economic evaluations: A systematic review of approaches for assessment and application. *ClinicoEconomics and Outcomes Research* 3: 89–104.

Goeree R., O'Reilly D., Hopkins R., Blackhouse G., Tarride J.E., Xie F., and Lim M. 2010. General population versus disease-specific event rate and cost estimates: Potential bias for economic appraisals. *Expert Review of Pharmacoeconomics and Outcomes Research* 10 (4): 379–384.

Goeree R., O'Reilly D., Hux J., Lim M., Hopkins R., Tarride J., Blackhouse G., and Xie F. 2009. Total and excess costs of diabetes and related complications in Ontario. *Canadian Journal of Diabetes* 33 (1): 35–45.

Grootendorst P., Marshall D., Pericak D., Bellamy N., Feeny D., and Torrance G.W. 2007. A model to estimate health utilities index mark 3 utility scores from WOMAC index scores in patients with osteoarthritis of the knee. *Journal of Rheumatology* 34 (3): 534–542.

Hopkins R.B., Garg A.X., Levin A., Molzahn A., Rigatto C., Singer J., Soltys G., Soroka S., Parfrey P.S., Barrett B.J., and Goeree R. 2011. Cost-effectiveness analysis of a randomized trial comparing care models for chronic kidney disease. *Clinical Journal of the American Society of Nephrology* 6 (6): 1248–1257.

Hopkins R.B., Goeree R., and Longo C.J. 2010. Estimating the national wage loss from cancer in Canada. *Current Oncology* 17 (2): 40–49.

Hopkins R.B., Pullenayegum E., Goeree R., Adachi J.D., Papaioannou A., Leslie W.D., Tarride J.E., and Thabane L. 2012. Estimation of the lifetime risk of hip fracture for women and men in Canada. *Osteoporosis International* 23 (3): 921–927.

Hopkins R.B., Tarride J.E., Leslie W.D., Metge C., Lix L.M., Morin S., Finlayson G., Azimaee M., Pullenayegum E., Goeree R., Adachi J.D., Papaioannou A., and Thabane L. 2013. Estimating the excess costs for patients with incident fractures, prevalent fractures, and nonfracture osteoporosis. *Osteoporosis International* 24 (2): 581–593.

Kagan A., Dawber T.R., Kannel W.B., and Revotskie N. 1962. The Framingham study: A prospective study of coronary heart disease. *Federation Proceedings* 21 (4)Pt 2: 52–57.

Kreiger N., Joseph L., Mackenzie T., Poliquin S., Brown J., Prior J., Rittmaster R., and Tenenhouse A. 1999. The Canadian Multicentre Osteoporosis Study (CaMos): Background, rationale, methods. *Canadian Journal on Aging* 18 (3): 376–387.

Lix L.M., Yogendran M.S., Leslie W.D., Shaw S.Y., Baumgartner R., Bowman C., Metge C., Gumel A., Hux J., and James R.C. 2008. Using multiple data features improved the validity of osteoporosis case ascertainment from administrative databases. *Journal of Clinical Epidemiology* 61 (12): 1250–1260.

Luyten J., Marais C., Hens N., De S.K., and Beutels P. 2011. Imputing QALYs from single time point health state descriptions on the EQ-5D and the SF-6D: A comparison of methods for hepatitis a patients. *Value in Health: The Journal of the International Society for Pharmacoeconomics and Outcomes Research* 14 (2): 282–290.

Melton L.J., III. 1996. History of the Rochester epidemiology project. *Mayo Clinic Proceedings* 71 (3): 266–274.

Mount Hood 4 Modeling Group. 2007. Computer modeling of diabetes and its complications: A report on the Fourth Mount Hood Challenge Meeting. *Diabetes Care* 30 (6): 1638–1646.

Mullins C.D., Seal B., Seoane-Vazquez E., Sankaranarayanan J., Asche C.V., Jayadevappa R., Lee W.C., Romanus D.K., Wang J., Hay J.W., and Smeeding J. 2010. Good research practices for measuring drug costs in cost-effectiveness analyses: Medicare, medicaid and other US government payers perspectives: The ISPOR Drug Cost Task Force report – Part IV. *Value in Health: The Journal of the International Society for Pharmacoeconomics and Outcomes Research* 13 (1): 18–24.

Mycka J.M., Dellamano R., Kolassa E.M., Wonder M., Ghosh S., Hay J.W., and Smeeding J. 2010. Good research practices for measuring drug costs in cost effectiveness analyses: An industry perspective: The ISPOR Drug Cost Task Force report – Part V. *Value in Health: The Journal of the International Society for Pharmacoeconomics and Outcomes Research* 13 (1): 25–27.

Ontario Case Costing Initiative (OCCI). 2011. Ontario Ministry of Health and Long-Term Care. http://www.occp.com/. Accessed on December 2, 2014.

Philips Z., Ginnelly L., Sculpher M., Claxton K., Golder S., Riemsma R., Woolacoot N., and Glanville J. 2004. Review of guidelines for good practice in decision-analytic modelling in health technology assessment. *Health Technology Assessment* 8 (36): iii–xi, 1.

Roberts M., Russell L.B., Paltiel A.D., Chambers M., McEwan P., and Krahn M. 2012. Conceptualizing a model: A report of the ISPOR-SMDM Modeling Good Research Practices Task Force – 2. *Value in Health: The Journal of the International Society for Pharmacoeconomics and Outcomes Research* 15 (6): 804–811.

Spiegelhalter D.J., and Best N.G. 2003. Bayesian approaches to multiple sources of evidence and uncertainty in complex cost-effectiveness modelling. *Statistic in Medicine* 22 (23): 3687–3709.

Stahl E., Lindberg A., Jansson S.A., Ronmark E., Svensson K., Andersson F., Lofdahl C.G., and Lundback B. 2005. Health-related quality of life is related to COPD disease severity. *Health and Quality of Life Outcomes* 3: 56.

Streiner D., and Norman G. 2008. *Health Measurement Scales. A Practical Guide to Their Development and Use*, 4th ed. New York: Oxford University Press.

Tarride J.E., Hopkins R.B., Leslie W.D., Morin S., Adachi J.D., Papaioannou A., Bessette L., Brown J.P., and Goeree R. 2012. The burden of illness of osteoporosis in Canada. *Osteoporosis International* 23 (11): 2591–2600.

Willan A.R., and Briggs A.H. 2006. *Statistical Analysis of Cost-Effectiveness Data*. West Essex: John Wiley & Sons Ltd.

Willan A.R., and O'Brien B.J. 1996. Confidence intervals for cost-effectiveness ratios: An application of Fieller's theorem. *Health Economics* 5 (4): 297–305.

Xie F., Hopkins R.B., Burke N., Habib M., Angelis C.D., Pasetka M., Giotis A., and Goeree R. 2014. Time and labor costs associated with administration of intravenous bisphosphonates for breast or prostate cancer patients with metastatic bone disease: A time and motion study. *Hospital Practice* 42 (2): 38–45.

Xie F., Hopkins R., Burke N., Tarride J.E., and Goeree R. 2012. Patient management, and time and health care resource utilization associated with the use of intravenous bisphosphonates for patients with metastatic bone disease: A Delphi study. *Hospital Practice (Minneap.)* 40 (2): 131–137.

Chapter 3

Meta-Analysis

Overview of Meta-Analysis

For a new drug that is being introduced, or if an older drug that is being applied to a new indication, regulatory approval requires one or two successful trials to establish clinical benefit given satisfactory safety. If only one trial is conducted, meta-analysis is not possible or necessary. However, if there are two or more trials, the results should be combined to establish an overall estimate of clinical effect. For a new drug that is approved where there are already established therapies, the benefit versus standard of care and all existing therapies are required for reimbursement. The absence of comparative effectiveness leads to a very high probability of rejection of the submission for reimbursement. For the first drug for a disease, a comparison to an existing therapy is not possible.

In addition, to build the economic model, meta-analysis should be conducted on all of the efficacy and safety outcomes from the trials, as well as other observational outcomes such as long-term effectiveness and safety. For all outcomes, the weighted estimate of effect estimated from a meta-analysis (or meta-analytic techniques) is required to produce a stronger conclusion than can be provided by any individual study.

In this chapter, we focus on combining the results of common drug–dose–outcome combinations versus common comparators, that is, a standard meta-analysis. The list of possible statistical software to perform a meta-analysis is long (Table 3.1), and we work through an example with STATA software (StataCorp 2009). In Chapter 4, we focus on indirect methods, and networks meta-analysis to combine evidence across outcomes for different

Table 3.1   Choice of Statistical Software to Conduct Meta-Analysis

A Note on Biostatistical Software to Conduct a Meta-Analysis
The brand names of software that can conduct meta-analysis continue to grow. There are single-purpose software designed only for meta-analysis, multi-purpose software with add-on packages to conduct meta-analysis and samples of raw code that will generate meta-analysis results for standard statistical software.
For most meta-analyses, the single-purpose recommended Cochrane collaboration software review manager [RevMan] will perform most of the standard types of meta-analysis. The software has the huge advantage that the entire systematic review protocol is structured so that filling in the blanks will create a final report or manuscript suitable submission for a peer-reviewed journal. The software conducts meta-analysis and creates forest and funnel plots, and can switch between fixed and random effects, or remove outliers, with a single click of a button. When further analysis, such as a statistical test of publication bias or meta-regression, is required, software such as STATA is available that has available add-on packages. When Bayesian analysis, is required, the BUGS software is the current software of choice. Also available to conduct meta-analysis is the free software 'R-project', which has add-on packages for most requirements.
For this book, we use STATA and BUGS examples, but the analysis can be repeated in many different software applications, and the reader should make their own choice.

drug–dose combinations and different comparators, by ensuring we use a systematic approach to consider all of the available evidence.

The objectives for a systematic review of clinical literature and subsequent meta-analysis are to

■ Systematically search for all available evidence.
■ Describe the different study characteristics that generate the clinical evidence.
■ Describe the patients that were enrolled in the clinical studies, demographics and medical history.
■ Increase the statistical power for primary and secondary endpoints by pooling the individual study results.
■ Provide an overall measure of benefit (relative risk [RR], mean difference [MD], etc.).
■ Assess the consistency of the results of the studies, in other words, to assess heterogeneity.
■ Explain variations across different studies in magnitude and direction of relative effect.

- Assess the overall strength of a body of evidence, by using a tool such as GRADE.
- Identify data gaps.
- Provide suggestions for future research.
- Highlight the merits for future research.

The list of objectives was taken from the *Cochrane Handbook* (Higgins and Green 2009), which is an important reference for an overview of systematic reviews and meta-analyses.

The overall quality of the systematic review and meta-analysis depends on the quality of the search strategy, which we previously mentioned should be conducted by an experienced information specialist with a peer-reviewed search strategy. In addition, the quality of the evidence depends ultimately on the quality of the trials or observational studies that were conducted. The trials that are required for regulatory approval for drugs may be high quality, whereas the trials or other evidence to evaluate educational programs may be less quality, where quality of each study is assessed by an appropriate checklist. Nonetheless, a systematic approach to identify the studies and a systematic approach to conduct the meta-analysis will establish to the reviewers the quality of the approach to evaluate the combined body of evidence.

Initial Steps before a Meta-Analysis

After the search strategy has been executed, there is usually a minimum of two major steps and a few minor steps that must occur to finalize the list of included studies before we can conduct the meta-analysis. After the search has been executed, the full citations, including abstracts, keywords and author affiliations, are entered automatically into an electronic database, such as Reference Manager, Refworks or Citation Manager.

The next step is to screen with two independent reviewers for inclusion criteria such as the specific drugs included and the study design e.g. randomized controlled trial (RCT). This level 1 screening is often conducted based on the title and abstracts only; any differences in reviewer's choice of included studies are resolved by consensus or third reviewer, and the Cohen's kappa statistic should be provided. This typically yields about 10%–20% of the publications that will move onto level 2 screening, which is a review of the full-text articles by two independent reviewers, with similar or more refined inclusion criteria, such as study population as well as drugs and study design.

After consensus review at level 2 screening of full-text articles, with kappa estimated, a few more small steps are helpful. First, there should a check of the references in each final approved article to see if there were any missed studies. Obtaining a few articles from the bibliographic citations is common, whereas finding many new articles indicates a weak search strategy or screening process. Next, the articles must be reviewed to see if there is duplication or overlap of clinical trials, to ensure that each piece of evidence provides unique information. For example, a large multicentre trial may produce one publication of the trial, and there may be separate publications of each centre's results, with the multicentre evidence being preferred for meta-analysis. In addition, some trials have publications for the results at different time points, for different subgroups or for different outcomes. Each of these publications can be used for sensitivity analysis for time period or subgroups, whereas the main results are obtained from the most clinically relevant time point and overall patient population.

After all the studies have been identified, the data can then be abstracted onto paper and then into Microsoft Excel or Access or similar review software, or directly into the software, with data entry being double checked for errors or omissions. One final step occurs before the analysis can begin, and that is to deal with missing data parameters such as missing mean effect or, more often, the missing standard deviations. Instead of omitting the study because of lack or relevant data, it is more conventional to apply different strategies for different situations to estimate the missing data parameters (see Chapter 9).

A Comment on Frequentist and Bayesian Approaches

After completing the above steps to identify the literature, there is a choice between the two distinct approaches to conducting meta-analysis: frequentist and Bayesian (Ades et al. 2006; Egger, Smith, and Phillips 1997). The frequentist approach combines the evidence, assuming that all of the evidence represents a collective guess for the unknown estimate for the benefit of treatments for the disease. Bayesian analysis, however, sees the new trial evidence as being additive to the collective knowledge that was established before the abstracted evidence was pooled and estimated. The collective knowledge (and not an estimate) that existed before the new study evidence could be clinical opinions, results from different types of studies such as observational evidence or from earlier trial evidence, or an acknowledgement that nothing is known. The past collective knowledge is referred to as a *prior*, and when combined with the new study evidence, referred to as *data*, it will create a *posterior* or final estimate.

The choice of the prior is a common and fair criticism of Bayesian methods, and only when there is transparency and justification of the prior, the results are possibly acceptable. Despite the potential for questionable use of priors, there are two important benefits of using Bayesian methods. The first benefit is that data from different sources can be combined, whereas the frequentist methods suggest only pooling similar evidence. For example, if there are large registries and small RCTs, the overall estimate can be derived using Bayesian methods. The second benefit of Bayesian methods is that the interpretation of the statistical results is stronger, as an estimate of the truth, and this along with a detailed explanation of Bayesian methods is discussed in Chapter 5.

Steps in a Meta-Analysis

Once the articles have been identified, the analytic steps to conduct the meta-analysis begin after we have compiled the study evidence. To communicate the breadth of evidence, it is customary to create 'Table 1: Study Design and Characteristics of Patients for Included Studies' (Moher 2009). This table (or appendix) should list important study characteristics (location, year, sample size, duration of follow-up, practice setting, etc.), patient characteristics (age, sex, risk factors for the disease such as duration of disease and wound size) and study inclusion and exclusion criteria. All of these data can be used later to conduct sensitivity analysis or risk-adjusted analysis.

As a practical rule, we also create a table of outcomes from the studies to identify commonality to guide our analytic strategy. This table is never reported in the clinical literature, but we find it very helpful for internal communication with our sponsors to provide the scope of analysis: the number of studies for each outcome, time point and study population. After the scope has been identified and confirmed, we can begin the steps of the analysis.

1. Define the type of data that is available for analysis for each outcome (e.g. continuous, categorical, binary [yes/no]), and if necessary re-estimate the study results to create data that can be meta-analysed.
2. Select the appropriate outcome measure (RR, MD, sensitivity, area under curve, etc.) (see Appendices I and II for formulas and examples).

3. Conduct the preliminary analysis with an assessment of heterogeneity.
4. Investigate the source of heterogeneity and make adjustments for heterogeneity as sensitivity analyses by performing subgroup analysis, removing influential outliers or risk-adjusted analysis with meta-regression.
5. Assess publication bias with visual plots and statistical tests, if there are a sufficient number of studies for each outcome.
6. Assess the overall strength of evidence and the strength of risk of bias for each study, by using an assessment tool such as GRADE (Brozek et al. 2009) or Cochrane's Risk of Bias or similar assessment tool (Armijo-Olivo et al. 2012).

Step 1: Identify the Type of Data for Each Outcome

There are many possible ways to classify data and we will try to decipher the multiple taxonomy to guide the choice of data to conduct a meta-analysis. One way to classify data is to specify that data can be either quantitative or qualitative, and our focus is on quantitative data. It is possible that qualitative data can be transformed into quantitative data for analysis, such as the presence of a comment or not, or choose from a list of factors. However, in order to combine the data across studies, we must have data that are quantitative or have been transformed into quantitative data.

At the next level of description of the types of data, we can specify that data are continuous or categorical, which are the common terms in economics or sociology. Continuous data are the common clinical measures such as blood pressure, weight or age, and include any variable that may have decimal places, whereas categorical data have multiple non-numeric responses. Examples of categorical data would be levels of pain: severe, moderate, mild or absent. Other examples would be ethnicity or hair colour with every individual falling into one of the categories (collectively exhaustive) and only one category (mutually exclusive). Also included in categorical analysis is the special case of a binary variable, which has only two categories, often yes or no, indicating presence or absence of an event or factor.

A finer taxonomy for data includes the NOIR set for nominal, ordinal, interval and ratio (Table 3.2) (Whitley and Ball 2002). Nominal values are categories that do not have order or rank and would include ethnicity, hair colour, genotype or address. When the categories can be ranked, data are considered ordinal, which would include levels of pain. When the data have

Table 3.2 NOIR Classification of Quantitative Variables

Data Category	Data Type (NOIR)	Description
Categorical	Nominal	No order of categories Example: genotype
	Ordinal	Categories can be ranked high to low Example: pain levels
Continuous	Interval	Equal distance between intervals Can have negative values Example: change scores
	Ratio	Interval plus zero means an absence Examples: weight, blood pressure

Note: Binary (yes/no) is a special case of a nominal categorical variable that is usually placed in the NOIR classification. All categories are mutually exhaustive (each subject's response can be in only one category) and collectively exclusive (all subjects' responses must fit into one of the categories). Standard meta-analysis can be conducted on interval, ratio and binary data.

equal difference between the categories so that the difference between two values is equally meaningful, data are considered interval. These include the variables of temperature or a change score where a negative value can occur. The final type of variable is called a ratio variable, and this occurs when zero indicates a true absence, such as with height, weight, serum load and cholesterol level.

One purpose to classify the data is to identify the appropriate measures of central tendency, which is most often reported as an arithmetic mean or median. Data that are nominal should not be reported as arithmetic mean or median because the order of the responses can be scrambled. When data are ordinal with a defined order, the mean should also not be reported because it assumes equal distances between all the responses. Instead the median can be reported, but even then the preferred measure is the frequency counts for each level of response.

For meta-analysis, the required measures must be available as binary (dichotomous) or continuous variables (interval or ratio) (Higgins and Green 2009). More advanced statistical techniques have been proposed to deal with the different types of data, but these techniques are rarely used. The key then is to change any variable into binary, interval or ratio. The continuous measures of interval and ratio scales are already available in the correct form, but the nominal and ordinal categories are a bit trickier. For nominal categories, a series of new binary variables can be created for each category or groups of categories. For example, if the variable was genotype and the unique responses were A, B, C and D, the four new variables for genotype A (Y/N), genotype B (Y/N) and so on can be created. If some of the categories can be grouped, for example, if A and C genotypes have a high risk of cancer, the new variable could be genotype A or C (Y/N). For ordinal categories, the usual method is to create a cut-off for the ranked levels, such as presence of category above the lowest level (Y or N), at a conventional level that has clinical meaning. For example, you can create a variable for presence or absence of 'severe pain', or presence or absence of 'severe or moderate pain', or presence or absence of 'any pain'. The choice of level of cut-off depends on the availability of data at each level and the clinical opinion that a negative or positive response is indicative of benefit of therapy.

Step 2: Select an Appropriate Outcome Measure

Once data have been converted to continuous or dichotomous variables, we need to specify the meta-analysis outcome to create in the meta-analysis. provide a discussion of confidence intervals in Chapter 9. For dichotomous outcomes, the options are RR, odds ratio or risk difference (RD) (Table 3.3) (Bland and Altman 2000), and for continuous measures, the options are MD and standardized mean difference (SMD). The calculation for dichotomous data is presented with probabilities, where $P1$ is the probability of the event in the new treatment group ($P1 = 10/100 = 0.10$ or 10%) and $P2$ is the probability of the event in the standard of care ($P2 = 8/100 = 0.08$ or 8%). Occasionally, the number needed to treat (NNT) is estimated by 1/RD.

The choice of the outcome in HTA research is limited by the purpose of providing an estimate of the relative effect between each treatment. Because of this requirement, the benefit of a new treatment relative to natural history can be easily estimated with an RR for dichotomous data.

There are differences between odds ratios and RRs, for magnitude of effect and width of confidence interval. Odds ratio will give a more extreme result than RR and have wider confidence intervals. If the RR for an analysis was 0.85, the odds ratio will be lower than that value. In the

Table 3.3   Different Summary Outcome Measures for Event Data

Single-Study Outcome Data		
	New Treatment (N = 100)	Standard of Care (N = 100)
Event (yes)	10	8
No event (no)	90	92
Summary Outcome	*Description*	
RR	P1/P2 (10/100)/(8/100) = 10/8 = 1.25	
OR	(P1/[1 − P1])/(P2/[1 − P2]) (10/90)/(8/92) = 0.111/0.087 = 1.28	
RD	P1 − P2 (10/100) − (8/100) = 10%−8% = 2%	

P1 = proportion of patient with event in new treatment = 10/100 = 10%.

P2 = proportion of patient with event in standard of care = 8/100 = 8%.

NNT = 1/RD = 1/2% = 50.

OR, odds ratio.

above example, the odds ratio was 1.28, which is more extreme than the RR of 1.25. In addition, the confidence interval for an odds ratio will be wider than the confidence interval at for an RR.

The use of RR and odds ratio for an overall effect and for subgroup effects should be examined for the problem of Simpson's Paradox. Simpson's Paradox refers to the situation that the overall effect can be completely different and outside the range of all subgroup analyses. For example, for two subgroups the new drug may look unfavourable compared to standard of care, but the overall effect can produce an overall pooled estimate that the new drug looks favourable compared to standard of care. Because there is a choice to present the overall effect, or selective subgroups, or all subgroups, there is an option to present a favourable estimate of effect for a new drug.

The biggest problem that occurs for dichotomous data is the presence of zeroes in the denominator of the ratio. For example, if the number of favourable events for the new drug was 5 out of 100 patients, and 0 event for 100 patients for the placebo group, the estimate of RR would be (5/100)/(0/100), which, because we are dividing by zero, is an undefined number. There are four options to deal with this. The first option is to change the outcome measure to patients without favourable events to create an RR of (95/100)/(100/100) = 0.95. This is the easiest to do, but harder to interpret, with the estimate suggesting that the new drug is less likely to not have the favourable event.

A second option is to apply a correction factor by adding 0.5 to each cell, generating an RR of (5.5/100.5)/(0.5/100.5) = 11. The problem with this method is that when the studies are small, adding 0.5 can create an unreasonably artificial large magnitude of effect. Alternatively, the correction factor can be a smaller fraction than 0.5, or ideally the expected average of the event rates in the placebo group, so that the rate for the placebo group for the trial with the zeroes will equal the other studies' average for the placebo group.

Another suggested method is to use the Peto odds ratio, which adjusts for zero effects, or if there are many studies with zero outcomes. The fourth way to deal with the problem is to change the outcome measure to the RD. Although this is not as easy to deal with in the economic model, it will produce an outcome that makes sense. The estimation of an RD allows the estimation of the NNT, which is 1/RD. In the above example, the NNT would be 1 divided by 2% = 50. This suggests that instead of treating 50 patients with Drug B, you could treat them with Drug A and this would lead to one less event for the 50 patients.

Outcomes for Continuous Data

There are two options for continuous data, MD and SMD. When all of the studies use the same scale, the pooled estimate of the MD makes sense. When the scales used to create the same clinical outcome are different, the SMD makes sense. For example, if there were two studies that reported pain but used different pain scales, one scale out of 30 and the other out of 100, each created with different questions, it is unlikely that the scales will be perfectly correlated and you cannot simply multiply one scale by a factor to derive the other scale, unless the mapping is well established. Instead, we can use the SMD that takes each measurement and creates the standardized score (z-score, i.e. number of standard deviations) as an outcome measure, which can then be pooled. The problem with the SMD is that the final measure cannot be converted back onto the original scale because the magnitude of effect will be different for each scale used. An SMD of 2.1

standard deviations will likely have a larger effect on the pain scale out of 100. Instead, the SMD is useful in detecting whether statistical significance is observed.

Step 3: Conduct the Preliminary Analysis with an Assessment of Heterogeneity

Weighting of Each Study

The estimate of relative effect is first created for each study and then the overall pooled effect is estimated with relative weighting for each study, where each study has a different impact on the overall result. If there was no special weighting, the overall effect is the simple average of effects, which is problematic because studies vary by study size and precision of the estimate. The default weighting for a meta-analysis is the inverse variance weighting, where each study is weighted by the inverse variance (1/variance).

In statistical jargon, inverse variance weighting of the mean effects produces an estimate that is considered a 'best linear unbiased estimator' or 'BLUE' of the overall mean. The best is the selection of the measure of central tendency, using the arithmetic mean versus a different outcome such as the median, which will produce the smallest overall level of variance, when we use inverse variance weighting. The estimate is *linear* because we are dealing with simple means, and being unbiased is assumed. However, a biased estimate can occur if there is heteroskedasticity, that is, the estimates for each study differ in the amount of variance that is produced and linearly related to one of the covariates. Similar to this is the term *heterogeneity*, which implies that the estimates differ between studies. Unless the heteroskedasticity (or heterogeneity) is dealt with in an appropriate manner, the overall mean effect may be biased. With heteroskedasticity, a correction in the weighting of each study is applied to create an unbiased estimate, but dealing with heterogeneity implies adding the variance that occurs between studies to create an overall effect, a random effects model.

Another option for weighting is the Mantel–Haenszel (M–H) weighting, which is similar to inverse variance weighting except that the weight for each study it is the harmonic mean between the two study treatment arms, whereas inverse variance applies an arithmetic weight for the variance for the two arms within a study. The result is that the M–H weighting will down-weight studies that have different sizes in each treatment arm and has the effect of giving more weight to smaller studies. When the studies being pooled have similar sizes, and the two arms of each study are of equal size, there is little difference between inverse weighting and M–H weighting.

Random or Fixed Effects

We suggest that meta-analysis should always be conducted with random effects model instead of fixed effects model (Dias et al. 2013; Higgins and Thompson 2002); however, some researchers may disagree (Grutters et al. 2013; Ramaekers, Joore, and Grutters 2013). A random effects model adds the between-study variance into the overall estimate to create an estimate with a wider confidence interval than a fixed effects analysis, and thus is always more conservative. A fixed effects analysis does not add the between-study variance into the overall estimate that creates smaller confidence intervals, and there is a greater chance of producing a statistically significant result.

Fixed effects analysis is very restrictive in assuming that the only difference in estimates between studies is strictly due to chance, which assumes that any slight variation in the PICO (ST) is not systematically important. Any variation in the patient's characteristics, how the intervention or comparators were applied, how the outcomes were measured, the setting and time are all not important. Random effects assumes that the studies can vary randomly by these factors that may lead to heterogeneity, which should be incorporated in the estimates. The variation in the effects follows a distribution called the random effects distribution.

The DerSimonian and Laird approach to estimating random effects is the most common method and was originally developed for dichotomous data. In this simplest version of random effects, each study receives an adjusted weight based on the amount of variance that the study has away from the central mean. The weight adjusted for random effects is

$$W(\text{adjusted}) = \frac{1}{(1/\text{weight}) - \text{tau}^2}$$

Tau^2 measures the variability between treatment effects. If tau$^2 = 0$, then the random effects are equivalent to fixed effects. It is simplest to think of this two-step process. In the first step, each study is weighted by its inverse variance, and the overall effect is pooled along with the overall estimate of variance. Each study's estimate of effect is then compared to the pooled mean effect; any variation between each study and the pooled effect is considered between-study variation, or tau^2, and this extra variation is estimated and applied to each study to create the new weight for random effects.

Testing for Heterogeneity

Two important statistics have been established to investigate heterogeneity, Cochran's Q and I^2. In fact, the two statistics are related but put on different scales (Higgins and Thompson 2002). Cochran's Q is an estimate of heterogeneity estimated with a chi-squared distribution, where the chi-squared value can be compared to expected chi-squared values to create a p-value. I^2 is simply [$(Q - \text{d.f.})/\text{d.f.}$], where d.f. is the difference of the number of studies and 1 (d.f. = $n - 1$) with I^2 ranging from 0% to 100% (Table 3.4).

The problem with the test statistic Q is that when a small number of studies are available, the test has low power to detect heterogeneity, and rules such as when $n < 5$ ignore Q, or $n < 15$ question the results of Q have been proposed. It is generally agreed that for the low-powered test, we should use a p-value of .10 instead of .05. In addition, when there are a large number of studies ($n > 30$), the Q test may have high power to detect heterogeneity which may not be clinically important.

Because of these issues, the Q statistic is still reported, but not relied upon (as much) for inference. Many researchers have switched to focusing on the I^2 statistic, which describes the percentage of variation across studies, which is due to heterogeneity rather than chance (i.e. how much heterogeneity). The value of I^2 depends on the magnitude and direction of effects and the strength of heterogeneity (chi-squared).

Table 3.4 Cochrane Handbook Levels of Heterogeneity Defined by I^2

I^2 Range	Heterogeneity Level
0% < I^2 < 40%	Low
30% < I^2 < 60%	Moderate
50% < I^2 < 90%	Substantial
75% < I^2 < 100%	Considerable

Note: Notice that the confidence intervals overlap. Classification of heterogeneity level should also take into consideration the number of studies, study size and study diversity.

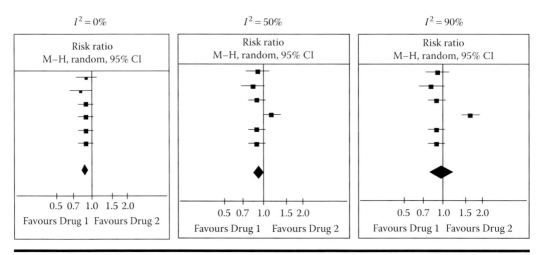

Figure 3.1 Forest plots with different I^2 values for low (left), moderate (middle) and considerable (right) heterogeneity. (CI, confidence interval.)

We can see in the example (Figure 3.1) that when we have 50% heterogeneity, there will be studies that have confidence intervals that do not overlap completely, whereas in this example, 90% heterogeneity suggests that the confidence intervals tend to separate. The degree of overlap and separation that leads to different levels of heterogeneity varies, but the broad rules of mostly overlapping, some overlapping and separation should be observed with low, moderate and high levels of heterogeneity. A further statistic that is becoming more common is the confidence interval for the I^2 statistic.

Step 4: Adjustment for Heterogeneity

Once heterogeneity has been measured, there are a few options on what to do next. One important consideration is that when the I^2 reaches greater than 90%, it is questionable if the studies should be pooled at all. This is important given the effect of the between-study variance on the estimate of I^2.

$$I^2 = \frac{\text{Between-study variance}}{\text{Between-study variance} + \text{within-study variance}}$$

When $I^2 = 100$, there is essentially little within-study variance, and all the variance is created by the between-study variance, suggesting that the studies vary too much to be pooled. Meanwhile, it is considered appropriate to

Table 3.5 Options on How to Deal with Heterogeneity

Ignore heterogeneity
Random effects model
Remove outliers
Subgroup analysis
Meta-regression adjustment

investigate the sources of heterogeneity when the I^2 above 50% and to make adjustment for the heterogeneity. At 50%, there is substantial or considerable heterogeneity, and there is an equal amount of between-study variability and within-study variability.

When heterogeneity is discovered, there are a few options (Table 3.5). First, we can simply ignore the heterogeneity, but this is not adequate with the statistical options that are available. If the heterogeneity is low, or when we have only two studies, nothing should be or can be done. When there is some low or moderate heterogeneity, we can incorporate heterogeneity into a random effects model. For substantial or considerable heterogeneity, we can remove outliers, conduct subgroup analyses or adjust for the heterogeneity in a meta-regression.

Finding a study, that is an outlier, that contributes to heterogeneity is an exercise in trial and error. Each study can be removed one at a time and placed back to assess each study sequentially. We then remove the study that contributed most to heterogeneity. If there is still moderate to severe heterogeneity, a new series of trial-and-error removals of studies will detect the source of the residual heterogeneity. After we have identified the outliers(s) that have contributed to heterogeneity, we must conduct a qualitative assessment of why the outlier is different from the other studies based on any apparent differences in 'Table 1: Study Design and Characteristics of Patients for Included Studies' (Moher 2009). We can continue to remove outliers until the I^2 is below 50%, which is an arbitrary number that we apply.

A rare occurrence is that the outlier that is removed may in fact be the most important influential study. This could occur when there are many poor-quality studies and there is only one high-quality pivotal study conducted, which then would be an outlier from the rest of the studies. Clinical opinion may be needed to identify if the studies that are removed to reduce heterogeneity are more important than the remaining studies.

After inspection of heterogeneity in the forest plot, we may find that a group of studies have different study results, and these studies are clearly different from the other studies in their study design or patient characteristics. We then could conduct a subgroup analysis on the remaining studies, and always on the composite, the studies removed. One important note for subgroup analysis in meta-analysis is that it is very difficult to pre-specify all potential subgroup analyses. We can pre-specify that in addition to the overall pooled estimates, we will conduct subgroup analysis selecting studies based on the study quality (according to a checklist), year of publication, study size or risk status of patients. More often than not, we do not have enough studies to conduct subgroup analysis based on all of the pre-specified choices, and an assessment of heterogeneity will guide us to detect the source of heterogeneity that was not pre-specified. Thus, *post-hoc* subgroup analysis is quite common and not penalized similar to *post-hoc* analysis in clinical trials.

A final set of procedures is available to adjust for heterogeneity, commonly called meta-regression (Dias et al. 2013; Higgins and Thompson 2004). Meta-regression is the technical term used for a regression conducted with data from a meta-analysis that includes a random effects (between-study variance) component. In a meta-regression, like all regressions, there are two functions of the regression: first, to test for a statistical significant effect and magnitude of a covariate, or second, to make a prediction that is risk adjusted. Most meta-analyses use meta-regression to test for significance of a covariate, but predictions for subgroups are important in an HTA context (Hopkins et al. 2008). We will demonstrate this, as part of our example. There are simple types of meta-regression, such as adding a single or few covariates, and more advanced types of meta-regression, such as hierarchical modelling.

Step 5: Assess Publication Bias

Publication bias occurs when publications that are available in the literature provide one side of a story, with journals often publishing new articles that have important statistical findings (Montori, Smieja, and Guyatt 2000). This would exclude studies that had non-significant study results. After all, who would want to read an article about a new type of drug, only to find that the conclusion of the study was that the drug may not work? Other than the presence of a statistical significant result increasing publication bias, there is also the chance that positive statistical findings will precede a confirmatory future study that creates an opposite result. In either case, there is a danger that the available published literature will not represent the true effect (Sutton et al. 2000). There are two ways to assess publication bias: either visually with plots, such as funnel or L'Abbe, or with a statistical test.

A funnel plot presents the overall treatment effect on the *x*-axis and a measure of weight on the *y*-axis. It assumes that the largest studies will be near the average and highest point, and small studies will be spread on both sides of the average. With the funnel plot, the overall symmetry around the main effect is investigated visually with the help of the 95% confidence intervals, and where a skewed distribution exits, publication bias may be present. The funnel plot requires a minimum of 10–15 studies to create a reasonable image that creates an overall pattern.

The L'Abbe plot presents a visual interpretation of the effect in the two treatment arms, with the *y*-axis usually representing the new treatment and the *x*-axis representing the standard of care arm. Each study is represented by a circle, with the size of the circle representing the study weight such as overall sample size. On the L'Abbe plot are a line of equality, where the two treatments are equal, and a line with the overall measure of effect, such as the pooled RR.

Any of the forest, funnel or L'Abbe plots may display publication bias and indicate outliers, given sufficient number of studies, but this is left to the research team's artistic ability to find the outliers or to detect the pattern of bias. To support any visual inspection, a statistical test is necessary. The formal test of publication bias is conducted with an Egger test for RR, or if there is imbalance between the sizes of treatment and control groups, Harbord test is conducted for odds ratio, or when there are large treatment effects, few events per trial, or all trials are of similar sizes (Egger, Smith, and Phillips 1997). Both apply a regression of the effect size (estimate divided by its standard error) against precision (reciprocal of the standard error of the estimate) and then test if the regression constant = 0. These tests are easily conducted in STATA.

Step 6: Assess the Overall Strength of Evidence

Regardless of whether, the analysis of included studies is narrative or quantitative, the *Cochrane Handbook* (Higgins and Green 2009) provides a general framework for synthesis by considering the four following questions:

1. What is the direction of effect?
2. What is the size of effect?

3. Is the effect consistent across studies?
4. What is the strength of evidence for the effect?

Meta-analysis can be used to address these four questions if comparisons being made in the primary study designs (e.g. case control, prospective cohort) are similar and the reported outcome measures (e.g. odds ratios, risk ratios) are consistent. If the studies are too diverse in terms of study design, study population, exposures and/or outcomes, meta-analysis may not be feasible. If meta-analysis is not appropriate, reviewers can perform a narrative synthesis using subjective (rather than statistical) methods to address questions 1–4. In a narrative synthesis, the method used for each stage should be followed systematically. Bias may be introduced if the results of one study are inappropriately stressed over those of another. The Economic and Social Research Council (ESRC) Methods Programme Guidance on the Conduct of Narrative Synthesis in Systematic Reviews is one example of a framework to conduct a narrative synthesis (Pope, Mays, and Popay 2006).

To assess the strength of evidence, it is customary to follow the GRADE checklist for each study and to provide an overall assessment of the strength of evidence. In addition, other measures, such as the risk of bias tool, provide a checklist of items that, if implemented in the RCT, would lead to a possible reduction in bias. If many studies miss one or more items, a reduction from high- to moderate- to low-quality evidence is stated.

An Example of Meta-Analysis

Consider the fake data for nine trials identified that compared Drug A with Drug B to prevent a bad event (such as myocardial infarction) (Table 3.6). The publications of the trials were reported from 1990 to 2014, and the size of the trials ranged from 200 (100 allocated to each drug) to 1800 patients (900 per drug). The table lists the study IDs for our meta-analysis, the study name (this could be Hopkins 1990) and a variable for risk. The risk variable, which can be used for subgroup analysis or risk-adjusted analysis, can be any measure such as the presence of a different inclusion/exclusion criteria or co-morbidity (prior history of disease, previous myocardial infarction, age, sex, other diseases). In our example, the risk variable was either 1 or 0, implying that all subjects for each study were either always with the risk or always without the risk. For Drug A and Drug B, we list the number of

Table 3.6 Data from Nine Studies Collected for the Purpose of Meta-Analysis

			Drug A		Drug B	
Studyid	*Name*	*Risk[a]*	*Events 1*	*Total Patients 1*	*Events 2*	*Total Patients 2*
1	Study-1 1990	1	10	100	10	100
2	Study-2 1994	0	10	200	30	200
3	Study-3 2000	0	30	300	40	300
4	Study-4 2010	1	10	100	50	400
5	Study-5 2012	1	60	500	30	500
6	Study-6 2001	0	60	600	90	600
7	Study-7 2010	0	60	700	100	700
8	Study-8 2014	1	75	800	70	800
9	Study-9 2009	0	60	900	100	900

[a] 1, risk factor present; 0, risk factor absent.

events and the total number of patients in each arm. Table 3.7 provides the STATA code that will do everything we need for the meta-analysis, and we will work through the code and output subsequently.

In our example, data reside in a Microsoft Excel worksheet in the top rows with no blank spaces above the data, and the variable labels are in the first row and the data begin in the second row. The import command can bring the data into STATA, or this can be accomplished with the Import tab in STATA. To complete the meta-analysis, we rely on the commands `metan`, `labbe`, `metafunnel`, `metareg` and `metabias` (Harris et al. 2008), which can be obtained within STATA if not already installed, by typing 'findit metan' and following the directions for free installation with Help menus for explanation and examples.

The code creates the variables that we need for the meta-analysis, and because we have events and total patients, we need to calculate the number of patients without events (NoEvents1, NoEvents2). We also need the natural log of the RR and its standard error, because the log transformation is required for better fit of the data for some of the tests. First, we conduct a meta-analysis with random effects and then with fixed effects, with M–H weighting. For inverse weighting, the options fixed must be switched to fixedi and random must be switched to randomi.

Table 3.7   STATA Code for Meta-Analysis

```
import excel "data.xls", sheet("Sheet1") firstrow

gen NoEvents1 = Total1-Events1

gen NoEvents2 = Total2-Events2

gen logRR = ln((Events1/Total1)/(Events2/Total2))

gen selogRR = sqrt(1/Events1 +1/Events2 -1/Total1 -1/Total2)

* random effects and fixed effects meta-analyses

metan Events1 NoEvents1 Events2 NoEvents2, rr random
textsize(150)

metan Events1 NoEvents1 Events2 NoEvents2, rr fixed

* construct a L'Abbe plot

labbe Events1 NoEvents1 Events2 NoEvents2, xlabel(0,0.25,0.5)
ylabel(0,0.25,0.5) null rr(.78)

* assess for outliers

metareg logRR, wsse(selogRR)

predict yhat1, xbu

qnorm yhat1, mlabel(STUDYID)

* make predictions after adjusting for covariates (Risk)

metareg logRR Risk, wsse(selogRR)

* unadjusted analysis

metan Events1 NoEvents1 Events2 NoEvents2 if Risk = =0, rr
random

metan Events1 NoEvents1 Events2 NoEvents2 if Risk = =1, rr
random

* adjusted analysis

metareg logRR Risk, wsse(selogRR)

predict yhat2, xbu

predict se, stdxbu

gen rr = exp(yhat2)

gen rr_upper = exp(yhat2+1.96*se)

gen rr_lower = exp(yhat2-1.96*se)

bysort Risk: sum rr rr_upper rr_lower
```

Table 3.7 (*Continued*) STATA Code for Meta-Analysis

```
* construct a Funnel plot and assess for publication bias
metafunnel logRR selogRR, egger
metabias Events1 NoEvents1 Events2 NoEvents2, egger
metabias Events1 NoEvents1 Events2 NoEvents2, harbord
```

Note: gen is the short acceptable form for generate, for generating a new variable.

Table 3.8 Summary of Results from Fixed Effects and Random Effects Meta-Analyses

Study	RR	95% Confidence Lower	95% Confidence Upper	Random Effects Weight (%)	Fixed Effects Weight (%)
1	1.000	0.435	2.297	2.04	6.90
2	0.333	0.167	0.663	6.12	8.35
3	0.750	0.480	1.171	8.16	11.38
4	0.800	0.421	1.521	4.08	8.87
5	2.000	1.314	3.045	6.12	11.71
6	0.667	0.491	0.906	18.37	13.20
7	0.600	0.443	0.812	20.41	13.25
8	1.071	0.785	1.462	14.29	13.15
9	0.600	0.442	0.815	20.41	13.20
Summary Estimate					
RR random	0.785	0.585	1.052	$p = .106$	
RR fixed	0.778	0.685	0.883	$p < .001$	

Note: Heterogeneity – Chi-squared 36.24 (d.f. = 8), $I^2 = 77.9\%$.

$p < .001$

RR, relative risk.

A few points emerge after the metan command was entered (Table 3.8). The relative study weights increase as the study sample size becomes larger, but there is an adjustment for precision. Study 6 has 1200 patients with a relative weight of 18.37% for random effects, whereas Study 3 has 600 patients with a relative weight of 8.16% (or 44% of the weight of Study 6).

Also, there are important differences between random effects and fixed effects analyses. First, the pooled meta-analytic overall estimate of RR was not significant for random effects ($p = .106$), whereas the result was significant for fixed effects ($p < .001$) and the difference in the magnitude of RR was almost zero (random effects RR = 0.785 versus fixed effects RR = 0.778). This is generally true that the confidence interval for fixed effects will be smaller than that for random effects, because tau² is added to the random effects variance. Second, the relative weights for each study differ for the random effects and fixed effects analyses. Fixed effects apply a near equal weight for each study, whereas random effects add back the tau² to weights. Our forest plot from Tau STATA for the random effects analysis is presented in Figure 3.2. A similar forest plot can be obtained with Review Manager software.

Outliers

From the forest plot, we see the individual study estimates as the small squares and lines represting the confidence intervals, with the large diamond showing the overall effect (middle of the diamond) and its confidence

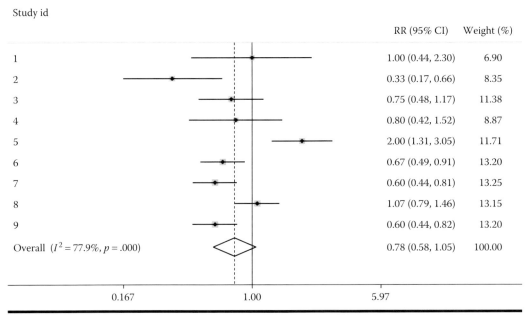

Figure 3.2 **Summary of forest plot. Each line represents a study, and the final line represents the overall effect, with the diamond representing the position of the overall effect and the 95% confidence interval (CI). Studyid 2 and 5 have CIs that are diverging from the other studies. Note: Weights are from random effects analysis.**

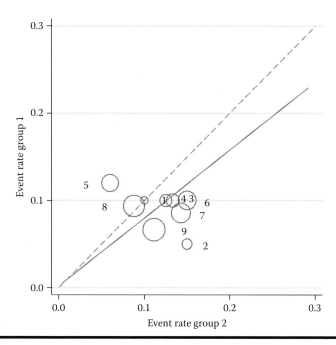

Figure 3.3 Summary of the L'Abbe plot. The dashed line indicates the line of equal effect between treatments 1 and 2. The solid line proceeds through the point of meta-analytic RR. Circle sizes represent the relative weights for meta-analysis.

interval. Two studies that appear to be different than the rest are studyid 2 and 5. Both of these studies may be contributing to an overall heterogeneity. A visual inspection for heterogeneity shows that the confidence intervals for both studies are not fully overlapping with the pooled effect.

The L'Abbe plot also confirms that studyid 2 and 5 are outliers from the other study results (Figure 3.3). Re-running the meta-analysis after removing studyid 2 or 5 should be conducted to see if the heterogeity falls from 77% to below 50%. Based on the qnorm plot, which assesses if each study follows a normal distribution relative to the mean effect, it appears that the studyid 5 may have a more important effect as an outlier (Figure 3.4).

Risk-Adjusted or Unadjusted Analysis

Because we have some heterogeneity, the reason why studyid 2 or 5 differs may be because of an explainable covariate such as risk. Studyid 5 has high-risk patients, whereas studyid 2 has low-risk patients. Then we should investigate whether the variable risk is an important covariate in a meta-regression (Harbord and Higgins 2008).

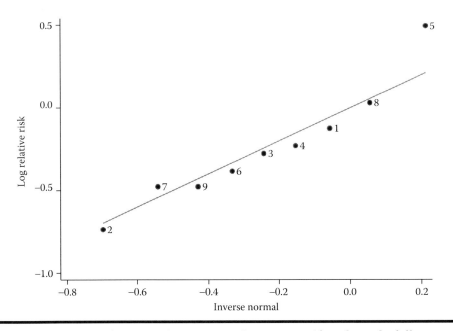

Figure 3.4 Summary of qnorm plot. qnorm plot assesses if each study follows a normal distribution relative to the mean effect. In STATA with meta-analysis, the qnorm plot's predicted values versus actual data when the study's estimates are ranked in order.

Based on this meta-regression (Table 3.9), it appears that risk is a significant predictor of the level of relative risk, $p = .011$. Because we are using aggregated study level data, we use a cut-off of 0.10 to assess the significance for covariates in a meta-regression. Moving from Risk level 0 to Risk level 1 increases the log of the RR (logRR) by 0.700.

The next steps after the `metareg` command are to make predictions and confidence intervals of RR for different levels of risk (Table 3.10). We then compare this result to the unadjusted results when we conduct subgroup analysis in the meta-analysis by risk. In this case, for the studies that have Risk = 0, the confidence intervals are narrower for the subgroup analysis than for the regression-adjusted analysis, whereas for Risk = 1, the confidence intervals are wider for the subgroup analysis than for the regression-adjusted analysis. The difference in the width of the confidence intervals is because the subgroup analysis still has heterogeneity within that category, which contributes tau² to the confidence interval. Thus, depending on the level of heterogeneity a stratified analysis may produce different widths of confidence intervals than regression-adjusted predictions. When the covariate is a continuous measure such as average patient BMI, years with disease, or publication date, the regression-adjusted prediction tends

Table 3.9 STATA Output from Meta-Regression Analysis, after Including Risk as a Covariate

Meta-regression number of observation = 9.

REML estimate of between-study variance tau^2 = 0.0239.

Percentage of residual variation due to heterogeneity I^2 = 41.55%.

Proportion of between-study variance explained adjusted *R*-squared = 85.89%.

With Knapp–Hartung modification.

logRR	Coefficient	Standard Error	t-Statistic	p-Value	95% CI Lower	95% CI Upper
Risk	0.701	0.202	3.46	.011	0.222	1.179
Constant	−0.497	0.122	−4.07	.005	−0.786	−0.208

logRR is the outcome of meta-regression, and the value of logRR without the risk factor is obtained from the constant. The total amount of between-study variance tau^2 is 0.0239, which in itself is not a meaningful estimate, such as I^2 = 41.55%. The adjusted *R*-squared is 85.89%, which will be high when the confidence intervals are narrow. The coefficient for risk and the overall effect are both significant, and the risk factor is positive, suggesting that the presence of the risk factor increases the relative risk.

CI, confidence interval; RR, relative risk.

Table 3.10 Comparison of RR with Subgroup Analysis and Risk-Adjusted Meta-Regression

	RR (95% CI) Risk = 0	RR (95% CI) Risk = 1
Subgroup analysis	0.615 (0.523, 0.724)	1.199 (0.797, 1.804)
Regression-adjusted analysis	0.609 (0.456, 0.814)	1.232 (0.877, 1.732)

Note: Unadjusted random effects overall RR: 0.785 (95% CI: 0.505–1.052).

CI, confidence interval.

to have a smaller width of the confidence intervals than for stratification subgroup analysis, which is useful for reducing uncertainty in the cost-effectiveness analysis (Table 3.10).

Publication Bias

The funnel plot of the standard error of logRR versus logRR suggests that there may be two outliers: one with a higher level of logRR and the other with a lower level of logRR, as we have seen earlier (Figure 3.5). The plot

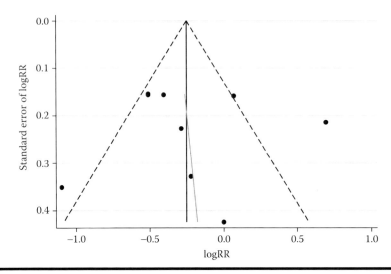

Figure 3.5   A funnel plot with pseudo 95% confidence intervals to assess publication bias (small-study effect). The peak of the triangle represents the point of the overall effect. There are two studies that are outside the 95% confidence intervals: one higher and one lower. The Egger line that is slanted backwards is indicating that the logRR increases as the weight decreases. This suggests that small studies may be more influential.

is mostly symmetrical (by quick inspection), but the Egger line is slightly slanted. The Egger line from the regression of selog RR versus logRR suggests that there is a slight increase in logRR (effect) with a decrease in selogRR (larger studies). The formal test of bias provides a p-value of .932 for the null hypothesis of small-study effects. A summary of important considerations is provided (Table 3.11).

Meta-Analysis of Diagnostic Accuracy Studies

The meta-analysis of diagnostic accuracy studies poses a unique statistical problem (Deeks, Bossuyt, and Gatsonis 2013), the possibility of four outcomes for any test subject. In most meta-analyses, we have the option of having an event or not having an event. With diagnostic accuracy, we have the result of the diagnostic test (positive or negative) and the true disease state (positive or negative). This creates four outcomes for a diagnostic test, listed in Table 3.12 as A, B, C and D.

Two events can happen with positive test result. Either a true positive (TP) (A) occurs when the test result is positive and the disease is true, or a

Table 3.11 Reviewer's Summary Notes on Proper Use of Meta-Analysis for Cost-Effectiveness Analysis

RR or odds ratio: RR is more directly applicable to cost-effectiveness analysis.
Random effects or fixed effects: Fixed effects assume that the PICO (ST) is near identical across studies, which is a rarely justified occurrence. Fixed effects may provide statistically significant findings, but the random effects estimate should also be provided.
High heterogeneity: Heterogeneity with $I^2 > 50\%$ should be explained by removing outliers or subgroup analysis.
Outliers: Outliers can be identified with a forest plot, a funnel plot, a L'Abbe plot or a qnorm plot.
Subgroups: Meta-regression can detect, with low power, if stratification should be conducted. The stratified results and the risk-predicted results may differ, and the confidence intervals may be larger or smaller.
Magnitude: A discussion of the magnitude of effect is essential, but is often overlooked. A statistically significant result is more likely to be published than a non-significant result, although an effect with sufficient magnitude is needed to justify changing clinical practice.

Table 3.12 Diagnostic Accuracy Outcomes

	Positive (+) Disease	Negative (−) Disease	Total
Positive (+) test	True positive (A)	False positive (B)	A + B
Negative (−) test	False negative (C)	True negative (D)	C + D
Total	A + C	B + D	A + B + C + D

Note: True positive (TP = A): the test result is positive and the disease is truly present.

False positive (FP = B): the test result is positive, but the disease is truly absent.

False negative (FN = C): the test result is negative and the disease is truly present.

True negative (TN = D): the test result is negative and the disease is truly absent.

The prevalence is the total number of positive cases = A + C.

The prevalence rate = (A + C)/(A + B + C + D).

false positive (FP) (B) occurs when the test result is positive but the disease is truly absent. Similarly, two events can happen with negative test results. Either a false negative (FN) (C) occurs when the test result is negative and the disease is true, or a true negative (TN) (D) occurs when the test result is negative and the disease is truly absent.

Table 3.13 Example of Diagnostic Accuracy Study

	Positive (+) Disease	*Negative (−) Disease*	*Total*
Positive (+) test	70	5	75
Negative (−) test	30	95	125
Total	100	100	200

The presence or absence of a disease is confirmed with a gold or reference standard, which is the highest quality established test for that disease, or by external adjudication of multiple factors, or in some cases ultimate tests such as an autopsy. In reality, the same statistical methods are applied when there is an absence of a gold standard, but the terminology and interpretation may differ. To summarize the relationship between test results and disease status, there are several summary measures each with a different purpose. For this, we will work through an example of 200 subjects given a new test and the presence of disease verified by a gold standard (Table 3.13).

Sensitivity (the proportion of persons with a disease who are correctly identified by the new test as having the disease) is $A/(A + C) = 70/(70 + 30) = 70\%$. Specificity (the proportion of persons without a disease who are correctly identified by the new test as not having the disease) is $D/(B + D) = 95/(95 + 5) = 95\%$. A test with high sensitivity is useful to rule out a disease, in that a high sensitivity would indicate that a negative test is likely to not have a disease (small C). Alternatively said, high sensitivity indicates that any true disease will likely be detected, and a negative test result is a strong result. A test with high specificity is useful to confirm a disease, in that there is little chance that a positive result will create a false positive (low B). Alternatively said, a high specificity indicates that any absence of disease will likely be detected, and a positive test result is a strong result. These suggestions for being a good test apply only when there are numerous positive and negative true cases, such as for a common disease. Sometimes there are two acronyms that are used to help remember diagnostic accuracy. A negative result with high sensitivity test will ensure ruling out a disease, with useful acronym SNout. A negative result with high specificity test will ensure ruling in a disease, with useful acronym SPin. However, a test with high sensitivity and poor specificity may be problematic for ruling a disease.

There are other measures that are useful for clinicians that are transformations of sensitivity and specificity, but these outcomes are not commonly pooled in a meta-analysis. These are listed in Appendices 1, 2 for reference only. One alternate measure that has become common in meta-analysis of diagnostic accuracy studies is the area under the curve (AUC) of a summary receiver operator curve (SROC). A receiver operator curve (ROC) can be created for every study and a meta-analysis generates an SROC. The math to create the SROC is a bit tricky, and we include this only as Appendix 1 for reference as well.

The AUC of the SROC is a non-specific measure of the ability of a test to diagnostic decision making. Consider three tests with equal AUC under the SROC but with different sensitivities and specificities (Table 3.14). Test 1 has high specificity, whereas Test 2 has high sensitivity and Test 3 has reasonable sensitivity and specificity. To be sure of the benefit of the new test's place in the diagnostic sequence, there are other diagnostic test measures that can be evaluated so that there is sufficient specificity for a high sensitivity and vice versa. In our example, the high positive predictive value (PPV) suggests that if positive test is found in Test 1, there is a 98.8% probability of the disease being positive (this is very high). For Test 2, if there is a negative result, there is 98.8% probability of the disease being absent (this is very high). Test 3 is inferior to either Test 1 or Test 2 for sensitivity or specificity, but Test 3 may be useful if it is a non-expensive, non-invasive test for a non-threatening disease, where confirmatory tests are expensive or invasive.

A meta-analysis of diagnostic accuracy studies will lead to a number of important decision impacts, which relate to the use of the diagnostic technology in practice. With increasing impact, we make decisions based on the following:

1. *Technical capacity*: Is the technology reliable across studies?
2. *Diagnostic accuracy*: What is sensitivity, specificity, and AUC of the SROC?
3. *Diagnostic impact*: Could the new test replace or is it an add-on to the current sequence of tests?
4. *Therapeutic impact*: Could the new test change treatment?
5. *Patient outcome*: Could the new test improve health outcomes?
6. *Cost-effectiveness*: Is the new test cost-effectiveness a replacement or add-on test?

The progression through the steps should be sequential (Newman et al. 2007).

One of the first assessments of the diagnostic test is the ability to be consistent. It would be worrisome for variations in diagnostic accuracy to occur across studies, which is detected with large confidence

Table 3.14 Three Tests with Similar AUC under the SROC

Test	True Positive	False Positive	True Negative	False Negative	Sensitivity (%)	Specificity (%)	AUC	Positive Predictive Value	Negative Predictive Value
1	80	1	99	20	80	99	0.895	0.988	0.832
2	99	20	80	1	99	80	0.895	0.832	0.988
3	89	10	90	11	89	90	0.895	0.899	0.891

Table 3.15   Diagnostic Accuracy and Economic Models

The diagnostic accuracy outcomes that are required to build an economic model are sensitivity and specificity, and disease prevalence. For every cell in the 2 × 2 table (true positive, false negative, true negative, false positive), the economic model must consider the cost and quality of life consequences. With every positive test result, there is a probability of receiving treatment (not always 100%) and a probability that the treatment will be successful (success is not always 100%). A poor assumption for economic models is that false negatives will never receive treatment, but in reality if the patient's disease progresses, the presence of the disease will be detected, treatment may occur and success may occur. The AUC of an SROC is nice to know for descriptive comparisons of two or more tests.

intervals for the estimates of diagnostic accuracy. Given consistent estimates, the next hurdle is to understand the place in therapy of the new test. If the new test has higher sensitivity or specificity, or reasonable diagnostic accuracy with lower costs, the test may replace an existing test or be used as a screening tool, respectively. To complete an HTA for a diagnostic test, the impact on costs and quality of life for all the four outcomes must be assessed. For positive cases that are identified (TP), there is a probability of receiving treatment and a probability of a successful treatment. It would be a weak economic model if it is assumed that all TP cases are treated and cured. Similarly, for the three other outcomes, FP, TN and FN, there are health consequences and probabilities of receiving treatment and probabilities of the treatment being successful. For example, for true cases that are not identified FN, there is a probability that the patient will go home and if symptoms become worse (before a negative outcome occurs), the patient will seek a second opinion or show up at the emergency room and receive more tests and subsequent medical care (Table 3.15).

Example of Meta-Analysis for Diagnostic Accuracy

In this example, we have 10 studies from which we have fake data to allow meta-analysis to derive the pooled estimates of sensitivity, specificity and AUC (Table 3.16). If the data exist as a Microsoft Excel file, we can import the data with the import function, assign the first row as the variable name and then conduct the analysis.

Table 3.16   Diagnostic Accuracy Outcomes from Included Studies, with Continuous Risk Factor (Effect Modifier)

Studyid	Risk	N	True Positive	False Positive	True Negative	False Negative
1	90	100	39	6	54	1
2	70	200	120	20	60	0
3	40	300	189	18	72	21
4	70	400	255	10	90	45
5	80	500	135	35	315	15
6	30	600	384	18	102	96
7	20	700	140	105	420	35
8	40	800	276	4	396	124
9	40	900	621	45	180	54
10	10	1000	702	88	132	78

Note: Risk factor is continuous measure with values between 0 and 100.

N, total number of patients.

STATA commands:

```
import excel "diag_accuracy_data.xls", sheet("Sheet1") firstrow
*Meta-analysis command
midas tp fp fn tn, res(all)
```

The statistical output using `midas` command with the results-all option, `res(all)`, provides a wealth of summary information (Table 3.17) (Dwamena 2007). First, we see that there are 10 studies, with 3330 positive disease cases (TP + FN) and 2170 negative disease cases (FP + TN), for an overall disease prevalence of 0.61.

Deviance, AIC, BIC and BICdiff are the measures of statistical fit of the overall model, and these measures are necessary if we wish to compare these results to a different model, such as removing an outlier, subgroup analysis or with meta-regression.

The weighted correlation between sensitivity and specificity was −0.54, indicating that as sensitivity increases, specificity will decline. For every 10-point rise in sensitivity, for example, from 80% to 90%, specificity will fall to 0.051%. Ideally, the specificity should rise as the sensitivity rises, according

Table 3.17   STATA Output from Diagnostic Accuracy Meta-Analysis from `midas` Command

Summary Data and Performance Estimates
Number of studies = 10
Reference-positive units = 3330
Reference-negative units = 2170
Pre-test probability of disease = 0.61
Deviance = 174.2
AIC = 184.2
BIC = 189.2
BICdiff = 295.7
Correlation (mixed model) = −0.54
Proportion of heterogeneity likely due to threshold effect = 0.29
Area under ROC, AUROC = 0.941 (0.876–0.973)
Heterogeneity (chi-square): LRT_Q = 275.553, d.f. = 2.000, LRT_p = 0.000
Inconsistency (I^2): LRT_I^2 = 99.3, 95% CI = (99.0–99.6)
Parameter estimate 95% CI
Sensitivity = 0.892 (0.824, 0.936)
Specificity = 0.861 (0.767, 0.921)
Positive likelihood ratio = 6.4 (3.8, 10.8)
Negative likelihood ratio = 0.13 (0.08, 0.20)
Diagnostic odds ratio = 51.3 (27.6, 95.5)

to a threshold level used to define a positive result. In this case, it is best to think of a laboratory test to detect a disease, such as *t*-score for bone mineral density. As the cut-off of the *t*-score is raised (more negative, because *t*-score is the number of standard deviations below normal for bone mineral density), this would lead to decreased sensitivity from setting a higher cut-off value, fewer disease cases and higher specificity, being easier to reject. For new tests, or redefining a new cut-off level based on new test equipment, this trade-off of sensitivity and specificity is captured in the ROC. The heterogeneity that exists across the sensitivity and specificity measures can be more related to a negative correlation than true heterogeneity within each scale ($0.29 = -0.54^2$). Not shown are the measures of between-study variability of sensitivity and specificity, because by themselves the numbers have no meaningful interpretation. Instead the correlations are used to estimate heterogeneity of I^2.

The overall measure of diagnostic accuracy is AUC that equals 0.941, and very high levels of heterogeneity $I^2 = 99.3\%$. Sensitivity analysis should be conducted to assess the importance that each study contributes to heterogeneity. The other estimates automatically reported are sensitivity = 0.892, specificity = 0.861, positive likelihood ratio = 6.4, negative likelihood ratio = 0.13 and diagnostic odds ratio = 51.3. Overall, the test appears to be of high quality with AUC = 0.941, but the test is similar to our example of Test 3 (from Table 3.14), where sensitivity and specificity are marginal, but the overall AUC is high. Also problematic are our LR+ of 6.4 where a value of 10 is an acceptable cut-off for positive confirmation of the disease and LR− = 0.13 where less than 0.10 is an acceptable cut-off for negative confirmation of the disease.

A closer look at the bivariate forest plot of sensitivity and specificity can be quickly conducted (Figure 3.6). Here, we can see that studyid 8 contributes to heterogeneity for sensitivity, whereas studyid 10 and 8 contribute to heterogeneity for specificity. The PPV is 91% and the negative predictive value (NPV) is 84%, suggesting that the test would be able to predict disease with a positive test and less sure with a negative result.

```
midas tp fp fn tn, id(STUDYID) ms(0.75) bfor(dss)
textscale(1.05)
```

The SROC is easily plotted with the `sroc(both)` option, where `both` refers to prediction and confidence intervals (Figure 3.7). We can identify our outliers studyid 10 and 8, and high sensitivity results of studyid 1 and 2.

```
midas tp fp fn tn, plot sroc(both)
```

In our dataset, there is a measure of risk, which is our covariate for different levels of a risk factor. This time, the covariate is a continuous measure, such as the mean pre-test probability of a disease ranging from 0 to 100. We run the `midas` command with `reg(Risk)` as the option.

```
midas tp fp fn tn, reg(Risk)
```

Data have been taken from the output and summarized in Table 3.18. In our assessment of risk as a covariate to explain diagnostic accuracy, the

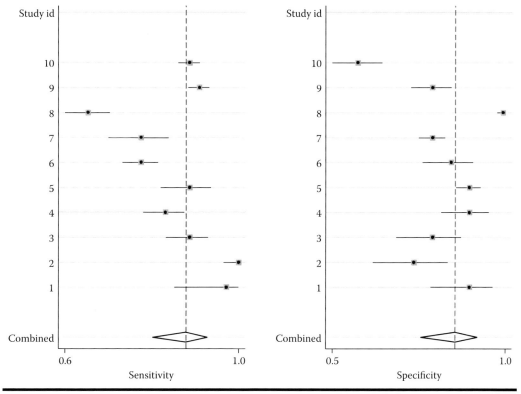

Figure 3.6   Bivariate summary of forest plot. The bivariate plot provides the summary of the evidence for sensitivity (left) and specificity (right). Notice that studyid 8 has low sensitivity and high specificity relative to the other studies.

meta-regression results estimated that risk was not a significant predictor of sensitivity ($p = .92$) or specificity ($p = .98$), but risk was a significant predictor for the joint measure ($p < .01$).

Hierarchical Summary Receiver Operator Curve

The `midas` command conducts the meta-analysis by fitting a regression bivariate model to separately estimate the pooled sensitivity and specificity. The estimate of AUC and the SROC plot are built upon the individual contributions of sensitivity and specificity. When we wish to model the diagnostic accuracy more formally as one model, we can specify the bivariate model with a hierarchical (mixed effects) SROC (HSROC). The HSROC estimation can be achieved with the `metandi tp fp fn tn` command. In the absence of a covariate, the `midas` and `metandi` commands produce equivalent results (Harbord and Whiting 2009).

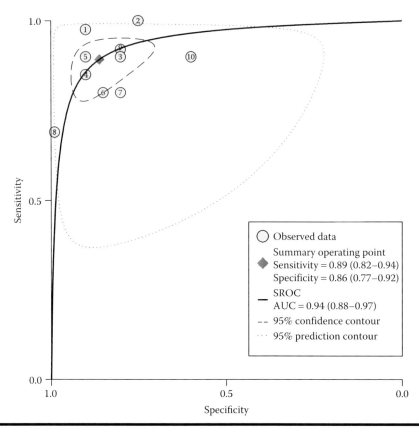

Figure 3.7 SROC with prediction and confidence contours. The solid line is the SROC that was created by the ROC regression. The diamond represents the point that is furthest to the top left and the maximum AUC point (0.94). The values of sensitivity and specificity correspond to the values derived from the bivariate forest plot.

Table 3.18 STATA Output from Diagnostic Accuracy Meta-Analysis from `midas` Command, with Risk Added as a Covariate

Measure	Value
Studies (*n*)	10
Sensitivity	0.89 (0.84–0.93)
p-Value for risk as a covariate for sensitivity	.96
Specificity	0.86 (0.78–0.92)
p-Value for risk as a covariate for sensitivity	.98
Joint model *I²*	0.83 (95% CI: 63, 100)
Joint model of *p*-value as a covariate	<.01

Summary

We have reviewed the traditional methods for conducting a meta-analysis where there are two or more studies that have similar PICO characteristics. The techniques that we have provided will handle most meta-analyses of clinical trial data. In Chapters 4 and 5, we introduce network meta-analysis and Bayesian methods to deal with the non-common problems of analyzing studies with different comparators and with different study designs.

References

Ades A.E., Sculpher M., Sutton A., Abrams K., Cooper N., Welton N., and Lu G. 2006. Bayesian methods for evidence synthesis in cost-effectiveness analysis. *PharmacoEconomics* 24 (1): 1–19.

Armijo-Olivo S., Stiles C.R., Hagen N.A., Biondo P.D., and Cummings G.G. 2012. Assessment of study quality for systematic reviews: A comparison of the Cochrane collaboration risk of bias tool and the effective public health practice project quality assessment tool: Methodological research. *Journal of Evaluation in Clinical Practice* 18 (1): 12–18.

Bland J.M., and Altman D.G. 2000. The odds ratio. *British Medical Journal* 320 (7247): 1468.

Brozek J.L., Akl E.A., Alonso-Coello P., Lang D., Jaeschke R., Williams J.W., Phillips B., Lelgemann M., Lethaby A., Bousquet J., Guyatt G.H., and Schunemann H.J. 2009. Grading quality of evidence and strength of recommendations in clinical practice guidelines. Part 1 of 3. An overview of the GRADE approach and grading quality of evidence about interventions. *Allergy* 64 (5): 669–677.

Higgins J., and Green S. (eds.) 2009. *Cochrane Handbook for Systematic Reviews of Interventions Version 5.0.2.* Copenhagen, Denmark: The Cochrane Collaboration. http://handbook.cochrane.org. Accessed on December 2, 2014.

Deeks J.J., Bossuyt P., and Gatsonis C. 2013. *Cochrane Handbook for Systematic Reviews of Diagnostic Test Accuracy Version 1.0.0.* The Cochrane Collaboration. http://srdta.cochrane.org/handbook-dta-reviews. Accessed on December 2, 2014.

Dias S., Sutton A.J., Welton N.J., and Ades A.E. 2013. Evidence synthesis for decision making 3: Heterogeneity – Subgroups, meta-regression, bias, and bias-adjustment. *Medical Decision Making* 33 (5): 618–640.

Dwamena B. 2007. *MIDAS: Stata Module for Meta-Analytical Integration of Diagnostic Test Accuracy Studies.* Boston College Department of Economics, Statistical Software Components. http://fmwww.bc.edu/repec/bocode/m/midas.pdf. Accessed on December 2, 2014.

Egger M., Smith G.D., and Phillips A.N. 1997. Meta-analysis: Principles and procedures. *British Medical Journal* 315 (7121): 1533–1537.

Grutters J.P., Sculpher M., Briggs A.H., Severens J.L., Candel M.J., Stahl J.E., De R.D., Boer A., Ramaekers B.L., and Joore M.A. 2013. Acknowledging patient heterogeneity in economic evaluation: A systematic literature review. *PharmacoEconomics* 31 (2): 111–123.

Harbord R., and Higgins J. 2008. Meta-regression in Stata. *The Stata Journal* 8 (4): 493–519.

Harbord R., and Whiting P. 2009. Metandi: Meta-analysis of diagnostic accuracy using hierarchical logistic regression. *The Stata Journal* 9 (2): 211–229.

Harris R., Bradburn M., Deeks J.J., Harbord R., Altman D., and Sterne J. 2008. Metan: Fixed- and random-effects meta-analysis. *The Stata Journal* 8 (1): 3–28.

Higgins J.P., and Thompson S.G. 2002. Quantifying heterogeneity in a meta-analysis. *Statistics in Medicine* 21 (11): 1539–1558.

Higgins J.P., and Thompson S.G. 2004. Controlling the risk of spurious findings from meta-regression. *Statistics in Medicine* 23 (11): 1663–1682.

Hopkins R., Bowen J., Campbell K., Blackhouse G., De R.G., Novick T., O'Reilly D., Goeree R., and Tarride J.E. 2008. Effects of study design and trends for EVAR versus OSR. *Vascular Health and Risk Management* 4 (5): 1011–1022.

Landis J.R., and Koch G.G. 1977. The measurement of observer agreement for categorical data. *Biometrics* 33 (1): 159–174.

Moher D., Liberati A., Tetzlaff J., and Altman D.G. 2009. Preferred reporting items for systematic reviews and meta-analyses: The PRISMA statement. *Annals of Internal Medicine* 151 (4): 264–269.

Montori V.M., Smieja M., and Guyatt G.H. 2000. Publication bias: A brief review for clinicians. *Mayo Clinic Proceedings* 75 (12): 1284–1288.

Newman T., Browner W., Cummings S., and Hulley S. 2007. Designing studies for medical tests. In *Designing Clinical Studies*, eds. S. Hulley, S. Cummings, W. Browner, D. Grady and T. Newman, Chapter 12, 183–206. Philadelphia, PA: Lippincott Williams & Wilkins.

Pope C., Mays N., and Popay J. 2006. How can we synthesize qualitative and quantitative evidence for healthcare policy-makers and managers? *Healthcare Management Forum* 19 (1): 27–31.

Ramaekers B.L., Joore M.A., and Grutters J.P. 2013. How should we deal with patient heterogeneity in economic evaluation: A systematic review of national pharmacoeconomic guidelines. *Value in Health: The Journal of the International Society for Pharmacoeconomics and Outcomes Research* 16 (5): 855–862.

StataCorp. 2009. *Stata Statistical Software: Release 11*. College Station, TX: StataCorp LP.

Sutton A.J., Song F., Gilbody S.M., and Abrams K.R. 2000. Modelling publication bias in meta-analysis: A review. *Statistical Methods in Medical Research* 9 (5): 421–445.

Whitley E., and Ball J. 2002. Statistics review 1: Presenting and summarising data. *Critical Care* 6 (1): 66–71.

Appendix I: Diagnostic Accuracy Measures

	Positive (+) Disease	*Negative (−) Disease*
Positive (+) test	True positive	False positive
Negative (−) test	False negative	True negative
Sensitivity TP/(TP + FN)	The proportion of persons with a disease who are correctly identified by a screening test, that is, a test with a high sensitivity is useful for *ruling out* a disease if a person tests negative	
Specificity TN/(TN + FP)	The proportion of persons without a disease who are correctly identified by a test. High specificity is important when the treatment or diagnosis is harmful to the patient	
Positive predictive value TP/(TP + FP)	The proportion of patients with positive test results who are correctly diagnosed	
Negative predictive value TN/(TN + FN)	The proportion of patients with negative test results who are correctly diagnosed	
Positive likelihood ratio (LR+) Sensitivity/(1 − specificity)	Indicates how much more likely it is to get a positive test in the diseased as opposed to the non-diseased group	
Negative likelihood ratio (LR−) (1 − sensitivity)/specificity	Indicates how much more likely it is to get a negative test in the non-diseased as opposed to the diseased group	
AUC (non-parametric Wilcoxon approximation)	Represents the probability that a randomly chosen diseased subject is correctly diagnosed with greater suspicion than a randomly chosen non-diseased subject	
Wilcoxon AUC = $(TN \times TP + 0.5 \times TN \times FN + 0.5 \times FP \times TP)/(N_N \times N_A)$		

Note: Likelihood ratio positive > 10, likelihood ratio negative < 0.1: exclusion and confirmation.

Likelihood ratio positive > 0, likelihood ratio negative > 0.1: confirmation only.

Likelihood ratio positive < 10, likelihood ratio negative < 0.1: exclusion only.

Likelihood ratio positive < 10, likelihood ratio negative > 0.1: no exclusion or confirmation.

AUC, area under the curve; FN, false negative; FP, false positive; LR, likelihood ratio; N_A, number of positive disease cases; N_N, number of negative disease cases; TN, true negative; TP, true positive.

Appendix II: Estimation of Cohen's Kappa Score

Consider the Level of Agreement between Two Reviewers (or between Two Tests)

		Rater 1		
		Positive	Negative	Total
Rater 2	Positive	48	6	54
	Negative	8	30	38
	Total	56	36	92

In percentages:

P_o = probability of observed agreement.

P_e = probability of expected agreement

Kappa = $(P_o - P_e)/(1 - Pe)$

Kappa = $([(48/92) + (30/92)] - \{[(56/92) * (54/92)] - [(36/92) * (38/92)]\})/(1 - \{[(56/92)*(54/92)] - [(36/92)*(38/92)]\}) = 0.6316$

According to Landis and Koch (1977), a kappa value 0 indicates poor agreement; 0.01–0.20, slight agreement; 0.21–0.40, fair agreement; 0.41–0.60, moderate agreement; 0.61–0.80, good agreement; and 0.81–1.00, excellent agreement.

Chapter 4

Network Meta-Analysis

Introduction

The use of network meta-analysis has become widespread with the advantage of answering research questions that were not answerable before. We prefer the term *network meta-analysis* as an overarching terminology that includes direct comparison of head-to-head trials, indirect comparison by linking with a common comparator, mixed treatment comparisons (MTCs) by combining direct and indirect evidence (Lu and Ades 2004) and network chain analysis (Table 4.1) (Coleman et al. 2012; Hoaglin et al. 2011; Jansen et al. 2011, 2014; Sutton et al. 2008).

Before network meta-analysis, when there are only two drugs and all of the RCTs have been between these two drugs, a standard meta-analysis would have allowed the estimation of a meta-analytic rate between the common comparators. With the development of network meta-analysis, different research questions can be answered in two situations. First, many new drugs have been approved for use based on placebo-controlled trials. Second, most reimbursement agencies wish to know the relative safety and efficacy of all comparators for treatment and not just the comparators of drugs in the trial that granted regulatory approval. Reimbursement submissions are considered incomplete if there is absence of relative efficacy between the new drug and standard of care and all available comparators.

Head-to-Head and Placebo-Controlled Trials

A head-to-head trial is the gold standard and the most scientifically rigorous method of hypothesis testing to establish causation (Table 4.2). Two

Table 4.1 Terminology for Indirect Meta-Analysis

Direct comparison	Estimates created from randomized comparators Example: Three *RCTs all with Drug A versus Drug B
Indirect comparison	Estimates created not from randomized comparators Example: Six RCTs—three trials with Drug A versus placebo and three trials with Drug B versus placebo. Can derive A versus B relative effect
Mixed treatment comparisons	Estimates created from both direct and indirect evidence Example: Three RCTs—A versus placebo, B versus placebo and A versus B. Creates direct evidence, indirect evidence and mixed treatment evidence
Network chain analysis	Estimates created from linking multiple studies to create a pairwise comparison Example: Three RCTs—Drug A versus Drug B, Drug B versus Drug C and Drug C versus Drug D. Can derive A versus D relative effect
Network meta-analysis	Estimates created from simultaneous synthesis of evidence of all pairwise comparisons Can include direct, indirect, mixed treatment and chained evidence
Generalized evidence synthesis	Combines different study types as well as different RCT evidence Can include direct, indirect and mixed treatment evidence from RCTs and observational data. Often reported as hierarchical meta-analysis

*RCT, randomized controlled trial.

sets of patients, who have equal chance of receiving the new therapy or a different active drug, are assumed to be equal for prognostic factors. With one set of patients receiving the new drug, the only difference in outcomes from the other set of patients must be due to the new drug, and this establishes causation. The guidelines to properly design an RCT have been consolidated by the FDA, Health Canada and EMA as the International Conference on Harmonisation of Technical Requirements for Registration of Pharmaceuticals for Human Use (ICH). The United States, Canada and the European Union, list identical guidelines on their websites. Given that a well-designed, executed and reported trial is the gold

Table 4.2   Hierarchy of Study Evidence

Level	Intervention Studies
I	A systematic review of Level II studies
II	A randomized controlled trial
III-1	A pseudo-randomized controlled trial (i.e. alternate allocation or some other method)
III-2	A comparative study with concurrent controls Non-randomized, experimental trial (including indirect meta-analysis) Cohort study Case–control study Interrupted time series with a control group
III-3	A comparative study without concurrent controls Historical control study Two or more single-arm studies Interrupted time series without a parallel control group
IV	Case series with either post-test or pre-test/post-test outcomes

standard, there are situations where a placebo-controlled trial is preferable to a head-to-head trial.

A common problem with head-to-head RCTs is that they are often more complex and expensive and require larger sample sizes than earlier phase II placebo-controlled trials (Boers 2002). The head-to-head studies are larger because the sample size that is powered to detect a benefit will be larger with smaller difference versus a drug than versus a placebo. However, there may be cases where a placebo-controlled trial is preferred, for reasons other than cost.

In a recent *The New England Journal of Medicine* debate on osteoporosis drugs, Stein (Stein and Ray 2010) argued that placebo-controlled trials are unethical because of the withholding of proven therapies in the placebo allocation, whereas Rosen (Rosen and Khosla 2010) argued that the therapies are only proven in high-risk patients (prior fracture, BMD < −3 or higher fracture risk assessment) and the inclusion criteria that possess true equipoise should only include individuals who are at low risk or are non-responsive to mild therapies. Government bodies such as the Tri-Council Policy Statement on the Ethical Conduct for Research Involving Humans in Canada suggest that placebo-controlled trials are acceptable to establish the existence of effect and adverse events of drugs with new pharmacological mechanisms (Canadian Institutes of Health Research, Natural Sciences and Engineering Research Council, and Social Sciences and Humanities Research Council of Canada [CIHR, NSERC, and SSHRC] 2010). That is, if the true benefit and safety and efficacy profile are unknown, only the placebo-controlled trial will demonstrate the safety and efficacy profile for the patients that were included.

Osteoporosis is a disease where most of the drugs that are available for therapy have been approved based on a placebo-controlled trials because each new drug has a different biological mechanism. The osteoporosis drugs include bisphosphonates (which bind to the surfaces of the bones and slow down the bone-resorping action of the osteoclasts), selective oestrogen receptor modulators (which replace the bone-building and maintaining activity of hormone oestrogen that is reduced in menopause), human monoclonal antibodies (which inhibit the development and activation of osteoclasts) and parathyroid hormone analogs (which activate the osteoblast [bone-building] cells). Each of these drugs has a unique mechanism, and any safety or efficacy effect must be quantified versus placebo. Interestingly, the disease is long term, and allowing the crossover to active treatment at the end of the main phase of the trial may have increased the chance of ethical approval. However, notice that when a reimbursement agent wishes to know the relevant efficacy to prevent an important patient outcome, the comparison between the many comparators can only be achieved with network meta-analysis.

The theoretical foundations of the network meta-analysis were provided in 1997 by Bucher et al. (1997) for the pairwise division of odds ratios to produce a common odds ratio thereafter referred to as the Bucher method (i.e. for two drugs A and C and placebo B, the odds ratio of A/B divided by odds ratio of C/B produces an odds ratio of A/C). Although head-to-head studies are the highest level of clinical evidence, there exists the rationale to use indirect treatment comparison (ITC) analysis where a head-to-head study is absent and not likely to be forthcoming (Bucher et al. 1997). Even if head-to-head evidence was available, indirect treatment evidence based on other trials may be useful because of differences in patient characteristics and study characteristics such as length of follow-up (Eddy, Hasselblad, and Shachter 1990).

A very important note on indirect methods is that the pooled estimate is considered lower quality evidence than a well-designed, powered, executed trial of one comparator directly to another. Whether a meta-analytic rate from an indirect analysis with adequate evidence is preferable to a single or group of poor-quality trials is worthy of debate. This dilemma should always be added as a limitation to the discussion of any indirect analysis results.

Another caveat is that the results from head-to-head studies may differ from network meta-analysis. A recent review of the results of head-to-head and indirect comparison analyses described that out of 44 meta-analyses that had both indirect comparison and head-to-head studies, the head-to-head effect was similar in all but three cases to the indirect estimates for the same drugs and outcomes (Song et al. 2003). Of the three cases where the results were statistically different, two cases had the relative clinical benefit in the same direction, whereas the third had differences in dosage regime in the studies. This result was also reported by Bucher et al. (1997) where the indirect comparison results were similar in direction as the head-to-head estimates. In addition, Bucher and Song both reported that the magnitude of the indirect comparison results was larger between comparators than that of the head-to-head comparisons, and the level of significance between comparators was less in indirect comparison than in direct comparison. Specifically, this says that an odds ratio to prevent a bad event will be lower (preferable) with indirect comparisons, but the confidence intervals (CIs) may be wider.

When we conduct an indirect meta-analysis, there are a series of steps that we can apply to ensure the robustness of the results. We will work through the steps (Table 4.3) by using examples of increasing complexity.

Table 4.3 Steps to Conduct an Indirect Treatment Comparison

1. Establish potential network diagram of linking studies.
2. Check for consistency in outcomes for common linking arms.
3. Conduct meta-analysis and assess heterogeneity within common studies.
4. Conduct indirect meta-analysis across comparators.
5. Conduct sensitivity and subgroup analyses.
6. Report indirect treatment comparison results.

Step 1: Establish Potential Network Diagram of Linking Studies

When we are conducting an indirect meta-analysis, we have already conducted a systematic literature review, including the data abstraction phase. Our research question should have identified all relevant comparators (for drugs and devices, and programs). The research question would dictate the screening process and then the data abstraction. Thus, by the time we are ready for the meta-analysis, we already know the possible comparators and the outcomes with data available. We still call them possible comparators with potential network linkages because data may not be available for all outcomes. It is ideal to search for all comparators separately to find any placebo-controlled and head-to-head evidence. Then, a network diagram is often created for the maximum possible linkages based on study designs, and network diagrams are created for each outcome that has available data.

The simplest and most common type of indirect network diagram is presented in Figure 4.1. There are two types of studies: Drug A versus placebo and Drug B versus placebo. The end result of the indirect analysis is to create the measure of comparative effectiveness between Drug A and Drug B.

When there are more than two drugs, the network diagram becomes more complicated. In another example (Figure 4.2), there are three drugs all with placebo comparators, and three comparisons between the drugs which can occur (A vs. B, B vs. C and A vs. C). If there are four drugs, there would be six comparisons, and if there are five drugs all with placebo comparators, there would be 10 possible comparisons. At this point, the network diagram can become large, and if all of the studies are placebo-controlled, the network diagram is not helpful. When the network involves a mixture

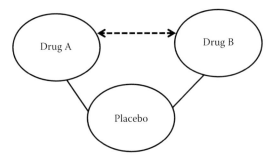

Figure 4.1 Simplest network diagram. There are two types of studies: Drug A versus placebo and Drug B versus placebo (indicated by the solid lines). The dashed line indicates the relative effect that we wish to estimate (Drug A versus Drug B).

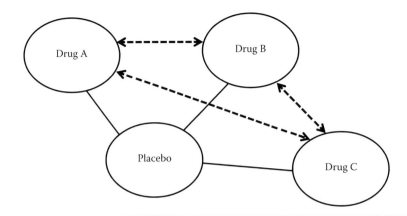

Figure 4.2   More than two comparators with placebo-controlled trials. There are three types of studies: Drug A versus placebo, Drug B versus placebo and Drug C versus placebo (indicated by the solid lines). The dashed line indicates the relative effect that we wish to estimate (Drug A versus Drug B, Drug A versus Drug C and Drug B versus Drug C).

of evidence that includes chains of trials, A versus B and B versus C, the network diagram becomes very helpful. At this point, the researchers' skills in using Microsoft Word or PowerPoint to create the visual display for the network diagram are tested.

A more complicated example would include a network of comparisons, where the comparison between two drugs may need to cross over more than one comparator (Figure 4.3). In this example, we have three groups of trials. In the first set of trials, Drug A is compared to Drug B; in the second set of trials, Drug B is compared to Drug C; and in the third set of trials, Drug C is compared to Drug D. We can link each of the trials to create some comparisons; if we combine A versus B with B versus C with B as the common comparator, we can derive an estimate for A versus C. If we want an estimate of D versus A, we need to link A to B, B to C, and finally C to D.

For diseases with established treatments, complicated network diagrams like Figure 4.4 are often created. This represents among the most complicated network diagrams and any more difficulty would be simple extensions of this example. The solid lines indicate that there is a trial with comparative evidence between the two circled names. We see that there are trials

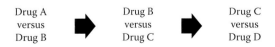

Figure 4.3   Chain of evidence for indirect comparisons—An extended chain where not all of the studies have a common comparator.

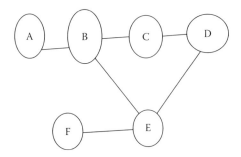

Figure 4.4 Complicated network diagram. The solid lines represent studies that have head-to-head comparators, such as Drug A versus Drug B and Drug B versus Drug E, but not Drug B versus Drug F. We can derive with all indirect pairwise comparisons of A, B, C, D, E and F.

between A and B (marked by the solid line), B versus C, C versus D and so on. However, we now have trials with different linkages to other comparators that allow the estimation of relative effect along different pathways. For example, we can estimate the relative effect between A and E by using the linkages A–B–C–D–E or A–B–E. The closed loop of B–C–D–E–B is a common example, where multiple pathways can be created, whereas analysis that includes F always proceeds through the open loop from E.

To provide a different estimate for the variety of pathways that can be created, the *Lumley method* provides an estimate of all of the comparators within the loop and an assessment of the coherence (e.g. consistency) of the estimates from using different pathways, for example, B–E and B–C–D–E. Any incoherence is incorporated into the confidence interval of the estimate between B and E, and B and D from B–C–D or B–E–D, and so on, for all comparisons. Although the Lumley statistical code was written for SAS software, we are unaware if the code has been created for other software. One limitation of the original SAS code is that it works only for closed loops and could only be used to compare drugs in the loop of B–C–D–E. Otherwise, the software tends to average across the multiple pathways.

Step 2: Check for Consistency in Outcomes for Common Linking Arms

In order to link the evidence, we need to demonstrate that it is appropriate to link the studies with a common comparator. The assumption of similarity of patients across the trials is often assumed, and a high-quality report would take the step to demonstrate that the patients are indeed similar.

The similarity of patients across the studies can be tested by comparing the rates of events in the linking arm. Consider 10 studies that include studies of Drug A versus placebo and 5 studies with Drug B versus placebo. The forest plot for the relative risk (RR) of the bad event is presented for Drug A versus placebo and Drug B versus placebo.

The first thing to check is whether we are comparing apples to apples, that is, are the patients similar across the studies? We notice that the trial with Study 3 for Drug A has much higher rates of events in the placebo arm (Table 4.4). The forest plot does not detect this directly, but a closer look shows that the events for Drug A intervention are also much higher than other trials with Drug A. This suggests that Study 3 has a different patient or study characteristic that the other studies and the results should not be used in the meta-analysis. In this case, excluding the outlier Study 3, all of the other studies have consistent placebo rates of events of 5%–6%.

There are two important notes. First, the assessment for the consistency of the rates of events or measures of change must be conducted separately for each outcome. We have experienced examples where only one of the outcomes seems problematic. However, there is no established consensus on whether to remove the study for that outcome or remove the study completely for all outcomes. Study 3 presents the case for possible effect modifier that raises the rates of events in the study, but when the events are raised only in the placebo control arm, this is problematic. When the level of events is higher in both the placebo and active comparator treatment arms, the effect modifier would explain the increased level of events, and essentially cancel each other out. Still we suggest sensitivity analysis with and without any similar studies. This leads to the second point that relates to the selection of the primary analysis and then sensitivity analysis. We suggest

Table 4.4   Rate of Events in Placebo Arm for Drug A and Drug B

	Drug A Trials Placebo			Drug B Trials Placebo	
	Events/N	Rate (%)		Events/N	Rate (%)
Study 1	11/200	5.5	Study 6	11/200	5.5
Study 2	10/200	5.0	Study 7	10/200	5.0
Study 3	36/200	18.0	Study 8	10/200	5.0
Study 4	12/200	6.0	Study 9	12/200	6.0
Study 5	13/200	6.5	Study 10	13/200	6.5

Table 4.5 Data for Indirect Comparisons for STATA

Drug	Events1	Total1	Events2	Total2
A	3	200	11	200
A	2	200	10	200
A	2	200	12	200
A	3	200	13	200
B	6	200	11	200
B	4	200	10	200
B	4	200	12	200
B	6	200	13	200

Note: The analysis is conducted with Study 3 and Study 8 excluded because of high rate of events in the placebo treatment group and because of high heterogeneity, respectively.

that a sensitivity analysis be conducted that does not exclude the outliers (Table 4.5), to prove that the findings from a systematic review are not dependent on arbitrary decisions.

Step 3: Conduct Meta-Analysis and Assess Heterogeneity within Common Comparators

The meta-analysis within common comparators follows the standard rules of traditional meta-analysis. For both sets of trials, Drug A versus placebo and Drug B versus placebo, we conducted a meta-analysis with a random effects model to estimate the RR of the bad events (Figure 4.5). Only Drug A had a statistical benefit of reducing the rate of bad events, as indicated by the diamond being to the left of the unity line (the RR and the 95% CI); for Drug B, the rate was not significant based on the position of the diamond, the estimate of the CIs crossed unity (0.28–1.51) and the p-value was greater than .05 ($p = .31$).

However, unique to Drug B versus placebo was the presence of heterogeneity, $I^2 = 0.74$, and to explain the high heterogeneity from an inspection of the forest plot, Study 8 appears to be an outlier. After removing Study 8 from the analysis, the heterogeneity reduced to $I^2 = 0$, and the RR was significant, RR = 0.44 (95% CI: 0.26–0.73). The rate of bad events was 12.5% in Study 8 treatment group, whereas all of the other studies had 1%–3% in their treatment groups.

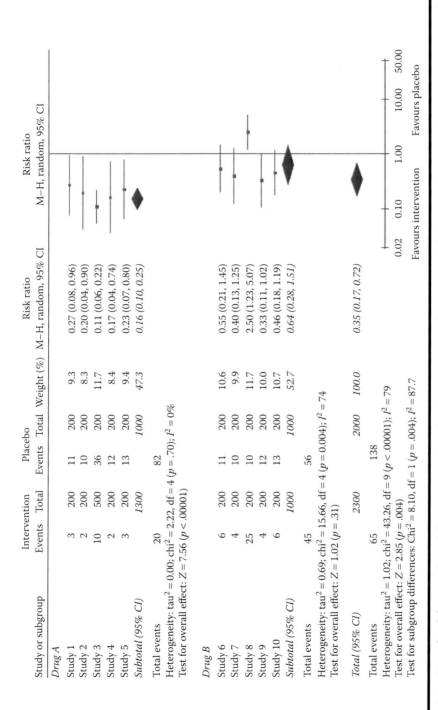

Study or subgroup	Intervention Events	Intervention Total	Placebo Events	Placebo Total	Weight (%)	Risk ratio M–H, random, 95% CI	Risk ratio M–H, random, 95% CI
Drug A							
Study 1	3	200	11	200	9.3	0.27 (0.08, 0.96)	
Study 2	2	200	10	200	8.3	0.20 (0.04, 0.90)	
Study 3	10	500	36	200	11.7	0.11 (0.06, 0.22)	
Study 4	2	200	12	200	8.4	0.17 (0.04, 0.74)	
Study 5	3	200	13	200	9.4	0.23 (0.07, 0.80)	
Subtotal (95% CI)		1300		1000	47.3	*0.16 (0.10, 0.25)*	
Total events	20		82				

Heterogeneity: $tau^2 = 0.00$; $chi^2 = 2.22$, df = 4 ($p = .70$); $I^2 = 0\%$
Test for overall effect: $Z = 7.56$ ($p < .00001$)

Study or subgroup	Intervention Events	Intervention Total	Placebo Events	Placebo Total	Weight (%)	Risk ratio M–H, random, 95% CI	Risk ratio M–H, random, 95% CI
Drug B							
Study 6	6	200	11	200	10.6	0.55 (0.21, 1.45)	
Study 7	4	200	10	200	9.9	0.40 (0.13, 1.25)	
Study 8	25	200	10	200	11.7	2.50 (1.23, 5.07)	
Study 9	4	200	12	200	10.0	0.33 (0.11, 1.02)	
Study 10	6	200	13	200	10.7	0.46 (0.18, 1.19)	
Subtotal (95% CI)		1000		1000	52.7	*0.64 (0.28, 1.51)*	
Total events	45		56				

Heterogeneity: $tau^2 = 0.69$; $chi^2 = 15.66$, df = 4 ($p = 0.004$); $I^2 = 74$
Test for overall effect: $Z = 1.02$ ($p = .31$)

Study or subgroup	Intervention Events	Intervention Total	Placebo Events	Placebo Total	Weight (%)	Risk ratio M–H, random, 95% CI	Risk ratio M–H, random, 95% CI
Total (95% CI)		2300		2000	100.0	*0.35 (0.17, 0.72)*	
Total events	65		138				

Heterogeneity: $tau^2 = 1.02$; $chi^2 = 43.26$, df = 9 ($p < .00001$); $I^2 = 79$
Test for overall effect: $Z = 2.85$ ($p = .004$)
Test for subgroup differences: $Chi^2 = 8.10$, df = 1 ($p = .004$); $I^2 = 87.7$

0.02   0.10   1.00   10.00   50.00
Favours intervention   Favours placebo

Figure 4.5   Standard forest plot of drug versus placebo for Drug A and Drug B. This forest plot provides an assessment of heterogeneity within drug type and an estimate of relative efficacy within each drug type. Study 8 contributes to the high level of heterogeneity and can be removed as an outlier.

Therefore, now we have a problem: which studies should be included in the network meta-analysis between Drug A and Drug B? The two problematic studies are Study 3 (different placebo rates and probably different risk status for the patients than all other studies) and Study 8 (an outlier that had common rates of events for the patients that received placebo, but higher rates of bad events in the treatment group). Interestingly, Study 3 had problematic rates of bad events for the placebo arms, but was not identified by an assessment of heterogeneity. The important thing to remember is that these problems could also exist in a standard type of meta-analysis. In the standard meta-analysis, we would conduct the primary analysis and sensitivity analysis and possibly risk adjustment.

The first thing we could do is to declare that Study 3 and Study 8 are outliers, and the indirect results should be reported without the outliers as the primary analysis, and the sensitivity analysis should include the outliers. An important step is to try to explain why there are outliers. The reasons why these two studies are often explainable by the differences across studies in the inclusion or exclusion criteria or by the differences in baseline characteristics of the patients. If explainable, a risk-adjusted analysis could occur, such as with meta-regression as explained in Chapter 3. This also reminds us to present the results as composites. For example, if Study 3 and Study 8 had an average age of 70 years, whereas all of the other studies had an average age of 80 years, you really have created two subgroups. The results of the remaining eight studies are presented as the primary case, and the results of the two outliers should also be reported as a subgroup.

There are other important measures that should be assessed before conducting the network meta-analysis, which are steps that are identical with a traditional meta-analysis. They include assessing for publication bias and assessing the strength of evidence with the GRADE approach.

Step 4: Conduct Indirect Meta-Analysis across the Comparators

Network Meta-Analysis Software

There are many different choices of statistical software to conduct indirect analysis. A clever programmer can provide code to run the analysis on any statistical package. However, because the reviewers of an indirect analysis wish to ensure that the analysis was done correctly, it is preferable that the analysis be conducted in software that has been verified as being useful.

We follow our favourite choices for most indirect meta-analyses: Wells Canadian Agency for Drugs and Technologies in Health (CADTH) software, STATA and WinBUGS. See the CADTH reference document for an explanation of some software choices and examples of source code (Wells et al. 2009).

By far, the simplest software to conduct a network meta-analysis is made possible by George Wells, a clever fellow in Ottawa, Canada, who developed the free CADTH software specifically designed for network meta-analysis. This software requires Windows XP or later versions of Windows can run in compatibility mode with a .DLL file transferred.

From our simple example with Drug A and Drug B, after removing the outliers, the result for Drug A versus placebo was RR = 0.22 (95% CI: 0.11, 0.43) and that for Drug B versus placebo was RR = 0.44 (95% CI: 0.26, 0.83). The indirect analysis result for Drug A versus Drug B was RR = 0.50 (95% CI: 0.213, 1.176), $p = .324$. The p-value is obtained by entering the data from the original forest plots, after typing in the arrow key and selecting 'derived'.

Alternatively, we can use STATA to conduct the network meta-analysis. This is quite handy because the data have already been entered to conduct the meta-analysis within each comparator. Data should be in the format of Table 4.5 in Microsoft Excel or entered directly into STATA (Table 4.6).

Table 4.6   STATA Code for Indirect Treatment Comparisons Using Meta-Regression

```
import excel "data.xlsx", sheet("Sheet1") firstrow clear
gen compb = 0
replace compb = 1 if DRUG = = "A"

* compute values of the four cells for each trial
gen noevent1 = Total1-Events1
gen noevent2 = Total2-Events2

* meta-analysis of all trials to compute logrr and se
metan Events1 noevent1 Events2 noevent2, rr random nograph notable
gen logrr = log(_ES)
gen se = _selogES
gen wt = 1/((se)^2)

* random effects meta-regression with indirect covariate (compb)
metareg logrr compb, wsse(se)
```

The exponentiation of the variable compb from −0.6894346 (95% CI: −1.754346, 0.3754772) would create an estimate of RR = 0.5019 (95% CI: 0.1730, 1.4557) with *p*-value = .164 (Table 4.7). This result is not meaningfully different than the Wells CADTH results. This is the general finding that the differences in magnitude of RR do not change meaningfully with different software packages, but the *p*-value may change slightly. It is our preference that the analysis be conducted with at least two different software packages to verify the results.

The STATA code is fairly straightforward for the comparison of two drugs, but when we add three or more drugs and wish to have an estimate of comparisons across drugs, the coding gets tricky. When we use the Wells CADTH software, it is easy to compare the results for two drugs versus placebo (Figure 4.6). When we have more drugs, and many outcomes, the manual entry of data can become labour intensive. However, the Wells CADTH software has an advantage over STATA for cases where there are network chains of evidence.

For our chain of events example, the Wells software has a huge benefit. We have three groups of trials. In the first set of trials, Drug A is compared to Drug B; in the second set of trials, Drug B is compared to Drug C; and in

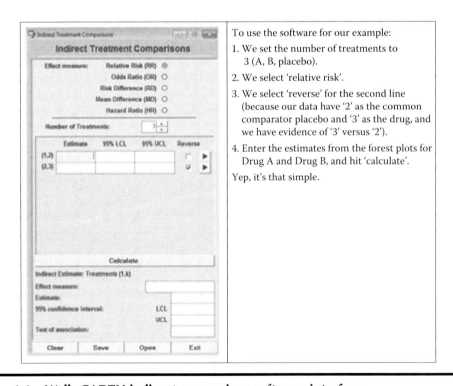

Figure 4.6   Wells CADTH indirect comparison software interface.

Table 4.7 Output from STATA for Indirect Comparison

Meta-regression number of obs = 8.

REML estimate of between-study variance tau^2 = 0.

Percentage of residual variation due to heterogeneity *I*-squared_res = 0.00%.

Proportion of between-study variance explained adjusted *R*-squared = .%.

With Knapp–Hartung modification.

logRR	Coefficient	Standard Error	t-Statistic	p-Value	95% CI Lower	95% CI Upper
compb	−0.689	0.435	−1.58	.164	−1.754	0.375
_cons	−0.825	0.264	−3.13	.020	−1.471	−0.179

CI, confidence interval.

the third set of trials, Drug C is compared to Drug D. We can link each of the trials to create some comparisons: if we combine A versus B with B versus C with B as the common comparator, we can derive an estimate for A versus C. If we want an estimate of D versus A, we need to leap across B and C, somehow linking all sets of studies. The Wells CADTH software does this nicely for us, with the sample data listed in Figure 4.7.

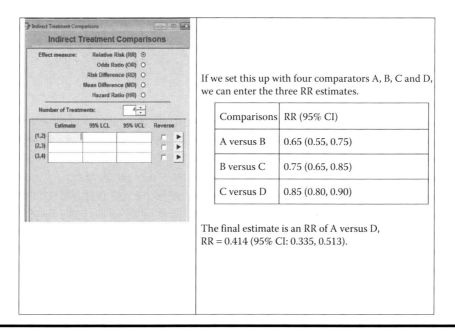

Figure 4.7 Wells CADTH indirect comparison software interface for a chain of evidence.

This is very helpful; however, if we are required to estimate the relative efficacy for all of the comparisons, this would be a total of three analyses: A versus C, B versus D and our A versus D. More complicated network analysis can be conducted simply with Bayesian network meta-analysis or often referred to in the Bayesian world as MTCs. We will present an introduction to the Bayesian meta-analysis at the end of this chapter.

Step 5: Conduct Subgroup and Sensitivity Analyses

The purpose of subgroup and sensitivity analyses is to assess the robustness of the findings. In statistical jargon, an estimate is robust when the main findings are not unduly affected by outliers or other small departures from model assumptions. The model assumptions are similarity of patients across studies (similar placebo rates within comparators and across comparators), homogeneity within all comparators and exchangeability (the relative efficacy of a treatment is the same in all trials included in the network meta-analysis). The word *consistency* has often been used instead of exchangeability. An example of inconsistency would be where some trials report statistically significant findings and others not (consistency of variance). Another example would be where the estimate of relative effect may vary across studies, that is, explainable or unexplainable by factors (consistency of effect). The inconsistency of effect may be detected by an assessment of heterogeneity, whereas the inconsistency of variance would only be detected by visual inspection of the forest plot.

The primary analysis should include similar patients with homogeneity within comparators, where the results are consistent within the comparators. If we removed outliers, three sets of results must be presented for our example with 10 studies: (1) the primary analysis without the outliers ($n = 8$), (2) the result of the outliers ($n = 2$) and (3) the sensitivity analysis with the results including the outliers ($n = 10$).

Similar to traditional meta-analysis, we would conduct pre-specified subgroup analysis for any differences in study design, patient risk status or study quality. It is preferable to pre-specify the subgroup analysis before conducting any meta-analysis, but in reality the differences in studies and patients are not made apparent until data abstraction, and assessment of similarity and consistency. Common pre-specified subgroup analysis includes, among others, study quality, year of publication, study size, location of study, multi-centre versus single centre and potential differences in pre-established prognostic or risk factors.

The often missing assessment of subgroup analysis is to compare the results across the subgroups. Here we assess if the results are biologically plausible (supported by external data), clinically meaningful or statistically meaningful. For network meta-analysis, there is usually a lack of sufficient number of studies to conduct and assess subgroup analysis, and quite often we simply move to assessing a risk-adjusted model such as within a meta-regression in STATA or with Bayesian MTC results.

Step 6: Report Network Meta-Analysis Results

A consensus document for conducting and reporting of a network meta-analysis has been generated by the ISPOR. We have provided a few of the main points mentioned in that document in Table 4.8.

The most salient point is the necessity to explain every step of the analysis, from how the researcher assessed similarity, consistency and heterogeneity to how violations of the assumptions are dealt with. If the steps that we have presented are followed and described, clarity will be achieved.

Table 4.8   Suggested Steps in Reporting Network Meta-Analysis (Reviewers' Notes)

1. Provide step-by-step descriptions of all analyses, including explicit statements of all assumptions and procedures for checking them.
2. Describe analytic features specific to network meta-analysis, including comparability and homogeneity, synthesis, sensitivity analysis, subgroup analysis and meta-regression and special types of outcomes.
3. Follow conventional guidelines for statistical model diagnostics.
4. Evaluate violations of similarity or consistency assumption in evidence network.
5. Consider use of meta-regression models with treatment–covariate interactions to reduce bias, if similarity or consistency is a problem.
6. Follow PRISMA statement for reporting of meta-analysis.
7. Provide graphical depiction of evidence network.
8. Indicate software package used in the analysis and provide code (at least in an online appendix).

Bayesian Mixed Treatment Comparisons

A recent innovation for network meta-analysis is the introduction of Bayesian MTC. MTC has been able to overcome the shortcoming that we have described earlier and many other that we know and we will list. However, first we should acknowledge David Spiegelhalter, another clever fellow, at the MRC Biostatistics Unit at the University of Cambridge, who in 1989 developed the Bayesian inference using Gibbs sampling (BUGS) software to conduct a Bayesian analysis. By 1997, Nicky Best contributed to the software group at the Imperial College, and the Windows version WinBUGS was launched. Since 1997, there has been a very wide expansion in the use of the free software and open sharing of different applications that could not have been previously solved.

MTC incorporates the generalized approach to evidence synthesis and can handle many different types of relationships between studies. Our list of where we have used MTC would include the following:

1. Chained networks, with open or closed loops
2. Incorporating the results of multiple arm studies
3. Incorporating evidence from placebo trials, with evidence from head-to-head trials
4. Incorporating risk adjustment
5. Incorporating different types of study designs

One key advantage that MTC has over other software is that all relevant comparators are simultaneously compared. One drawback is the requirement of pre-specifying the priors, which we will discuss in Chapter 5.

Network Meta-Analysis Example

In one of the author's PhD thesis (RH), Chapter 2 was dedicated to the network meta-analysis of the benefit of osteoporosis drugs to prevent fractures. The outcomes were the rates of vertebral, non-vertebral, hip and wrist fractures. In the first step, a table was provided, Table 1 'Characteristics of Included Studies' (Hopkins et al. 2011) to describe the study characteristics (country, numbers of study centres and patient follow-up in years) and the baseline patient characteristics (age in years, years since menopause, BMD of the hip reported as g/cm² and history of fractures).

For every outcome, the different rates versus placebo were reported and the rates versus each other drug. For each outcome, the odds ratio was derived by combining the odds ratio of each comparator versus a common group (i.e. odds ratio of A/C = odds ratio of A/B divided by odds ratio of C/B), and 95% credibility intervals (CrIs) for fracture versus placebo were estimated. In addition, the odds ratio between each drug comparator was estimated along with its 95% CrI.

The primary statistical analysis was a Bayesian network meta-analysis estimate of relative efficacy versus placebo and other drugs. More detail is provided for this example in Chapter 5. In addition to Bayesian methods, the analysis was conducted with the Wells CADTH software and STATA. In addition, the effect size was estimated for each drug versus placebo, where the effect size was defined as the ratio of the odds ratio for fracture of placebo versus drug to the standard error of the estimate of the odds ratio. A higher effect size indicates that the drug has lower odds for fractures than placebo and/or that the standard error is small.

Assessing Robustness: Homogeneity and Consistency of Evidence

A number of steps were taken to assess the integrity of the ITC analysis. The assessments included (1) assessing homogeneity in meta-analysis of each comparator and across comparators, (2) checking the consistency of the ITC analysis between Bayesian and classical software packages and (3) checking the consistency of the ITC analysis with head-to-head studies, if available. If there was homogeneity within drugs and across drugs, and the ITC evidence was consistent across methodologies or with head-to-head evidence, the ITC evidence is considered strong and free of bias (Glenny et al. 2005).

Homogeneity with each drugs and across all drugs was assessed with Review Manager 5 software (The Cochrane Collaboration 2011). Heterogeneity was assessed with I^2, with greater than 50% being moderate heterogeneity and greater than 70% being considerable heterogeneity, as suggested by the *Cochrane Handbook of Systematic Reviews of Interventions* (Higgins and Green 2009). Consistency of evidence was assessed by comparing the results of the Bayesian analysis with Wells CADTH software (Wells et al. 2009). Checking consistency of ITC evidence versus head-to-head evidence was conducted by a search for meta-analysis of head-to-head evidence.

Adjustment for Difference in Baseline Characteristics

Finally, differences in patient characteristics were checked across drugs contributing to the relative efficacy estimates in the network meta-analysis. We estimated the odds ratios for fracture reduction with classical meta-analysis with meta-regression, with the log of the odds ratio as the dependent variable, and dummy variables were added for each of the drugs. Following the unadjusted results, we adjusted the network meta-analysis estimates with meta-regression to include the age in years, BMD in gcm^2 and percentage of subjects with history of a vertebral fracture. Meta-regression was conducted with STATA version 11.0 using the command `metareg` (StataCorp 2009). The methods, statistical code and final results are provided in Chapter 2, which was published by BioMed Central, London (Hopkins et al. 2011).

Network Meta-Analysis of Diagnostic Accuracy

The network meta-analysis of diagnostic accuracy data adds a further level of trickiness to the methodology. The most common diagnostic outcomes are sensitivity, specificity or area under the curve, and all three outcome measures are bounded by 0%–100%. However, if two sets of studies reported a sensitivity relative to a common gold standard, one test will have a higher relative sensitivity than the other (second) test. For example, if the sensitivity of Test 1 with reference to the gold standard was 95%, and the sensitivity of Test 2 was 85%, Test 1 has a relative sensitivity of 95%/85% = 1.12, or 112%.

In a recent report (Assasi et al. 2013), we conducted the network meta-analysis of high- and low-sensitivity troponin T (hs-cTnT and ls-cTnT) and high- and low-sensitivity troponin I (hs-cTnI and ls-cTnI) for the rapid diagnosis of acute coronary syndrome.

The analysis of the diagnostic performance involved two steps. In the first step, the direct comparison was generated, which compared the test, such as hs-cTnI, to the reference standard for the diagnosis of acute myocardial infarction (AMI) for each study. Then, the results of similar tests (hs-cTnI for AMI) were pooled to create one estimate. The pooling of the estimates was conducted with two different methods. In the preferred method, where there were at least four different studies that reported the same outcome, and data were diverse enough to allow statistical convergence, a random effects meta-analysis for diagnostic tests was conducted in STATA with the command `midas tp fp fn tn`. If there were fewer than five studies ($N < 5$), a fixed effects analysis was conducted with a simple sum of the elements in the 2 × 2 tables.

In the absence of head-to-head evidence of tests such as hs-cTnT versus hs-cTnI, the second step was a network meta-analysis to provide a comparative estimate between the two tests. The comparative estimates were compared as pairwise comparisons derived from the Wells CADTH software. The method used by the CADTH software has been referred to as the Bucher method. One caveat with this analysis of the pairwise estimates, such as for sensitivity, was that the estimation was conducted under the assumption of normality that creates CIs not bounded by 1.0, which was observed in the data. In particular, the CIs for sensitivity or specificity were never above 1.0. This is different than the CI for sensitivity or specificity alone, which are bounded by 1.0 because of the use of binomial CIs. The estimates from the network meta-analysis were interpreted as a ratio of estimates (relative sensitivity, relative specificity, relative area under the curve).

References

Assasi N., Blackhouse G., Campbell K., Hopkins R., and Goeree R. 2013. *High-Sensitivity Cardiac Troponin for the Rapid Diagnosis of Acute Coronary Syndrome in the Emergency Department: A Clinical and Cost-Effectiveness Evaluation [Science Report]*. Ottawa, ON: Canadian Agency for Drugs and Technologies in Health.

Boers M. 2002. EMEA guidelines for trials in osteoporosis: Design implications. The *Netherlands Journal of Medicine* 60 (8): 310–314.

Bucher H.C., Guyatt G.H., Griffith L.E., and Walter S.D. 1997. The results of direct and indirect treatment comparisons in meta-analysis of randomized controlled trials. *Journal of Clinical Epidemiology* 50 (6): 683–691.

Canadian Institutes of Health Research, Natural Sciences and Engineering Research Council, and Social Sciences and Humanities Research Council of Canada (CIHR, NSERC, and SSHRC). 2010. *Tri-Council Policy Statement: Ethical Conduct for Research Involving Humans*. www.pre.ethics.gc.ca/pdf/eng/tcps2/ TCPS_2_FINAL_Web.pdf. Accessed on December 2, 2014.

Coleman C.I., Phung O.J., Cappelleri J.C. Baker W.L., Kluger J., White C.M., and Sobieraj D.M. 2012. *Use of Mixed Treatment Comparisons in Systematic Reviews*. Rockville, MD: Agency for Healthcare Research and Quality (US). August. Report No.: 12-EHC119-EF. http://www.ncbi.nlm.nih.gov/books/n/ methresmix/pdf. Accessed on December 2, 2014.

Eddy D.M., Hasselblad V., and Shachter R. 1990. A Bayesian method for synthesizing evidence. The confidence profile method. *International Journal of Technology Assessment in Health Care* 6 (1): 31–55.

Glenny A.M., Altman D.G., Song F., Sakarovitch C., Deeks J.J., D'Amico R., Bradburn M., and Eastwood A.J. 2005. Indirect comparisons of competing interventions. *Health Technology Assessment* 9 (26): 1–134, iii–iv.

Higgins J., and Green S. 2009. *Cochrane Handbook for Systematic Reviews of Interventions Version 5.0.2*. Copenhagen, Denmark: The Cochrane Collaboration.

Hoaglin D.C., Hawkins N., Jansen J.P., Scott D.A., Itzler R., Cappelleri J.C., Boersma C., Thompson D., Larholt K.M., Diaz M., and Barrett A. 2011. Conducting indirect-treatment-comparison and network-meta-analysis studies: Report of the ISPOR task force on indirect treatment comparisons good research practices: Part 2. *Value in Health: The Journal of the International Society for Pharmacoeconomics and Outcomes Research* 14 (4): 429–437.

Hopkins R.B., Goeree R., Pullenayegum E., Adachi J.D., Papaioannou A., Xie F., and Thabane L. 2011. The relative efficacy of nine osteoporosis medications for reducing the rate of fractures in post-menopausal women. *BMC Musculoskeletal Disorders* 12: 209.

Jansen J.P., Fleurence R., Devine B., Itzler R., Barrett A., Hawkins N., Lee K., Boersma C., Annemans L., and Cappelleri J.C. 2011. Interpreting indirect treatment comparisons and network meta-analysis for health-care decision making: Report of the ISPOR task force on indirect treatment comparisons good research practices: Part 1. *Value in Health: The Journal of the International Society for Pharmacoeconomics and Outcomes Research* 14 (4): 417–428.

Jansen J.P., Trikalinos T., Cappelleri J.C., Daw J., Andes S., Eldessouki R., and Salanti G. 2014. Indirect treatment comparison/network meta-analysis study questionnaire to assess relevance and credibility to inform health care decision making: An ISPOR-AMCP-NPC good practice task force report. *Value in Health: The Journal of the International Society for Pharmacoeconomics and Outcomes Research* 17 (2): 157–173.

Lu G., and Ades A.E. 2004. Combination of direct and indirect evidence in mixed treatment comparisons. *Statistics in Medicine* 23 (20): 3105–3124.

Rosen C.J., and Khosla S. 2010. Placebo-controlled trials in osteoporosis – Proceeding with caution. *The New England Journal of Medicine* 363 (14): 1365–1367.

Song F., Altman D.G., Glenny A.M., and Deeks J.J. 2003. Validity of indirect comparison for estimating efficacy of competing interventions: Empirical evidence from published meta-analyses. *British Medical Journal* 326 (7387): 472.

StataCorp. 2009. *Stata Statistical Software: Release 11*. College Station, TX: StataCorp LP.

Stein C.M., and Ray W.A. 2010. The ethics of placebo in studies with fracture end points in osteoporosis. *The New England Journal of Medicine* 363 (14): 1367–1370.

Sutton A., Ades A.E., Cooper N., and Abrams K. 2008. Use of indirect and mixed treatment comparisons for technology assessment. *PharmacoEconomics* 26 (9): 753–767.

The Cochrane Collaboration. 2011. *Review Manager (RevMan) [Computer Program]*. Version 5.1. The Nordic Cochrane Centre. Copenhagen, Denmark: The Cochrane Collaboration.

Wells G.A., Sultan S.A., Chen L., Khan M., and Coyle D. 2009. *Indirect Evidence: Indirect Treatment Comparison in Meta-Analysis*. Ottawa, ON: Canadian Agency for Drugs and Technologies in Health. http://www.cadth.ca/en/publication/884. Accessed on December 2, 2014.

Chapter 5

Bayesian Methods

Introduction

In order to explain the Bayesian philosophy, it would be important to first recap the philosophy of the more common traditional frequentist approach (Bland 1998). Consider the case of a trial that was conducted with the frequentist approach. When analyzed, the relative risk of having a bad event is estimated between the two comparators, and a confidence interval for that estimate is generated. In the frequentist philosophy, the true relative risk is always an unknown quantity (a parameter), and all we can do is to come up with an estimate of the parameter (a statistic). Technically speaking, in the frequentist world, it is incorrect to state the parameter value, and instead, the correct erudition is to state 'the estimate for the parameter value is …' In the case of a single trial, we did not include all patients who had the same exact indication and who were measured the same exact outcome, in the same exact setting. Because trials are only a sample of patients, we can never be 100% sure of what the true value is. Even for estimates that we think we are 100% certain, you can also come up with a set of possible reasons why the estimate is not the absolute truth.

Another important feature of the frequentist philosophy is the concept of the confidence interval, which is often misinterpreted. A long-winded definition could be 'If the experiment were repeated an infinite number of times under similar conditions, then there would be a 95% probability (or 95 out of every 100 trials) that the mean estimate would lie somewhere within the confidence interval, assuming normality'. This says that we are only 95% sure that the mean would fall within the confidence interval if we could repeat the trial an infinite number of times. In other words, we are not sure of the true value of the mean estimate (e.g. relative risk), but we are confident that the mean estimate would fall somewhere in the confidence interval.

In the frequentist philosophy, we also use the conventional choice of 5% for the level of significance and the concept of statistical power. The 5% level of significance comes for the work of Fisher who called the finding *significant* if the derived *p*-value was less than 0.05% and weakly significant if the *p*-value was less than 10%, where the latter seems to have been abandoned. The rule is arbitrary, and like driving on the right side of the road (not left side, sorry Londoners), if everyone agrees that it is a good idea, we are okay. Bayesians think that the *p*-value is a value that is worth discussing, as the probability of a null effect.

Statistical power is the ability of the test or study to detect a statistical difference, if the difference truly exists. In statistical jargon, this is the probability of rejecting the null hypothesis (of no difference), when there is a true difference. Power is not used in the Bayesian sense, because we have updated all of the data to create the posterior distribution, which is a summary of all of the data that are available, and the sample size calculation may not require the extra power component (Claxton 1999; O'Hagan and Stevens 2001). With a frequentist approach, the power is the long-run probability that if more data are collected (replication probability) and the truth was that there was a difference, the study should reject the null hypothesis. In other words, the power describes the ability to repeat the study and discover that there was a difference, and a well-powered study indicates that the current study will have 80% or 90% probability of detecting a difference when there is truly a difference.

Study Power for Trials of Rare Diseases

One unfortunate aspect of the frequentist and perhaps Bayesian philosophies is that trials may not be conducted for rare diseases. Increased statistical power and detecting statistical significance relies on a large sample size. With rare diseases and small number of subjects available, there would never be a large enough sample to create a confidence interval to prove statistical significance to conduct a trial, to be adequately powered, and later perform meta-analysis.

The concept of statistical power is a problem for randomized controlled trials (RCTs) that are conducted to test for differences in interventions. For any trial, we estimate the required sample size such that the estimated statistical benefit is 95% confidence that is just enough to be statistically significant. The source of the measure of effect size can come from previous studies, previous meta-analysis, clinical opinion on the meaningful clinically important difference or 0.5 standard deviations (SDs) if the distribution is known. Beyond having a sample size that is sufficient to make our effect size statistically significant, the sample size estimations add in an additional increase in the sample size to create sufficient power.

The sample size formula is in the general form:

$$n = \frac{(\text{confidence} + \text{power})^2}{\text{Effect size}}$$

Typically, with 95% confidence and 90% power, the equation becomes

$$n = \frac{(1.96 + 1.282)^2}{\text{Effect size}}$$

Thus, the additional sample size that we require to adjust for power would be 2.9 times larger than if the power requirement was set to zero. For rare diseases, the probability of conducting subsequent trials that would achieve different significant findings is small because any trial that was conducted for rare diseases would already enrol many of the current patients, and their results would already be known. Thus, the concept of adequate statistical power is already achieved when most of the patients with a disease are already enrolled, and the probability of finding a different result is unlikely. Further research that leads to new rules for rare diseases for designing trials and conducting cost-effectiveness analysis will become increasingly important as we move to introduce drugs based on non-universal genetics (biologics).

Interpretation of Bayesian Results

Finally, we can talk about Bayesian philosophy, which interprets means and confidence intervals differently. Instead of thinking that there is one true mean value for an estimate, the Bayesian philosophy claims that there is a distribution of the parameter which we can estimate, and this becomes our current knowledge. With the Bayesian's estimate of the distribution of the parameter, this leads to the ability to state that there is a probability of 95% and that the population value lies within the 95% confidence interval. To remind researchers that the confidence interval is interpreted differently, Bayesians use the term *credibility interval* instead of *confidence interval*. The underlying

Bayesian philosophy is that researchers are continually updating the estimate of the credibility interval, in other words, our current state of knowledge.

Bayesian Theorem

We provide a diagram for the Bayesian theorem and avoid using formula where it is not necessary to understand the concept (Figure 5.1). The Bayesian theorem and philosophy start off with the assumption that we have a current belief about the distribution for our parameter, and this distribution is referred to as a prior distribution, or more informally, *prior*. Then, new data are obtained from a new trial or study, and when we update our belief after incorporating (combining) the new evidence, we generate a posterior distribution, or simply called a *posterior*. In the frequentist world, the new data are evaluated in isolation, and we generate a *p*-value of the new data alone. Another way to think of Bayesian analysis is that we have previously conducted a meta-analysis (generated a prior), we have found a new study (new data) and we have updated our meta-analysis (generated a posterior) (Briggs 1999).

For a review of how to design Bayesian studies, we will refer you to Brad Carlin, another clever fellow, at the University of Minnesota, Minneapolis, Minnesota for his website (http://www.biostat.umn.edu/~brad/) and textbook (Carlin and Louis 2008), and hope that you attend one of his seminars, for he makes it seem so easy and exciting (honestly!). For evidence synthesis such as meta-analysis, we follow the work of another nice clever fellow Sir David Spiegelhalter in his textbook (Spiegelhalter, Abrams, and Myles 2004) and his web page (http://www.statslab.cam.ac.uk/Dept/People/Spiegelhalter/davids.html). We highlight the steps of a Bayesian analysis (Table 5.1) and will humbly work through a simple example and later provide two advanced examples.

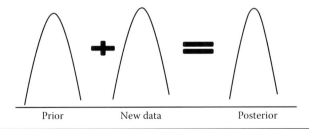

Figure 5.1 **Bayesian theorem. A *prior* distribution (a belief or from previous information) is updated with *new data* (a new trial or other data source) to create a *posterior* (a current estimate).**

Table 5.1 Steps for a Bayesian Meta-Analysis

1. Specify the model.
2. Assign the prior(s).
3. Conduct the simulation.
4. Assess convergence.
5. Interpret and report the results.

Step 1: Specify the Model

When we conduct a meta-analysis, there is an upfront choice to decide on the statistical outcome that we are attempting to estimate, similar to frequentist analysis. In addition, we need to upfront specify the explanatory variables (the data) and the mechanism that links the data to the final outcome. One tricky aspect of running WinBUGS for meta-analysis or cost-effectiveness analysis is the necessity to write the code to run the model, which includes stochastic nodes and arrays (Lunn et al. 2000).

For an example of indirect treatment comparison (network meta-analysis), we can work through an example that was Chapter 3 in a PhD thesis and later published with open access (Hopkins et al. 2011). The example was an indirect comparison of different drugs to prevent fractures for post-menopausal women. We looked at nine different drugs: alendronate, denosumab, etidronate, ibandronate, raloxifene, risedronate, strontium, teriparatide and zoledronic acid. We estimated the odds ratio of four different types of fractures: hip, non-vertebral, vertebral and wrist fractures. The advantage of this topic was that where a large number of studies (NS) (30) with numerous drugs and numerous outcomes, we had the opportunity to assess different methods for conducting the indirect meta-analysis and highlight some biostatistics issues. The different methods were using different software: STATA, WinBUGS and Wells CADTH software. The choice of software was not an important feature with the results differing only slightly when the meta-analysis results were not significant. This was a positive finding because, according to the US National Institute of Standards and Technology (NIST) registry, the choice of statistical software can produce different results for some statistical problems.

For the WinBUGS model (Table 5.2), we first direct our attention to lines 24–28, which are footnotes in the code (begin with the # sign) that list our variables in the model, which are simple enough.

Table 5.2 Bayesian WinBUGS Model

Line Number	Indirect Treatment Comparisons WinBUGS Model for Vertebral Fractures
1	`model {`
2	`for (i in 1:N) {logit(p[i])<-mu[s[i]]+delta[i] * (1-equals(t[i],b[i]))`
3	`    r[i]~dbin(p[i],n[i])`
4	`    delta[i]~dnorm(md[i],tau)`
5	`    md[i]<-d[t[i]] - d[b[i]] }`
6	
7	`for (j in 1:NS) {mu[j]~dnorm(0,.001)}`
8	`d[1]<-0`
9	`for (k in 2:NT) {d[k] ~dnorm(0,.001)}`
10	`sd~dunif(0,2)`
11	`tau<-1/pow(sd,2)`
12	
13	`for (i in 1:N) {mu1[i]<-mu[s[i]]*equals(t[i],1)}`
14	`for (k in 1:NT) {logit(T[k]) <- sum(mu1[])/23+d[k]}`
15	
16	`# ranking and probability {treatment is most effective}`
17	`for (k in 1:NT) {rk[k] <-rank(T[],k)`
18	`best[k]<-equals(rk[k],1)}`
19	
20	`# all pairwise odds ratios`
21	`for (c in 1:(NT-1)) {for (k in (c+1):NT) {or[c,k] <- exp(d[k]-d[c])}}`
22	`}`
23	
24	`# s[] indicates study`
25	`# t[] treatment`
26	`# r[] numerator`
27	`# n[]denominator`

Table 5.2 (*Continued*)   Bayesian WinBUGS Model

Line Number	Indirect Treatment Comparisons WinBUGS Model for Vertebral Fractures
28	# b[] comparator treatment for that trial, b[i]< = t[i] (= 1 if all placebo based)
29	
30	# treatment
31	# 1 placebo
32	# 2 alendronate
33	# 3 etidronate
34	# 4 ibandronate
35	# 5 raloxifene
36	# 6 Risedronate
37	# 7 Teriparatide
38	# 8 ZA
39	# 9 Denosumab
40	#10 Strontium

```
Data
list(N = 46, NS = 23, NT = 10)
s[]    t[]    r[]    n[]    b[]
1      1      0      49     1
1      2      0      95     1
. . . . . . . .
END (hard return)
(hard return)
```

Each study has a number *s*[], where *s*[1] is the first study and *s*[2] is the second study, and when we wish to run all studies, we use *s*[*i*] from 1 to NS.

Each treatment has a number *t*[], where *t*[1] is the first treatment and so on, which are all listed in lines 31–40. When we wish to use all treatments, we use the expression *t*[*k*] for *k* from 1 to number of treatments (NT).

Because we are dealing with events, the probability of an event is the number of events *r*[] divided by the number of patients *n*[].

For every study, we select the common comparator, *b*[], which is equal to 1 for placebo trials. For mixed treatment comparison, when we have placebo trials and active treatment comparators, we can use a value other than 1 for the comparator.

The model includes all of the lines from 1 to 22, with the model starting with the statement, model { (*hard return*), and then finishing on line 22 with } (*hard return*). These two points are both necessary and elegant.

The data file structure is listed at the end of the program.

We have 46 lines of data, with each line providing the study number (from 1 to 23 studies), the treatment number (from 1 to 10 treatments, with 1 being placebo), the number of events in each arm (*r*), the number of patients in each arm (*n*), and the linking group for each study, *b* = 1 for placebo.

Each line of this model is described as follows:

Line 2: It is working with log odds ratio (logit) of the difference (delta) between each treatment versus a common linking arm. The log of an odds ratio creates a difference function. If OR = *A/B*, log(OR) = log(*A*) − log(*B*).

Line 3: By assuming that the rates follow a binomial probability distribution, given r and n, we can find p, the probability.

Line 4: The delta is trial-specific odds ratio that is distributed normally with a random effects assumption (tau), with an overall mean of md.

Line 5: md is the median difference between all treatments t[] versus the comparator b[].

Lines 7–11: These lines are the priors for the model, more on this later.

Lines 13 and 14: These lines create the average of the effects across the treatments (NT), for all studies (N).

Lines 15–21: These lines produce the results that we want to rank the best treatments, to estimate the probability of being the best treatment and to provide the pairwise odds ratios between all treatments.

Lots of examples and extensions are provided by the leaders in this field, at the School of Social and Community Medicine, University of Bristol, Bristol (http://www.bris.ac.uk/social-community-medicine/projects/mpes/mtc/).

Step 2: Assign the Prior(s)

Priors need to be assigned for all parameters in the Bayesian indirect comparison example. If we think logically about the analysis, we will proceed through a series of steps. First, we have priors for all common linking estimates of effect, comparators mu [] on line 7. In addition, we need a prior for all estimates of odds ratio versus placebo for all treatments, listed on line 9 for *k* treatments. These priors are with both a mean of zero and a very small precision (0.001). The variance of the prior is 1/precision, which translates into a variance of 1000 (very uncertain for an odds ratio).

The tau is the precision (or 1/variance) of the random effects, and every variance also has a mean of the variance (0) and an estimate of the precision of the variance. In this case, we assumed that the prior for tau was distributed with a power distribution with a mean of SD (which was the distributed uniformly with mean 0 and precision 2) and a precision of 2. In our analysis, we ran the analysis after changing the priors to verify that the priors were non-informative, which means that the final results are driven by the data.

The ability to use different priors is a fair criticism of Bayesian methods. In our example, the use of non-informative priors ensured that the final results (posterior) were generated only from the data. In reality, using non-informative priors produces the same estimates that would have been created with a frequentist software. Using Bayesian software WinBUGS increases the versatility to combine evidence simultaneously. For most analyses, priors are non-informative and should be tested with different specifications to verify that they do not affect the final results. It is highly transparent when the authors indicate the points at which the priors would become informative.

Informative priors can be used only when we are combining evidence from different sources. For example, we may wish to conduct a meta-analysis that combines new data with any type of prior such as low-quality or previous RCTs or observational studies. In this case, the priors are all specified based on the previous results. Another general example for WinBUGS is when we have a prior that generates a natural history for patients with a disease, and then our new data would include the effect of the treatment for us to generate the updated life profile.

Step 3: Conduct the Simulation

In WinBUGS, the simulation is conducted by checking the model, loading the data, specifying the number of chains and initial values for each chain, running the model and checking for convergence (Figure 5.2). The simplest example of the steps required to run our model is provided with the code

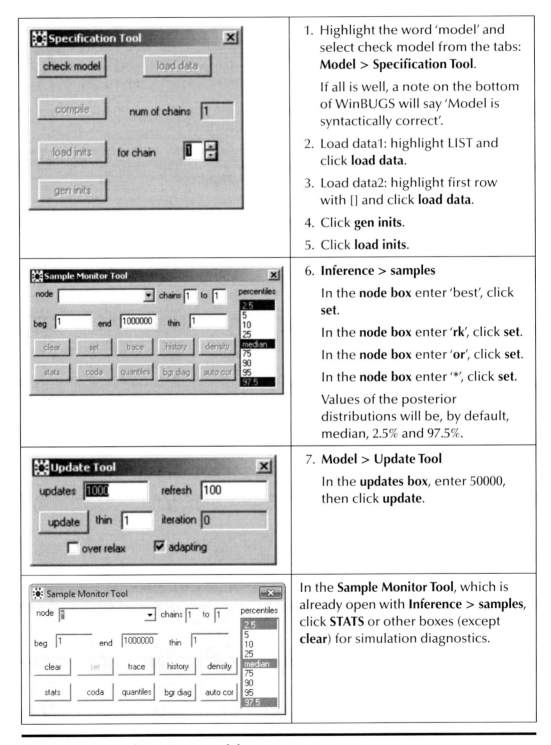

	1. Highlight the word 'model' and select check model from the tabs: **Model > Specification Tool.** If all is well, a note on the bottom of WinBUGS will say 'Model is syntactically correct'. 2. Load data1: highlight LIST and click **load data.** 3. Load data2: highlight first row with [] and click **load data.** 4. Click **gen inits.** 5. Click **load inits.**
	6. **Inference > samples** In the **node box** enter 'best', click **set.** In the **node box** enter '**rk**', click **set.** In the **node box** enter '**or**', click **set.** In the **node box** enter '*', click **set.** Values of the posterior distributions will be, by default, median, 2.5% and 97.5%.
	7. **Model > Update Tool** In the **updates box**, enter 50000, then click **update.**
	In the **Sample Monitor Tool**, which is already open with **Inference > samples**, click **STATS** or other boxes (except **clear**) for simulation diagnostics.

Figure 5.2 **Executing a Bayes model.**

written and stored as a WinBUGS file, with the data listed in Table 5.3. (A code file must be opened from within the program).

Step 4: Assess Convergence

One common learning block for users of Bayesian methods is that the answer to the simulation is a distribution and not an estimate of the true value. We have found that the best way to explain this is by using an analogy. In the standard Gibbs sampling, we liken the detection of the posterior distribution to the searching the top of a tree for a squirrel. The squirrel uses each of its four legs and leg-by-leg reaches out and detects the level of the terrain in all four directions. Whichever direction produces the highest climb, that is, the direction that the squirrel goes, the squirrel takes a big jump in that direction. In the new position, the terrain (posterior distribution) is assessed for a slope, and then the squirrel jumps in the direction with the highest increase in slope. The squirrel does this about 50,000 times or until the squirrel spends almost all of its time around a certain area (distribution). First, notice that the squirrels take a big jump every time to ensure that the full landscape is covered (all possible parameter values are assessed for fit). This also means that the squirrel will always keep jumping and not land exactly in one spot on the top of a tree. Second, the squirrel will occasionally jump away from the tree if the terrain is uneven, which would occur when correlations between data exist, or when the solution is spread over a large period (non-significant findings with broad confidence intervals) and will come back to the same area sometimes slowly. Finally, we can define convergence as finding a stationary process, which mathematically states that as the number of iterations is increased, the probability is also increased that the next iteration (jump) will come from the existing distribution.

There are different ways of assessing whether we have achieved an acceptable level of convergence to derive the final posterior distribution. The simplest approach is to specify two or more chains, where each chain represents a unique simulation. If the different chains lead to the same final posterior distribution, and different starting values were specified for each chain, then we have some reassurance that we may have achieved convergence.

A bit more sophisticated assessment of convergence is to look at a visual display of the simulation. This includes looking at the autocorrelation plot, the trace plot and the density plot. The autocorrelation plot assesses the correlation of the value for each of the past 50 iterations values. The lower the correlation the better the value, which means each new sampling draw is closer to being randomly assigned within the posterior distribution than being related to previous draws. However, high autocorrelation will only indicate that convergence will be slow and is not a true test.

A second easy graph to assess is the trace, which indicates the mean value of the posterior distribution that is estimated after each new iteration. As there are more iterations, the mean value should stabilize to a certain value. A trace that has not come to a stabilized value is problematic, and more iterations are necessary. The density plot is simply the plot of the mean value, including all iterations. If the graph has a narrow confidence interval, the mean value is fairly certain.

Beyond graphs, we can check the value of the Monte Carlo (MC) error, which should be less than 1%–5% of posterior SD. By running the model with increasing numbers of iterations: 20,000, then 30,000 and so on, if more iterations reduce the MC errors, more iterations are appropriate.

More formally, we should assess convergence with a statistical test. Formal examples of convergence are Gelman–Rubin, Raftery–Lewis, Geweke and Heidelberger–Welch (Table 5.3).

Briefly, the Gelman–Rubin test is really a plot of how well two independent chains are mixing. In the graph that is created, we assess the within-chain variance and the between-chain variance as well as the total variance. This is similar to random effects. We wish to have more within-chain variance and small amounts of between-chain variance. If the variance is high between the chains, there are two separate chains with different answers, instead of approaching one common posterior distribution. The graph produces three lines: blue, green and red. The blue line is the average width of 80% intervals within runs (measures within-run variability). The green line is the width of 80% interval of pooled runs (measures total variability), whereas the red line is the ratio of green to blue line (total vs. within-chain variability). To signal possible convergence, we look for the blue and green lines to stabilize and the red line to be close to 1.

The Raftery and Lewis test evaluates how well you can estimate the different quantiles of the posterior distribution in terms of convergence to stationarity and accuracy of estimation. For a specific quantile, create a two-state chain (above/below quantile), estimate the minimum lag such that states are roughly independent and estimate how many iterations it takes to burn in.

Table 5.3 Assessing Convergence with BOA

Step 1: Install BOA

BOA (Bayesian Output Analysis) is a package for use in Splus/R for convergence diagnostics

You will need to download R and install (www.r-project.org)

Then add the package 'boa'

Packages -> Install packages

Select Canada(ON) mirror, then boa

Type library(boa) in the Console window

Step 2: Assess files from WinBUGS

Run your chain as usual, then press 'coda' on the Sample Monitor Tool

The top window is the index file. Select it and save as file1.ind (with type plain text)

Select it again and save as file2.ind (type = plain text)

Save the contents of the next window as file2.out (type = plain text)

Save the contents of the last window as file1.out (plain text)

Step 3: Start BOA

Enter in the command line in R > **boa.menu()**

The following pops up:

```
    1: File      >>
    2: Data      >>
    3: Analysis  >>
                    Select: 5
    4: Plot      >>
    5: Options   >>
    6: Window    >>
```

Step 4: Select global options

BOA MAIN MENU

GLOBAL OPTIONS MENU

```
    1: Back
    2: -----------+
```

(Continued)

Table 5.3 (*Continued*) Assessing Convergence with BOA

```
     3: Analysis...      |

     4: Data...    |

     5: Plot...    |          Select: 4

     6: All...     |

     7: -----------+
```

Step 5: Import data

Enter 1 at the next prompt

You're now back at the main menu

Enter 1 for the file menu

FILE MENU

```
     1: Back

     2: ---------------------+

     3: Import Data     >> |

     4: Load Session    |
                                Select: 3
     5: Save Session    |

     6: Exit BOA  |

     7: ---------------------+
```

Step 6: Specify data file type

IMPORT DATA MENU

```
     1: Back

     2: ------------------------+

     3: CODA Output Files        |

     4: Flat ASCII File          |
                                    Select: 3
     5: Data Matrix Object       |

     6: View Format Specifications |

     7: Options...                |

     8: ------------------------+
```

Table 5.3 (*Continued*)   Assessing Convergence with BOA

Step 7: Select data files

Enter filename prefix without the .ind or .out extension

The data is now loaded in

Enter 1 twice to get back to the main menu

Enter 3 for analysis

Enter 4 for convergence diagnostics

Step 8: Select convergence analysis

ANALYSIS MENU

```
    1: Back
    2: -------------------------+
    3: Descriptive Statistics  >> |        Select: 4
    4: Convergence Diagnostics >> |
    5: Options...                 |
    6: -------------------------+
```

Step 9: Select method of convergence diagnostics

CONVERGENCE DIAGNOSTICS MENU

```
    1: Back
    2: ---------------------+
    3: Brooks, Gelman & Rubin |
    4: Geweke                 |
    5: Heidelberger & Welch   |
    6: Raftery & Lewis        |
    7: ---------------------+
```

To exit:

Type 1 until you are back at the main menu

Choose the File option (enter 1)

Enter 6 to exit

The Geweke test treats the convergence as a time series of the posterior estimates. The idea is to compare the first set of estimates with the later generated estimates and test if the means are the same. The standard output for this test also tells us how many of the first few iterations need to be discarded until the posterior distribution is discovered.

The Heidelberger and Welch test consists of two parts: a stationary portion test and a half-width test. The whole chain is first tested for being stationary (no drift), but if drift appears, the first, second or by every 10% is dropped consecutively until a stationary distribution is found. The second part of the test examines if the width of the confidence is smaller than a specified value. Thus, the test provides two estimates: (1) the number of iterations that are required for burn-in which can be discarded and (2) the number of iterations that are needed to estimate the posterior mean sufficiently accurately.

Each of these tests is unique and will test for convergence differently. One slight problem with the formal statistical tests is that they are not conducted within the WinBUGS interface. Data need to be exported into different software for analysis. The simplest for us to assess convergence has been the R-project software download BODA addon. To get started with WinBUGS, a video on how to use WinBUGS is available online, search 'WinBUGS the movie'.

Step 5: Report the Findings

The comprehensive reporting of Bayesian results has led to two well-known checklists: reporting of Bayes used in clinical studies (ROBUST) and BayesWatch. The Bayesian reporting of clinical trials is suggested according to the ROBUST criteria (Sung et al. 2005) (Table 5.4). The reporting of Bayesian analysis is governed by BayesWatch (Spiegelhalter et al. 2000). We are unaware of a checklist for reporting of Bayesian meta-analysis. However, because we are using Bayesian analysis for a meta-analysis, we need to follow the PRISMA checklist and create a PRISMA diagram (Moher et al. 2009). The ROBUST criteria list includes the items that are expected to be reported over and above the PRISMA checklist. They include seven items grouped into three categories: (1) the prior distribution (specification, justification and sensitivity analysis), (2) the analysis (specification of the statistical model and analytic technique) and (3) the presentation of results (central tendency and SD or credible interval).

Table 5.4   Suggested Items for Reporting Bayesian Meta-Analysis

All PRISMA items (27 items)*
ROBUST (seven items)
The prior distribution (specification, justification and sensitivity analysis)
The analysis (specification of the statistical model and analytic technique)
The presentation of results (central tendency and standard deviation or credible interval)
Methodological details of Bayesian analysis (seven items)
Details of software, for example, WinBUGS, R-project
If Markov chain Monte Carlo used: Gibbs sampling, Metropolis–Hastings
Choice of starting values (identify that different values were assessed)
Number of chains
Burn-in iterations discarded
Number of iterations
Convergence diagnostics

*Prisma Checklist (Moher 2009).

We have found that the analysis section can often be improved, and as reviewers, we would like to see more than the minimum information and the inclusion of other items: number of iterations, thinning, burn-in and details of convergence diagnostics. These items are covered in BayesWatch (details of software, and if Markov chain Monte Carlo used, choice of starting values, number and length of runs and convergence diagnostics and choices justified), but did not make the final seven items. The graphical presentation of Bayesian data is often messy, and graphs used to assess convergence or final density plots tend to add to the confusion and simple forest plot type graphs are more transparent.

Advanced Bayesian Models

Once a beginner has managed to run a WinBUGS model, the same steps to running advanced models exist (Eddy, Hasselblad, and Shachter 1990). In this sense, we are lucky that there has been an open educational role played by the University of Bristol and users. Most WinBUGS codes have been published, or if not published, the authors make references to other open code. In addition, the WinBUGS website has a user group that includes open discussion of fixes and assistance with coding. Next, we provide the description of a few advanced examples.

Advanced Example 1: Combining RCTs and Observational Data

Consider a situation where there are a few trials, where the characteristics of the patients in the trial do not fully represent (generalize to) the patient population. However, there are large observational studies that provide all the relevant outcomes with generalizable patient characteristics, or similarly, with longer study duration. There are two ways to analyze this situation. One way to analyze the data is the frequentist approach, which would be to conduct the meta-analysis of the RCTs and then conduct the meta-analysis of the observational data. If the results are consistent, there are no issues, but if the results differ then selective interpretation is required. For example, the RCTs may be in mildly ill patients, and the observational results may have come from a regression-adjusted or propensity-adjusted analysis with a derived relative effect from moderate or severe risk patients. Alternatively, the patient populations could look similar, and the results are still different. A Bayesian approach would use the observational data as prior distributions, and then the RCT would be the data to derive the posterior final result (McCarron et al. 2009; Spiegelhalter and Best 2003). The advantage of this method is that one final answer is created; however, there is still scepticism of combing data from different resources (Fryback, Chinnis, and Ulvila 2001).

Advanced Example 2: Covariate Adjustment

Consider the case where there are abundant RCTs, but there is wide variability in patient characteristics or in the study design across the RCTs. The frequentist solution would be to conduct a meta-regression with the patient characteristics and study design as covariates.

In the Bayesian world, this can also be conducted as a meta-regression. The advantage would be that it would include priors about known effects and covariates would be included. The addition of weakly informative priors would add to our model, which might decrease the variance that can be explained by the treatment effect. In other words, the confidence intervals for our treatment effect would be smaller if we added in weakly informative priors.

For example, if we had studies that estimated the risk of hip fracture, and we had some studies on patients with low bone mineral density (weak bones), for those studies, the risk of fracture would be higher. A meta-regression that included bone mineral density as a covariate may affect the relative risk estimate, and a Bayesian model that incorporated bone mineral density as a covariate with a weakly informative prior of how low bone mineral density leads to fractures would further improve on the estimate of relative risk. Because there are established risk equations relating bone mineral density to the 10-year risk of fracture, the FRAX equation that is available for most countries, we can incorporate this relationship between bone mineral density and fracture risk as a prior to reduce the uncertainty in the overall results. Alternatively, the effect that bone mineral density has on average for hip fracture would come from separate studies, either administrative data or requiring a systematic review of the relationship between the risk factor and the outcome.

A second example of adjustment form covariates would be from our meta-analysis with endovascular repair, where time was the covariate (Hopkins et al. 2008). Time was considered an important covariate because the use of this technology followed a learning curve (increasing skill for each task) and an experience curve (increased success over time). The success of surgery increased with the number of procedures performed and also with better selection of ideal candidates (EVAR). When we included time (year of publication), we saw that the new technology improved over time. Surprisingly, the standard of care surgical technology also improved over time due to the effect of the experience curve.

Advanced Example 3: Hierarchical Outcomes

Another recent example that we encountered was RCTs that included hierarchical (nested) outcomes. For psoriasis trials, the Psoriasis Area Severity Index (PASI) score is reported as the primary outcome to express the severity of symptoms, often reported as PASI 50, PASI 75 and PASI 90. PASI is an index to represent the level of symptoms that ranges from 0 (least severe) to 72 (worst), whereas PASI 75 represents an improvement of at least 75% in PASI score versus baseline for the patient in the trial. The outcomes are nested, with a patient who achieved 90% improvement (PASI 90) would automatically have achieved PASI 75 (75% improvement) and PASI 50 (50% improvement). In other words, we need to account for double counting (nesting), by using an ordered probit model (Reich et al. 2012).

The WinBUGS code that is available adjusts for the nesting effect, as well as imputes the expected results of data that are not provided for all of the levels for each study.

There is a similar problem when you conduct a review of rheumatoid arthritis drugs, where an American College of Rheumatology (ACR) score of ACR 20, ACR 50 and ACR 70 represents 20%, 50% and 70% improvements, respectively, in the number of tender joints and swollen joints, and improvements in at least three of five scales: C-reactive protein (CRP), erythrocyte sedimentation rate (ESR), Patient Global Assessment, Physician Global Assessment or Health Assessment Questionnaire (HAQ). The PASI case seems straightforward if all studies always report all three measures of PASI 50, PASI 75 and PASI 90. And of course, because they don't, we need to model the missing values, if we wish to simultaneously meta-analyse all three outcomes to improve on the meta-analysis of looking at each outcome separately.

The meta-analysis of nested ACR data has the same problem as the meta-analysis of PASI scores of not having all of the outcomes being reported for all of the trials. In addition, the specific improvements that lead to 50% improvement for one patient may be different for each drug. Specifically, the ACR 50 could have been derived from 50% improvement in CRP, ESR and Patient Global Assessment, whereas another study with similar ACR 50 rates had 50% improvement in Patient Global Assessment, Physician Global Assessment and HAQ. This source of variation contributes to heterogeneity, and imputing the missing ACR 20 might add more uncertainty than if the ACR 20 was provided.

Summary

Bayesian analysis offers versatility for conducting evidence synthesis because of the ability to combine multiple sources of data, as well as builds assumptions into the analysis. We can incorporate covariates and nest hierarchical outcomes, and combine multiple sources of evidence to produce one final estimate. With Bayesian analysis, the final estimate is dependent on the choice of the prior, which must be justified, including why this prior was chosen among alternatives, and provides the cited evidence to support this prior. Priors based on opinions that are unjustified can be seen as weak, and not demonstrating that different priors were tested to assess the impact of the prior is also incomplete.

Given the versatility of Bayesian analysis, there is an increased need to be able to conduct Bayesian analysis in different software. Bayesian analysis can be conducted in most software packages such as STATA or R-project, although the overwhelming choice of software is WinBUGS, or simply BUGS for non-Windows users. There is a small learning curve with WinBUGS, and workshops or working through available examples on the WinBUGS site or the examples that are provided within the free WinBUGS software are suggested.

In this chapter, we did not discuss Bayesian shrinkage factors that provide a technique to reduce the variance for a subgroup analysis. Briefly, the shrinkage factors have been applied to multinational data where the evidence generated from the combined international level helps to reduce the variance of each country's estimate compared to each country alone (Willan et al. 2005). In other words, the confidence interval of the estimate for each country will be smaller after applying the shrinkage factor than if the evidence of each country was estimated alone. The shrinkage factors can also be applied to a meta-analysis for a subgroup analysis, or from a multi-variate meta-analysis, where more than one outcome is simultaneously estimated, allowing for reduced variance for each outcome compared to investigating each outcome alone. The technique of shrinkage factors has been established but perhaps underutilized. In Chapters 6 through 8, we focus on the estimation of the parameters that are required for cost-effectiveness analysis: survival analysis costs and quality of life.

References

Bland J.M.A. 1998. Bayesians and frequentists. *British Medical Journal* 317 (7166): 1151–1160.

Briggs A.H. 1999. A Bayesian approach to stochastic cost-effectiveness analysis. *Health Economics* 8 (3): 257–261.

Carlin B., and Louis T. 2008. *Bayesian Methods for Data Analysis, Third Edition.* Boca Rotan, FL: Chapman & Hill/CRC Press.

Claxton K. 1999. The irrelevance of inference: A decision-making approach to the stochastic evaluation of health care technologies. *Journal of Health Economics* 18 (3): 341–364.

Eddy D.M., Hasselblad V., and Shachter R. 1990. A Bayesian method for synthesizing evidence: The confidence profile method. *International Journal of Technology Assessment in Health Care* 6 (1): 31–55.

Fryback D.G., Chinnis J.O., Jr., and Ulvila J.W. 2001. Bayesian cost-effectiveness analysis. An example using the GUSTO trial. *International Journal of Technology Assessment in Health Care* 17 (1): 83–97.

Hopkins R., Bowen J., Campbell K., Blackhouse G., De R.G., Novick T., O'Reilly D., Goeree R., and Tarride J.E. 2008. Effects of study design and trends for EVAR versus OSR. *Vascular Health and Risk Management* 4 (5): 1011–1022.

Hopkins R.B., Goeree R., Pullenayegum E., Adachi J.D., Papaioannou A., Xie F., and Thabane L. 2011. The relative efficacy of nine osteoporosis medications for reducing the rate of fractures in post-menopausal women. *BMC Musculoskeletal Disorders* 12: 209.

Lunn D.J., Thomas A., Best N., and Spiegelhalter D. 2000. WinBUGS—A Bayesian modelling framework: Concepts, structure, and extensibility. *Statistics and Computing 4:* 325–337.

McCarron C.E., Pullenayegum E.M., Marshall D.A., Goeree R., and Tarride J.E. 2009. Handling uncertainty in economic evaluations of patient level data: A review of the use of Bayesian methods to inform health technology assessments. *International Journal of Technology Assessment in Health Care* 25 (4): 546–554.

Moher D., Liberati A., Tetzlaff J., and Altman D.G. 2009. Preferred reporting items for systematic reviews and meta-analyses: The PRISMA statement. *Annals of Internal Medicine* 151 (4): 264–269, W64.

O'Hagan A., and Stevens J.W. 2001. Bayesian assessment of sample size for clinical trials of cost-effectiveness. *Medical Decision Making* 21 (3): 219–230.

Reich K., Burden A.D., Eaton J.N., and Hawkins N.S. 2012. Efficacy of biologics in the treatment of moderate to severe psoriasis: A network meta-analysis of randomized controlled trials. *British Journal of Dermatology* 166 (1): 179–188.

Spiegelhalter D., Abrams K., and Myles J. 2004. *Bayesian Approaches to Clinical Trials and Health-Care Evaluation*. West Sussex: John Wiley & Sons Ltd.

Spiegelhalter D.J., and Best N.G. 2003. Bayesian approaches to multiple sources of evidence and uncertainty in complex cost-effectiveness modelling. *Statistics in Medicine* 22 (23): 3687–3709.

Spiegelhalter D.J., Myles J.P., Jones D.R., and Abrams K.R. 2000. Bayesian methods in health technology assessment: A review. *Health Technology Assessment* 4 (38): 1–130.

Sung L., Hayden J., Greenberg M.L., Koren G., Feldman B.M., and Tomlinson G.A. 2005. Seven items were identified for inclusion when reporting a Bayesian analysis of a clinical study. *Journal of Clinical Epidemiology* 58 (3): 261–268.

Willan A.R., Pinto E.M., O'Brien B.J., Kaul P., Goeree R., Lynd L., and Armstrong P.W. 2005. Country specific cost comparisons from multinational clinical trials using empirical Bayesian shrinkage estimation: The Canadian ASSENT-3 economic analysis. *Health Economics* 14 (4): 327–338.

Chapter 6

Survival Analysis

Introduction

Consider this situation wherein here are two drugs, Drug A and Drug B, both are intended to prevent heart attacks after a specific diagnosis, and assume for the moment that the heart attacks for this patient population always lead to death, while the actual risk of death is 2%–5% for the general population for first heart attack. Next consider the trial that estimated the two-year rate of heart attack at 60% for Drug A and 50% for Drug B, and the result was more than the minimal clinically important difference and was statistically significant. The study was well-powered, had generalizable patient selection, was well designed and well reported, and is generally considered as high-quality evidence. If you were a patient with the specific diagnosis, which drug would you choose? we would choose Drug A. If you know why we might even be considering choosing Drug A, you can skip this chapter. Otherwise, let's work through an example.

Survival analysis adds an important dimension that affects the patient beyond the rates of events; the dimension is time where a delay in the occurrence of an event is meaningful. When we care about how many events occurred and when the events occurred, we need to conduct survival analysis. Survival analysis is often conducted in cancer trials, sometimes in cardiac trials and rarely elsewhere. The survival analysis is often conducted for the events of survival, progression-free survival (days until cancer progression), or with heart attacks or strokes. Secondary outcomes and safety events are rarely investigated with survival analysis, but they could be, and should be if we wish to extrapolate the future.

Kaplan–Meier Analysis

The starting point for all survival analysis is to use Kaplan–Meier analysis to create survival curves (Clark et al. 2003a). A curve is created for each drug, and a visual inspection offers many insights on the survival pattern. In order to conduct a Kaplan–Meier analysis, we need for each patient the starting day of the trial, the day of an event if an event happened and last day the patient's status was known. For most trials, we have a problem of right censoring where patients are lost to follow-up such as being unable to be reached, so that the last day the patient's status was known occurs before the end of the study period.

To conduct Kaplan–Meier analysis in STATA, we create a one-record line for each patient that contains a unique patient identification number, the treatment the patient was randomized, the patient's last known status either dead or alive, the date of their last known status or end of the follow-up period.

When the data are in the format of Table 6.1, we can use the code from Table 6.2 to conduct the Kaplan–Meier analysis and create the survival curves (Figure 6.1). Some functions for the analysis of survival in STATA use numeric values and other functions are okay with text. The two-year Kaplan–Meier survival estimate for Drug A is 27%, while for Drug B, it is 23%. In total, the number of events in Drug A for a proportion of patients that had an event was 60 out of 100 patients (60/100) or 60% and the annualized rate was 30%, and for Drug B the proportion of patients that had an event was 50 out of 100 patients (50/100) or 50% and the annualized rate was 25% (Table 6.3). There are often a few values that should be reported for survival analysis, such as average length of follow-up. For Drug A, patients were followed on average for 221 days and the mean time for events was 121 days. For Drug B, patients were followed on average for 490 days and the mean time for events was 429 days. We often use medians to represent days to events; in this case, for Drug A, the median follow-up was 107 days, and the median event time was 67 days. For Drug B, the median follow-up was 449 days, and the median event time was 404 days.

It is not common to statistically compare the differences between the groups in the duration of follow-up, but it can be reported as a descriptive statistic. Instead, people rely on judgement on whether the mean or median difference between the groups could be important. Still, reporting means, medians as well as some measure of variance is helpful, either $q1$ and $q3$ quartiles or 95% confidence intervals can be presented. Similarly, it is not

Table 6.1   Data Format to Conduct Survival Analysis in STATA

PatientID	Time	Censor	Treat	TREAT
1	485	1	1	Drug A
2	274	0	1	Drug A
3	123	0	1	Drug A
4	30	1	1	Drug A
5	297	1	1	Drug A
6	135	0	1	Drug A
7	48	1	0	Drug B
8	502	1	0	Drug B
9	133	0	0	Drug B
10	387	0	0	Drug B
11	10	1	0	Drug B
12	221	0	0	Drug B

Note: PateintID—Unique ID for each patient.

Time—Last day since the beginning study for each patient, where the status of death or alive was known.

Censor—1 = death, 0 = alive.

Treat—1 = Drug A, 0 = Drug B.

TREAT: The text variable for Drug A or Drug B.

Table 6.2   STATA Code to Conduct Kaplan–Meier Survival Analysis, Including Creating the Curves

```
stset Time, failure(censor)

sts test TREAT, logranksts graph, by(TREAT) xlabel(0(365)730) ///
plot1opts(lpattern(dash)) plot2opts(lpattern(solid))

sts list, by (TREAT)
```

Note: ///indicates that the syntax allows the code to continue on the next line.

common to compare the average time to events, because the time to events is considered along with the rates of events in Kaplan–Meier analysis.

So far we have some competing statistics, with Drug A having more events than Drug B, but the events occur earlier for Drug A. According to the Kaplan–Meier analysis, the chance of survival at two years is slightly

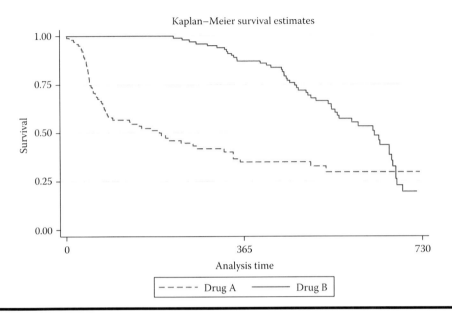

Figure 6.1   Kaplan–Meier survival estimates for Drug A and Drug B. At two years, the predicted survival for Drug A and Drug B was 27.25% and 23.25%, respectively.

Table 6.3   Proportions, Percentages and Rates

	Drug A	*Drug B*
Proportion	60/100	50/100
Percentage	60%	50%
Rate	30% per year	25% per year

Note: Rates always have a time component (per year or per lifetime)

Hazard rate for patients who received Drug A is 30% per year, or 60% for the study period.

Hazard ratio is the comparison of Drug A versus Drug B, 30% divided by 25% = 1.20, a 20% increase in the hazard ratio.

higher for Drug A. In addition, the area that exists under a survival curve is a measure of life expectancy, and based on the Kaplan–Meier curve, patients who received Drug B had more life expectancy.

More confusing for a reviewer is that the test for differences between two Kaplan–Meier curves can be conducted with one of three available tests: log-rank, Cox test of equality and Wilcoxon (Wilcoxon–Breslow–Gehan) test (Luke 1993). There are other tests that have been used to test the difference between survival curves, and perhaps the use of these tests should only be used if properly justified (Ohno-Machado 2001; Willett and Singer 1991). They include the Tarone–Ware, Peto–Peto–Prentice and the generalized Fleming–Harrington tests (Fleming and Lin 2000; Mathew, Pandey, and Murthy 1999). Each of the tests has a different assumption, and while the log-rank is the most common test, there are situations where the log-rank is not the best choice. Given that the three main test statistics can produce different p-values, there is a potential to selectively report favourable or unfavourable results. Of all the possible tests of differences in survival curves, justification should be provided for the method chosen, and even then a reviewer should ask for the simple log-rank result, as a sensitivity analysis.

Among the three common tests, the log-rank is most appropriate when the hazard functions are thought to be proportional across the groups, if they are not equal. This test statistic is constructed by giving equal weights to the contribution of early events and late events over the duration of the study. The Cox test of equality is often used with an adjusted analysis, and if there were no significant covariates, the Cox test is identical to the log rank test. Alternatively, the Wilcoxon test gives more weight to earlier events when the number of patients being followed is higher.

Another important and necessary analysis is to estimate the relative survival of Drug A versus Drug B, and this is estimated with the simple `stcox` command to estimate the Cox regression (Andersen 1991).

```
. stcox treat
```

This command produces the hazard ratio 3.23 (95% CI: 2.18–4.77), $p < .001$, which suggests that the difference between Drug A and Drug B is a 3.23 increase in the hazard rate for Drug A relative to Drug B.

A simplified version of what the Cox model does relates back to the Kaplan–Meier estimate. The Kaplan–Meier curve re-evaluates the estimate of survival whenever there is an event. Logically, this is like figuring out the probability of having an event for each day, if events occur in the first day and if more events occur in the next day, a separate probability of having an event is calculated for the first and second day and so on. Then to calculate the overall survival, the day 1 and day 2 probabilities are multiplied together. A new probability is estimated for every day that events occur, separately for each treatment until the end of the study. Every day that an event occurs, the Kaplan–Meier curve dips, and if no further events occur, the line flattens out.

The Cox model tries to explain the dips in the Kaplan–Meier curve with covariates, such as with treatment only or with treatment coefficient and some prognostic variables. A necessary test for using the Cox proportional hazard model is the proportional hazard assumption. This assumption requires that the differences in the rates of events that occur for the two treatments are roughly consistent during the study, that is, the hazard is proportional over time. This is necessary because we want dips in the Kaplan–Meier curves to be near the same time period for both patients who are receiving each of the drugs. This is very important because of our loss to follow-up. If a few events occurred late in the study period in one treatment, the size of the dip will be large because there are few patients being followed and the rates of events per remaining patients would be large. Conversely, if in the other treatment, the events occurred early or if there were more follow-up, the size of those dips would be smaller. Thus, trying to predict the size of dips between treatment groups requires that the events occur at similar intervals and the loss to follow-up to be similar across groups.

The proportional hazard assumption is often conducted with a visual assessment of one of two plots, easily constructed with the `stphplot` or `stphtest` commands. The first curve is the log–log plot of survival, and plots-log{-log(survival)} versus log(time). The proportional-hazards assumption is violated in our case because the curves are not roughly parallel (Figure 6.2). The second curve is the proportional-hazards assumption on the basis of Schoenfeld residuals after fitting a model with `stcox`. In our case, the line is not flat indicating that the proportional-hazards assumption is violated, and the relative hazard drifts over time (Figure 6.3).

```
stphplot, by(treat) plot1(msym(oh)) plot2(msym(th))
stphtest, plot(treat) msym(oh)
```

To recap so far, the relative survival of patients that take Drug A is estimated to be lower than for patients who take Drug B after we compared the following: rates of events, difference between Kaplan–Meier curves estimated for life expectancy and with the log-rank, Cox or Wilcoxon tests, and Cox regression estimate of the hazard ratio, but not the Kaplan–Meier projected endpoints (Table 6.4). But, we are not done.

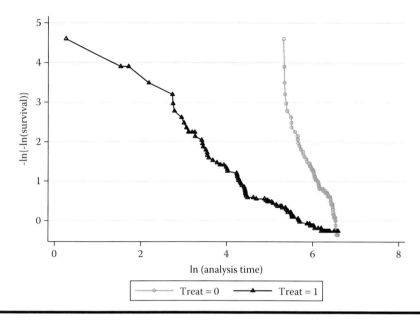

Figure 6.2 **Assessment of the proportional hazard assumption with a log–log plot. The line for Drug A or treat = 1 (on the left) is not parallel with the line for Drug B or treat = 0. The proportional hazard assumption of the rate of events between the two drugs being constant over time does not hold. The Cox proportional hazard regression model should not be used.**

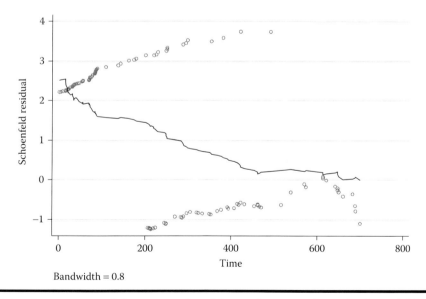

Figure 6.3 **Assessment of the proportional hazard assumption of Schoenfeld residuals. The line of the Schoenfeld residuals is not flat, and the hazard function is not proportional over time and drifts downward. The Cox proportional hazard regression model should not be used.**

Table 6.4 Recap of Possible Estimates for Differences in Survival

	Drug A	*Drug B*
Rate of events per year	30%	25%
Kaplan—Meier estimate of survival	27.25%	23.25%
p-value	.678	
Log-rank of survival functions: (non-direction)	31.78	78.22
p-value	<.001	
Cox equality of survival curves Relative hazard	2.3011	0.7127
p-value	<.001	
Wilcoxon (non-direction) Sum of ranks	4953	−4953
p-value	<.001	
Cox proportional hazard estimate of hazard ratio (95% CI)	3.22 (95% CI: 2.18–4.77)	1 (reference)
p-value	<.001	

Exponential, Gompertz and Weibull Models

Since we are comparing two drugs that may have a lifetime of benefit for patients, a lifetime economic model built on survival extrapolation is appropriate (Guyot et al. 2011). With lifetime extrapolation, we should conduct extrapolation (a prediction outside the study time period) instead of using prediction (explaining what occurred during the study period), with three different assumptions (Bradburn et al. 2003a, 2003b; Clark et al. 2003a, 2003b; Davies et al. 2013). One assumption is that the benefit that was created by the survival analysis using Kaplan–Meier curve be extended into future periods. In other words, we assume that there will be no more events occurring and the Kaplan–Meier curves will be flat over the subsequent years.

A second assumption about the survival pattern is that until the end of the lifetime for all patients, the survival curves will converge and the final survival endpoint will be equal. This assumes that the benefit that was derived for Drug B is not maintained and the benefit will slowly fall over time until the survival rates for the drugs are equal.

A third assumption is that we can predict the future survival pattern using a regression model with the two years trial data. When we make the extrapolations, we easily state that a straight line is a bad idea since straight lines always predict a negative survival area. Instead, we need a survival curve that can extrapolate well into the future and still predict survival that is reasonable. One very important assumption that we have already assessed for the survival patterns is that the proportional hazard assumption does not hold, and because of this failure we need to create survival curves for each drug.

There are a few rules for extrapolation. First, the survival curves should be estimated separately for each treatment to satisfy the lack of proportional hazards and to improve the fit of each model. Second, different functional forms and models should be tested to see which model fits the data best and provides the most logical and reasonable long-term predictions. Third, a decision to split the model into two phases can be made with clinical input. For example, if we look at deaths after a heart attack, many deaths occur within days or weeks following the heart attack. However, if the causal factors for a heart attack are not modified, the risk of second heart attack increases and a later heart attack with death will occur. In this case, we may need to have two periods: three months, and after three months. In our case, all of the events for patients who received Drug A occurred in the first year and no events occurred in the second year, while most of the events for patients who received Drug B occurred in the second year. If we split the survival curves into two periods, the first year and the future years including the second year, the survival curve for Drug A would be flat and the survival curve for Drug B would be very steep predicting complete loss of survival quickly.

For most situations the choice of regression model for extrapolated survival curves is the one-parameter model with constant hazard (exponential) or the two-parameter models that allow for increasing, decreasing or constant rates of hazard, e.g. Weibull or Gompertz (Table 6.5) (Bull and Spiegelhalter 1997; Lee and Go 1997). Although the Weibull is a two-parameter model, the exponential model is really a special case of Weibull curve, where one of the parameters equals a special value. Meanwhile, the exponential curve is simpler and easier to explain. These models are referred to as parametric models, while the Kaplan–Meier is nonparametric and the Cox is semi-parametric with added covariates to explain the nonparametric pattern (Clark et al. 2003b).

Table 6.5   Different Types of Survival Models: Nonparametric, Semi-Parametric and Parametric

Model	*Type*
Kaplan–Meier	Nonparametric
Cox proportional hazard model	Semi-parametric
Exponential	Parametric (one parameter)
Weibull	Parametric (two parameters)
	One parameter for hazard rate—increasing, decreasing or constant
	Second parameter to adjust scale for fit
Gompertz	Parametric (two parameters)
	One parameter for hazard rate—increasing, decreasing or constant
	Second parameter to adjust scale for fit

To select the appropriate survival regression model from the choice of three, we typically use post-estimation tests for goodness of fit. The tests include Akaike's Information Criterion (AIC), Cox–Snell residual plots and comparing the extrapolation predictions to external data sources (Davies et al. 2013). AIC essentially tests the R-squared (R^2) of the regression model, where R-squared is the proportion of variation of the outcome that can be explained by variation in the covariates including treatment and the estimates of survival curve parameters, after adjusting for the number of covariates. When comparing two regression models, the model with the lower (more negative) AIC value is the poorer fit. In addition, 95% confidence intervals are provided to assess if one curve is statistically superior to the other curves.

The Cox–Snell residuals are created with the following commands:

```
stcox treat
predict cox_snell_resid, csnell
stset cox_snell_resid, failure(censor)
sts generate H = na
line H cs cs, sort
```

which creates the variable cox _ snell _ resid and then plots the residuals versus time to allow a visual assessment of deviations from a 45° line. These plots can be compared between the different models. Finally, the use of secondary data such as a large cohort study or from administrative data may be available to estimate the survival for patients with the disease who are receiving usual care. These data are available in Canada by contracting with an academic group who can assess data from the Canadian Institute for Health Information for any disease that requires emergency room visits or hospital admissions.

We have included the STATA code to create the results from the different models for our example, and we have created a plot that displays all of the models together (Table 6.6). Based on Figure 6.4, the hazard rate of mortality

Table 6.6 STATA Code to Produce Instantaneous Hazard Rates at Each Time Point during the Study Period

```
stset Time, failure(censor)

streg if treat = =1, d(exponential)
predict Haz_A_exp, hazard
label var Haz_A_exp "Drug A exponential"

streg if treat = =0, d(exponential)
predict Haz_B_exp, hazard
label var Haz_B_exp "Drug B exponential"

streg if treat = =1, d(weibull)
predict Haz_A_weibull, hazard
label var Haz_A_weibull "Drug A Weibull"

streg if treat = =0, d(weibull)
predict Haz_B_weibull, hazard
label var Haz_B_weibull "Drug B Weibull"

streg if treat = =1, d(gompertz)
predict Haz_A_gomp, hazard
label var Haz_A_gomp "Drug A Gompertz"

streg if treat = =0, d(gompertz)
predict Haz_B_gomp, hazard
label var Haz_B_gomp "Drug B Gompertz"
```

(Continued)

Table 6.6 (*Continued*) STATA Code to Produce Instantaneous Hazard Rates at Each Time Point during the Study Period

```
label var _t "Study Duration"

twoway (line Haz_B_exp _t, sort lwidth(small)) (scatter Haz_A_ ///
exp _t, sort msize(vsmall)) (line Haz_B_gomp _t, sort ///
lwidth(medium)) (scatter Haz_A_gomp _t, sort msize(small)) ///
(line Haz_B_weibull _t, sort lwidth(thick)) (scatter Haz_A_ ///
weibull _t, sort msize(medium))
```

Note: /// indicates that the syntax allows the code to continue on the next line.

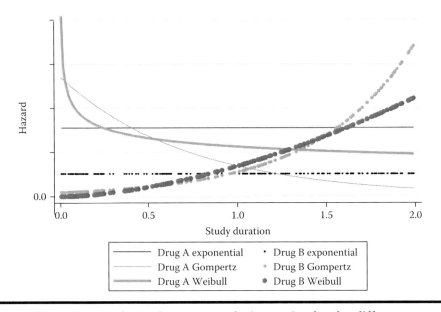

Figure 6.4 Instantaneous hazard rates at each time point for the different parametric models. Instantaneous hazard rates vary from 0.0 to 0.008 for each day in the study period. The hazard for Drug A drifts down, while the hazard for Drug B drifts upward.

over the two-year study period is declining for Drug A and increasing for Drug B, except for the exponential curves where the constant hazard rate is higher for Drug B. The curves that have the most curvature are the Weibull model for Drug A and the Gompertz model for Drug B. When we look at the survival curves over the two-year period using the STATA code in Table 6.7 to create Figure 6.5, we see that all of the survival curves for Drug B are below the survival curves for Drug A. When we used the regression models to extrapolate into the future for an additional eight years for a total of 10 years, almost

Table 6.7   STATA Code to Estimate Survival Curves for the Study Period

```
gen Time_yr = Time/365
stset Time_yr, failure(censor)

streg if treat == 1, d(exponential)
predict Surv_A_exp, surv

label var Surv_A_exp "Drug A exponential"

streg if treat == 0, d(exponential)
predict Surv_B_exp, surv
label var Surv_B_exp "Drug B exponential"

streg if treat == 1, d(weibull)
predict Surv_A_weibull, surv
label var Surv_A_weibull "Drug A Weibull"

streg if treat == 0, d(weibull)
predict Surv_B_weibull, surv
label var Surv_B_weibull "Drug B Weibull"

streg if treat == 1, d(gompertz)
predict Surv_A_gomp, surv
label var Surv_A_gomp "Drug A Gompertz"

streg if treat == 0, d(gompertz)
predict Surv_B_gomp, surv
label var Surv_B_gomp "Drug B Gompertz"

label var _t "Study Duration"

twoway (line Surv_B_exp _t, sort lwidth(small)) (scatter ///
Surv_A_exp _t, sort msize(vsmall)) (line Surv_B_gomp _t, ///
sort lwidth(medium)) (scatter Surv_A_gomp _t, sort ///
msize(small)) (line Surv_B_weibull _t, sort lwidth(thick)) ///
(scatter Surv_A_weibull _t, sort msize(medium))
```

Note: ///indicates that the syntax allows the code to continue on the next line.

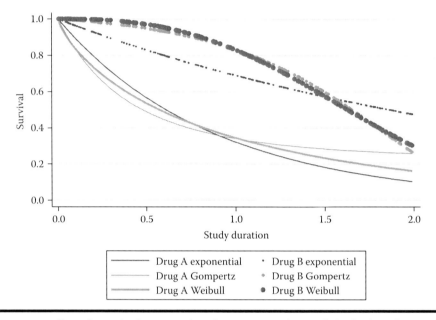

Figure 6.5 Predicted survival curves for the paramertic models during the study period.

all of the survival curves quickly reach 0% (Table 6.8). The exceptions are the exponential curve for Drug A which requires 10 years to reach 0%, while the survival curve that is extrapolated with the Gompertz model for Drug A indicates that the survival curve levels off at 24% (Figure 6.6; Table 6.9). In addition, the Gompertz model for Drug A has the lowest AIC (best fit).

Based on the extrapolations of the survival curves, and selecting the regression models with the best goodness-of-fit measure, we would estimate a survival benefit for Drug A. For the final recap, we discovered that the relative survival of patients that take Drug A is estimated to be lower than for patients who take Drug B after we compared the rates of events, difference between Kaplan–Meier curves estimated with log-rank, Cox or Wilcoxon tests and Cox regression estimate of the hazard ratio. But when we extrapolate to the longer time period, which would be required for populating a lifetime economic model, we would incorporate a survival benefit for Drug A.

Establishing and Using Risk Equations

Building a lifetime economic model is a difficult undertaking, with every disease and its progression being different. When trials are conducted with chronic diseases, there is never enough time to evaluate the occurrence

Table 6.8   STATA Code to Estimate Survival Curves beyond the Study Period

```
gen Time_yr = Time/365
stset Time_yr, failure(censor)

streg if treat = =1, d(exponential)
predict Surv_A_exp, surv
capture stcurve, surv range(0 10) outfile(exp_A, replace)
label var Surv_A_exp "Drug A exponential"

streg if treat = =0, d(exponential)
predict Surv_B_exp, surv
capture stcurve, surv range(0 10) outfile(exp_B, replace)
label var Surv_B_exp "Drug B exponential"

streg if treat = =1, d(weibull)
predict Surv_A_weibull, surv
capture stcurve, surv range(0 10) outfile(weib_A, replace)
label var Surv_A_weibull "Drug A Weibull"

streg if treat = =0, d(weibull)
predict Surv_B_weibull, surv
capture stcurve, surv range(0 10) outfile(weib_B, replace)
label var Surv_B_weibull "Drug B Weibull"

streg if treat = =1, d(gompertz)
predict Surv_A_gomp, surv
capture stcurve, surv range(0 10) outfile(gomp_A, replace)
label var Surv_A_gomp "Drug A Gompertz"

streg if treat = =0, d(gompertz)
predict Surv_B_gomp, surv
capture stcurve, surv range(0 10) outfile(gomp_B, replace)
label var Surv_B_gomp "Drug B Gompertz"

label var _t "Study Duration"
```

(Continued)

Table 6.8 (*Continued*)   STATA Code to Estimate Survival Curves beyond the Study Period

```
twoway (line Surv_B_exp _t, sort lwidth(small)) ///
(scatter Surv_A_exp _t, sort msize(vsmall)) ///
(line Surv_B_gomp _t, sort lwidth(medium)) (scatter ///
Surv_A_gomp _t, sort msize(small)) (line Surv_B_weibull _t, ///
sort lwidth(thick)) (scatter Surv_A_weibull _t, sort ///
msize(medium)), xscale(range(0 10))

TO PRODUCE THE CURVE WITH APPROPRIATE LABELS:

use gomp_B, clear
rename surv1 gomp_B
save "gomp_B.dta", replace
use gomp_A, clear
rename surv1 gomp_A
save "gomp_A.dta", replace
use exp_B, clear
rename surv1 exp_B
save "exp_B.dta", replace
use exp_A, clear
rename surv1 exp_A
save "exp_A.dta", replace
use weib_B, clear
rename surv1 weib_B
save "weib_B.dta", replace
use weib_A, clear
rename surv1 weib_A
save "weib_A.dta", replace

use weib_A, clear
merge 1:1 _t using "weib_B.dta", nogenerate
merge 1:1 _t using "exp_A.dta", nogenerate
merge 1:1 _t using "exp_B.dta", nogenerate
merge 1:1 _t using "gomp_A.dta", nogenerate
merge 1:1 _t using "gomp_B.dta", nogenerate
```

Table 6.8 (*Continued*)   STATA Code to Estimate Survival Curves beyond the Study Period

```
label var weib_A "Drug A Weibull"
label var weib_B "Drug B Weibull"
label var exp_A "Drug A Exponential"
label var exp_B "Drug B Exponential"
label var gomp_A "Drug A Gompertz"
label var gomp_B "Drug A Gompertz"
label var _t "Survival time"

capture save survival_predictions, replace

twoway (line exp_B _t, sort lwidth(small)) (scatter exp_A _t, ///
sort msize(vsmall)) (line gomp_B _t, sort lwidth(medium)) ///
(scatter gomp_A _t, sort msize(small)) (line weib_B _t, ///
sort lwidth(thick)) (scatter weib_A _t, sort msize(medium)), ///
xscale(range(0 10))

List
```

Note: /// indicates that the syntax allows the code to continue on the next line.

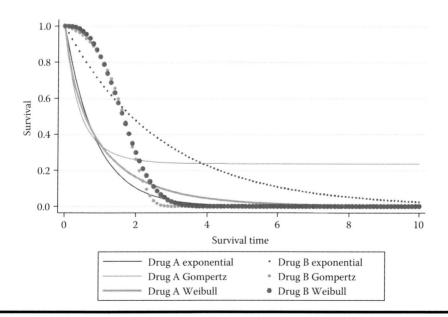

Figure 6.6   Predicted survival curves for the parametric models that were extrapolated beyond the study period. Only Drug A has a predicted long-term survival benefit.

Table 6.9 Survival Predictions for Three Parametric Models

Time (years)	Drug A Survival			Drug B Survival		
	Exponential	Gompertz	Weibull	Exponential	Gompertz	Weibull
0	1.00	1.00	1.00	1.00	1.00	1.00
1	0.32	0.34	0.34	0.69	0.83	0.83
2	0.10	0.26	0.16	0.48	0.26	0.30
3	0.03	0.24	0.08	0.33	0.00	0.03
4	0.01	0.24	0.04	0.23	0.00	0.00
5	0.00	0.24	0.03	0.16	0.00	0.00
6	0.00	0.24	0.01	0.11	0.00	0.00
7	0.00	0.24	0.01	0.07	0.00	0.00
8	0.00	0.24	0.01	0.05	0.00	0.00
9	0.00	0.24	0.00	0.04	0.00	0.00
10	0.00	0.24	0.00	0.02	0.00	0.00

Only Drug A has a predicted long-term survival benefit.

of the progression of all events for the full lifetime. To estimate the long-term benefit of a drug, we would need to follow a patient for a period that may be meaningless. Over time, there will be new drugs introduced, there may be a refinement in patient selection who would benefit the most from receiving the drug, there may be contraindications that create exclusion criteria, discovery of drug interactions that would prevent combination therapy, or the drug itself can be modified by delivery system such as enteric coating and slow-release activation. Instead, we are left with the problem of using an approximation of the typical long-term progression of patients, and then we can only predict how to modify the long-term progression based on a short-term change of therapy. We know how to modify the initial portion of the long-term progression based on evidence from the clinical trial but the expected long-term progression must come from other data sources.

To make long-term predictions of future events, we rely on using well-established risk equations that make predictions based on current and ongoing clinical factors. One example would be the risk of cancer that comes for smoking cigarettes (Klein 2002). If you smoke 10 cigarettes today, nothing will happen to you except maybe you will cough, your eyes will water and you may experience nausea, but there is no immediate cancer risk. If you smoke for 20 years we can provide you with an estimate of your average cancer risk. We also know what the reduction in cancer risk would be if you were a smoker and stopped today and never smoked again. With this cancer risk equation that incorporates the known impact from smoking, we can estimate the long-term health benefit of an intervention that leads to smoking cessation.

This is a lot of work and there are many assumptions that go into making this prediction. First, we need a long-term observational data set that follows patients with a known risk factor and follows them long enough to make a reasonable prediction of the outcome. If we had a prospective study, we can specify the risk factor in great detail, asking for the number of cigarettes smoked, or if the risk factor was a clinical lab value, such as A1c for blood glucose, we could measure it periodically. The most common types of prospective studies are well known and well used in the literature: Wisconsin Epidemiologic Study of Diabetic Retinopathy (Lecaire et al. 2014), United Kingdom Prospective Diabetes Study (Stratton et al. 2000), Framingham Heart Study (Ho et al. 2014), Rochester Epidemiology Project (Rocca et al. 2012) and so on.

Canada has an absence of many risk equations, except the osteoporosis from the Canadian Multicentre Osteoporosis Study (Kreiger et al. 1999) or the Recognizing Osteoporosis and its Consequences in Quebec study (Bessette et al. 2008). In these community-based prospective studies, patients have been followed for more than 10 years and periodically assessed for risk factors and outcomes, and risk equations have been created.

However, for community based studies, if the events are rare, or the risk factors are difficult to capture such as behaviour, and are not lab values, we may need to use retrospective analysis to create risk equations. This is often rated as lower-quality evidence for good reasons, because of the reliance of recall or lack of the availability to measure the risk factors. However, we can still identify lung cancer patients and ask if they have smoked, and accordingly can estimate the relationship between smoking and cancer.

The biggest hurdle beyond availability of data is the ability to capture all the important factors that may impact the prediction of the long-term outcome. Other than primary causal factors, such as smoking leading to cancer, we have effect modifiers and confounders including time varying confounding. The effect modifiers, like their name, modify the effect of a risk factor. The easiest way to detect effect modifiers is to conduct a subgroup analysis for two groups, with and without the modifier such as sex, and see if the casual relationship between smoking and cancer has the same magnitude.

If the relationships are different, when assessed by magnitude of the covariates, there is an effect modifier. The effect modifiers need to be inserted into the long-term risk equations, and ideally with an interaction term between the risk factor and the effect modifier.

Confounding occurs when the relationship between the casual factor and the outcome is distorted by the presence of another variable, which does not lie on the causal path between the casual factor and outcome. For example, obesity is associated with smoking and may also be correlated to cancer. The confounder of obesity must also be inserted in the long-term equation to adjust for the competing risk factor. The assessment for identification of effect modifiers and confounding can also be achieved with case-control studies.

One problem with risk equations and extrapolations is that we assume that everything stays the same over time. The patients may have changed their smoking volume over time, changed exercise habits, diet, left a stressful job and so on. As a result, some risk equations either have time-varying risk factors to account for predicted changes in risk factors or have simply shortened the time that the risk equation predicts. An example of the shorter time frame is the fracture risk assessment tool (FRAX) model that predicts the 10-year risk of fracture, after adjusting for known risk factors of fracture (Leslie et al. 2014; Silverman, Komm, and Mirkin 2014). With consensus, it was decided that predicting fracture risk beyond 10 years was too variable with many of the risk factors being able to change over time, the treatment will change and the 10-year time frame was long enough to incorporate typical clinical trials (generally 3–5 years) and a reversal phase when treatment is stopped.

Diabetes Modelling

The projection of long-term outcomes is an active area of research for diabetes, where a change in behaviour or drugs may take decades to provide benefit. Most long-term modelling studies of diabetes apply risk equations that incorporate risk factors and changes in intermediate markers or endpoints, such as age, A1c, sex, systolic blood pressure, race, smoking status, total cholesterol, duration of diabetes, obesity, lipids and fasting glucose, which lead to many predicted complications such as myocardial infarction, ischemic heart disease, stroke, congestive heart failure, amputation, blindness and renal failure (Tarride et al. 2010).

Diabetes is not unique in that there are many different prediction models, but diabetes is unique in that there is desire to validate the existing long-term outcome models. The Mount Hood Challenge Meetings have been held regularly since 2000 and provide a forum for computer modellers of diabetes to discuss and compare models and to identify key areas of future development. The Fourth Mount Hood Challenge was the first to ask participating modellers to perform simulations based on published clinical trials, thereby allowing comparison of all eight participating models against *real-life* data (Mount Hood 4 Modeling Group 2007). The working hypothesis for the Mount Hood Challenge was that this process of standardized comparison is the best method to identify differences between models as well as assessing the models' reliability in terms of projecting the *real-life* situation (clinical trials).

Acceptability of Surrogates

Given that the occurrence of diabetes complications may take a long time to develop, it is not surprising that trials are designed with intermediary endpoints as the primary outcome and not based on the long-term final outcomes. In these situations, the intermediary endpoints can be called surrogates. Surrogate outcomes have been more formally defined as, 'a laboratory measurement or a physical sign used as a substitute for a clinically meaningful endpoint that measures directly how a patient feels, functions or survives, and that is expected to predict the effect of the therapy' (Temple 1999). Studies often use surrogates as primary outcomes because the trials will be smaller, shorter and less invasive (Wieczorek et al. 2008). In order to be an efficient estimator (small errors) and a consistent estimator (leads to true result) of the long-term outcome, the surrogate must be associated with clinical benefit, be highly correlated with the final outcome, have a biologically plausible basis and have a comprehensive predictive ability to the final outcome so that effect modifiers and confounders can be incorporated.

Another important role of surrogates is for diseases where there is an absence of hard final outcomes disease such as stroke, heart attack, cancer progression or death. Instead, for some diseases, especially chronic disease, symptom relief or change in lab value is the important outcome for the patient's prognosis or the individual's assessment of disease severity.

Unfortunately, the acceptability of surrogates is elusive. From our recent review of 34 methodological guidelines and 140 HTA reports from decision-making HTA agencies, we could not find a list or catalogue of acceptable and validated surrogate outcomes (Rocchi et al. 2013). About half of the HTA reports assessed the acceptability of surrogates and all assessments of acceptability were conducted prospectively. Less than 5% of the HTA reports and economic analysis used surrogate outcomes exclusively, and all were diagnostic technologies.

The trade-off between approving drugs based on surrogate outcomes that require subsequent long-term follow-up studies to report the final outcomes, which may lead to different conclusions, versus withholding effective therapies suggests that caution is wise. On the one hand, the requirement for additional long-term studies or registries for drugs approved based on surrogates seems wise, although expensive and resource intensive, the additional studies later discovered the lack of benefit or increased harm leading to withdrawal of approval. On the other hand, the 'accelerated approval procedure' of the US Food and Drug Administration was introduced in 1993 for the possibility to base early approval of drugs for life-threatening conditions currently lacking of treatment options on surrogate endpoints (Carroll 2006).

A worthy exercise to help with the approval of drugs that had trials based on surrogate outcomes is to conduct a validation study prior to submitting the reimbursement request. The validation study can be a literature review to identify studies that provide evidence for the association of the surrogate and the final endpoint, or to use administrative databases to demonstrate the association, or to create consensus within a clinical community that the surrogate is a meaningful predictor of the final outcome by using a survey or Delphi panel.

Survival Adjustment for Crossover Bias

Survival analysis allows for the adjustment of the analysis when not all patients have completed their therapy or have not had complete follow-up. A further problem for survival analysis is when patients switch therapy during the study. We could restrict choice of therapy but this may not be ethical. When a new drug is being evaluated for regulatory approval, the option for a patient who has failed progression-free survival to switch to active treatment from placebo control is ethically justified and is often mandated as part of the study protocol. Luckily, decision-makers have accepted recent survival adjustment (crossover) methods in reimbursement submissions.

To attempt to remedy the potential crossover bias, two types of survival adjustment methods have been implemented for the analysis of trials and their associated economic evaluations: rank preserving structural failure time (RPSFT) and inverse probability of censoring weighting (IPCW). RPSFT assumes that every day on active treatment provides a delay to death of similar magnitude for patients assigned to active treatment and patients that switched, a *common treatment effect*. IPCW removes crossover patients from the analysis, and the frequency weights of the remaining patients in the placebo group are inflated by the degree of similarity in characteristics to crossover patients. The choice between IPCW or RPSFT depends on six properties: common treatment effect, true treatment effect, crossover percentage, disease severity, time dependence of treatment effect and crossover mechanism (Table 6.10) (Hopkins et al. 2014).

The common treatment effect assumes that for patients that have crossed over, the magnitude of benefit from the active treatment will be equivalent for patients which are randomly assigned to active treatment. Specifically, the outcomes of patients who switched therapies should not be different than the outcomes for patients who were randomly assigned to active treatment.

The factors relative treatment effect and disease severity are similar. When there is little difference between therapies with a hazard ratio near 1, or if

Table 6.10 Properties of Trials That Affect Choice between Inverse Probability of Censoring Weighting and Rank Preserving Structural Failure Time

Property of Trial	IPCW	RPSFT
Common treatment effect absent	Better	Worse, if >20% reduction in treatment effect for crossovers
True treatment effect (low hazard ratio)	Worse	Better, more variable only when treatment effect weak
Crossover % high	Worse	Better
Disease severity (low independent hazard rates)	Not important, unless small trial	Not important
Time dependence of treatment effect is high	Better, if crossovers <90%	Worse
Crossover mechanism (not explainable)	Worse	Better

IPCW, inverse probability of censoring weighting; RPSFT, rank preserving structural failure time.

the active treatment and placebo groups experience few events with independent hazard rates near 0%, the potential for a biased estimate of survival will be low regardless of the method. Simulation studies have attempted to estimate the limits of the hazard ratio and independent hazard rates where the choice between crossover methods became important.

Similarly, there will be a lower limit on the crossover percentage beyond which the choice of method begins to become not important. There also may be an upper limit, where if too many patients crossover, there will be insufficient data within the characteristics of the non-crossover patients to model the crossover mechanism for IPCW.

A factor affecting the modelling of RPSFT is the time dependence of treatment effect, which is an estimate of how long a patient must be on active treatment before they will receive a benefit. Specifically, if the active treatment benefit begins immediately, the time when crossing over will not matter. But, if a patient is required to be on active therapy for a longer period to receive benefit, for example, six months, crossing over late in a study with less than six months remaining will only have a partial effect on survival.

The final factor is the ability to explain the crossover mechanism, which is essential for IPCW analysis to incorporate the crossover mechanism, that is, why patients crossover, as a covariate in the analysis. Clear examples of a time-dependent covariate to predict and explain why a crossover could occur would be failure of progression-free survival, if designed as part of the study protocol.

The factors can be assessed as follows:

1. The rate of crossover can be reported as a percentage.
2. The disease severity can be assessed by rates of events for placebo and active treatment.
3. The true treatment effect can be assessed by the hazard ratio for intention-to-treat and per-protocol as treated. The intention-to-treat analysis assigns any benefit received for the crossover patients to the placebo group, and the per-protocol as treated is the other extreme where all of the treatment benefit from crossing over is assigned to the active treatment.
4. The common treatment effect can be assessed by Kaplan–Meier curves for active treatment arm and for crossover patients from placebo using the time of crossover as their starting time point. The Kaplan–Meier curves for the patients that crossed over should follow

the Kaplan–Meier curve for the active treatment group, if the common treatment effect holds.

5. The time dependence of treatment effect can be assessed as the time profile of the cumulative life expectancy differences between the Kaplan–Meier for active treatment patients versus placebo excluding crossovers.

6. The mechanism of crossover can be tested for regression goodness of fit, or it can be assumed true if the reason for crossover was progression-free survival failure, which is often related to tumour size in cancer trials.

Finally, a comparison of the results of different crossover methods should be reported with Cox regression analysis hazard ratios.

In a literature review that we conducted for evidence where both RPSFT and IPCW were used in survival analysis, the findings of the empirical evidence for relative performance demonstrated the following: intention-to-treat analysis always provided a higher estimate of the hazard ratio (closer to 1.0) and was therefore more conservative; per-protocol analysis provided the lowest estimates of the hazard ratio, and the IPCW and per-protocol results were similar in one trial and the use of RPSFT generates the lowest more favourable hazard ratio and increased the level of statistical significance when provided (Latimer et al. 2012; Morden et al. 2011). Finally, the empirical evidence suggests that the benefit for adjusting the hazard ratio translates into a more favourable cost-effectiveness ratio. The survival adjustment analyses can be conducted easily using STATA with the command `strbee` (White, Walker, and Babiker 2002).

Building a Life Table from Cross-Sectional Data

Sullivan's method is a very simple method to estimate life expectancy and lifetime risk of events, including being the primary method for estimating life expectancy at the national level, which gives us the estimate that life expectancy from birth is 84 years in Canada (Statistics Canada 2007).

The estimate of life expectancy simply begins by estimating the number of people that were alive at the start of the year for every year of age and estimating the number of deaths that occur during the year for each year of age. We then can derive the probability of death for each year of life, and then combine the probabilities for each year to estimate the lifelong probability of death, similar to a Kaplan–Meier analysis. The life expectancy is often estimated separately for men and women and can be estimated for any disease that data on prevalence and risk of death exist for each year. The same method can be used to estimate the lifelong risk of a clinical event such as a hip fracture, foot ulcer or other major event. The life table can also be adjusted for quality of life, if the effect on quality of life is known for each year of the disease. From this latter analysis, we can estimate the total life expectancy, disability-free life expectancy or quality-adjusted life expectancy (Glasziou, Simes, and Gelber 1990).

As an example of estimating the lifetime risk of an event, we estimated the lifetime risk of a hip fracture after making a few adjustments (Hopkins et al. 2012). We used Canadian national administrative for emergency room and hospital admissions to identify unique patients that experienced a hip fracture. To estimate the lifetime risk, we generated the age- and gender-specific rate of having a hip fracture and the number of fractures per population at risk from national census data. Next, using the life table method we summed the probability of survival at each age multiplied by the probability of a hip fracture to create lifetime risk.

The lifetime risk of hip fracture was estimated first without and then with adjustments for trends in mortality, for current trends in rates of hip fracture and for recurrent hip fractures. Both trends in mortality and number of hip fractures were derived with Poisson regression for national data. Linear trends were also investigated, and based on regression diagnostics, the linear regression predictions fit the data as well as Poisson regression trends, but the predictions were not sensible. Finally, to account for the chance that a person may experience two hip fractures during their lifetime, we estimated the lifetime risk of a first hip fracture. National data on the rate of second hip fractures are not available. To account for second hip fractures, we applied the literature values from one study from Sweden that provided rates of second hip fracture by age and sex. The percentage of hip fractures that are first fracture is almost 100% up to age 65 years and declines to about 80% for ages 85+. These rates were used to reduce the rates of hip fractures to estimate the lifetime risk of first hip fractures.

The results of crude lifetime risk of hip fracture for women and men were 12.1% (95% CI: 12.1, 12.2%) and 4.6% (95% CI: 4.5, 4.7%), respectively. When trends in mortality and hip fractures were both incorporated, the lifetime risk of hip fracture for women and men was 8.9% (95% CI: 2.3, 15.4%) and 6.7% (95% CI: 1.2, 12.2%), respectively, and the lifetime risk for first hip fracture for women and men was 7.3% (95% CI: 0.8, 13.9%) and 6.2% (95% CI: 0.7, 11.7%), respectively. A final conclusion was that the adjustments for trends in mortality and rates of hip fracture with removing second fractures produced non-significant differences in estimates and may not be necessary.

Summary

In this chapter, we demonstrated that there are many different ways to present survival analysis, and a reviewer should be cautious on interpreting a single estimate. For survival analysis, we prefer to see the unadjusted Kaplan–Meier curves, as well as tests for the proportional hazards assumptions. If a regression model was created, we would like to see the extrapolations of different models, as well as the results of statistical tests between competing models. We provided some guidance on how to adjust for crossover bias. Finally, we provide some suggestions on how to build the backbone of the lifetime model, by building a natural history model with risk equations or with cross-sectional data.

References

Andersen P.K. 1991. Survival analysis 1982–1991: The second decade of the proportional hazards regression model. *Statistics in Medicine* 10 (12): 1931–1941.

Bessette L., Ste-Marie L.G., Jean S., Davison K.S., Beaulieu M., Baranci M., Bessant J., and Brown J.P. 2008. Recognizing osteoporosis and its consequences in Quebec (ROCQ): Background, rationale, and methods of an anti-fracture patient health-management programme. *Contemporary Clinical Trials* 29 (2): 194–210.

Bradburn M.J., Clark T.G., Love S.B., and Altman D.G. 2003a. Survival analysis part II: Multivariate data analysis – An introduction to concepts and methods. *British Journal of Cancer* 89 (3): 431–436.

Bradburn M.J., Clark T.G., Love S.B., and Altman D.G. 2003b. Survival analysis Part III: Multivariate data analysis – Choosing a model and assessing its adequacy and fit. *British Journal of Cancer* 89 (4): 605–611.

Bull K., and Spiegelhalter D.J. 1997. Survival analysis in observational studies. *Statistics in Medicine* 16 (9): 1041–1074.

Carroll J. 2006. FDA keeps open mind about potential of surrogate endpoints. *Biotechnology Healthcare* 3 (3): 11–12.

Clark T.G., Bradburn M.J., Love S.B., and Altman D.G. 2003a. Survival analysis part I: Basic concepts and first analyses. *British Journal of Cancer* 89 (2): 232–238.

Clark T.G., Bradburn M.J., Love S.B., and Altman D.G. 2003b. Survival analysis part IV: Further concepts and methods in survival analysis. *British Journal of Cancer* 89 (5): 781–786.

Davies C., Briggs A., Lorgelly P., Garellick G., and Malchau H. 2013. The 'hazards' of extrapolating survival curves. *Medical Decision Making* 33 (3): 369–380.

Fleming T.R., and Lin D.Y. 2000. Survival analysis in clinical trials: Past developments and future directions. *Biometrics* 56 (4): 971–983.

Glasziou P.P., Simes R.J., and Gelber R.D. 1990. Quality adjusted survival analysis. *Statistics in Medicine* 9 (11): 1259–1276.

Guyot P., Welton N.J., Ouwens M.J., and Ades A.E. 2011. Survival time outcomes in randomized, controlled trials and meta-analyses: The parallel universes of efficacy and cost-effectiveness. *Value in Health: The Journal of the International Society for Pharmacoeconomics and Outcomes Research* 14 (5): 640–646.

Ho J.E., Larson M.G., Ghorbani A., Cheng S., Coglianese E.E., Vasan R.S., and Wang T.J. 2014. Long-term cardiovascular risks associated with an elevated heart rate: The Framingham heart study. *Journal of the American Heart Association* 3 (3): e000668.

Hopkins R.B., Campbell K., Burke N., Levine M., Thabane L., Duong M., Shum D., and Goeree R. 2014. Survival crossover adjustment and cost effectiveness analysis: An empirical and methodological review with application (poster). *Value Health* 17 (3): A202. *ISPOR 19th Annual International Meeting*, Montreal, QC, Canada.

Hopkins R.B., Pullenayegum E., Goeree R., Adachi J.D., Papaioannou A., Leslie W.D., Tarride J.E., and Thabane L. 2012. Estimation of the lifetime risk of hip fracture for women and men in Canada. *Osteoporosis International* 23 (3): 921–927.

Klein J.P. 2002. Survival analysis methods in cancer studies. *Cancer Treatment and Research* 113: 37–57.

Kreiger N., Joseph L., Mackenzie T., Poliquin S., Brown J., Prior J., Rittmaster R., and Tenenhouse A. 1999. The Canadian Multicentre Osteoporosis Study (CaMos): Background, rationale, methods. *Canadian Journal on Aging* 18 (3): 376–387.

Latimer N., Lambert P., Crowther M., Abrams K.R., Wailoo A.J., and Morden J.P. 2012. Methods for estimating survival benefits in the presence of treatment crossover: A simulation study. *Value in Health* 15 (4): A462.

Lecaire T.J., Klein B.E., Howard K.P., Lee K.E., and Klein R. 2014. Risk for end-stage renal disease over 25 years in the population-based WESDR cohort. *Diabetes Care* 37 (2): 381–388.

Lee E.T., and Go O.T. 1997. Survival analysis in public health research. *Annual Review of Public Health* 18: 105–134.

Leslie W.D., Morin S.N., Lix L.M., and Majumdar S.R. 2014. Does diabetes modify the effect of FRAX risk factors for predicting major osteoporotic and hip fracture? *Osteoporosis International* 25 (12): 2817–2824.

Luke D.A. 1993. Charting the process of change: A primer on survival analysis. *American Journal of Community Psychology* 21 (2): 203–246.

Mathew A., Pandey M., and Murthy N.S. 1999. Survival analysis: Caveats and pitfalls. *European Journal of Surgical Oncology* 25 (3): 321–329.

Morden J.P., Lambert P.C., Latimer N., Abrams K.R., and Wailoo A.J. 2011. Assessing methods for dealing with treatment switching in randomised controlled trials: A simulation study. *BMC Medical Research Methodology* 11: 4.

Mount Hood 4 Modeling Group. 2007. Computer modeling of diabetes and its complications: A report on the fourth Mount Hood challenge meeting. *Diabetes Care* 30 (6): 1638–1646.

Ohno-Machado L. 2001. Modeling medical prognosis: Survival analysis techniques. *Journal of Biomedical Informatics* 34 (6): 428–439.

Rocca W.A., Yawn B.P., St Sauver J.L., Grossardt B.R., and Melton L.J., III. 2012. History of the Rochester epidemiology project: Half a century of medical records linkage in a US population. *Mayo Clinic Proceedings* 87 (12): 1202–1213.

Rocchi A., Khoudigian S., Hopkins R., and Goeree R. 2013. Surrogate outcomes: Experiences at the common drug review. *Cost Effectiveness and Resource Allocation* 11 (1): 31.

Silverman S.L., Komm B.S., and Mirkin S. 2014. Use of FRAX-based fracture risk assessments to identify patients who will benefit from osteoporosis therapy. *Maturitas* 79 (3): 241–247.

Statistics Canada. 2007. *Life Expectancy at Birth and at Age 65 by Sex and by Geography, CANSIM Table 102-0512.* Statistics Canada, Ottawa, Canada.

Stratton I.M., Adler A.I., Neil H.A., Matthews D.R., Manley S.E., Cull C.A., Hadden D., Turner R.C., and Holman R.R. 2000. Association of glycaemia with macrovascular and microvascular complications of type 2 diabetes (UKPDS 35): Prospective observational study. *British Medical Journal* 321 (7258): 405–412.

Tarride J.E., Hopkins R., Blackhouse G., Bowen J.M., Bischof M., Von K.C., O'Reilly D., Xie F., and Goeree R. 2010. A review of methods used in long-term cost-effectiveness models of diabetes mellitus treatment. *PharmacoEconomics* 28 (4): 255–277.

Temple R. 1999. Are surrogate markers adequate to assess cardiovascular disease drugs? *Journal of the American Medical Association* 282 (8): 790–795.

White I.R., Walker S., and Babiker A. 2002. Strbee: Randomization-based efficacy estimator. *Stata Journal* 2 (2): 140–150.

Wieczorek A., Rys P., Skrzekowska-Baran I., and Malecki M. 2008. The role of surrogate endpoints in the evaluation of efficacy and safety of therapeutic interventions in diabetes mellitus. *Review of Diabetic Studies* 5 (3): 128–135.

Willett J.B., and Singer J.D. 1991. Applications of survival analysis to aging research. *Experimental Aging Research* 17 (4): 243–250.

Chapter 7

Costs and Cost of Illness Studies

Based on reviewing many cost-effectiveness analysis, a common error that we see is the under-reporting of the costs of clinical events, such as reporting only the cost of a hospital visit. In Canada, the cost of a clinical event is made of many *silo* budgets, including regional payments to hospitals, in-hospital drugs, provincial budgets to pay for clinician fees, community budgets to pay for care after discharge, a separate provincial budget to pay for outpatient drug prescriptions for seniors and based on need, and a separate provincial budget to pay for devices for mobility.

As just one of many examples, the average cost of a hospital visit for a hip fracture is approximately 70% for the hospital portion, which is often derived from case costing at hospitals, and 30% for physician fees, if we only include the initial acute care episode. When we follow the patient over the year following the fracture, the cost of return visits to the hospital to assess healing, physician fees, rehabilitation services and with additional nurse-based help at home or in nurse-based residency, the cost of a hip fracture becomes closer to about 40% hospital, 20% physician fees and 40% follow-up costs. In total if we only included the initial cost of the hospitalization, the cost would be under-reported by more than $50,000 per fracture. If we then apply the full cost of a fracture to a cost-effectiveness analysis, the ICER would shift by thousands or tens of thousands of dollars, in favour of a new therapy that provided a reduction in the number of fractures. We therefore think it is worth some time identifying all of the possible sources of costs for clinical events, or for increased disease severity, in order to more fully make the case for new interventions that reduce harmful clinical events.

From Clinical Events to Resource Utilization to Costs

The objective of a cost-effectiveness analysis is to compare the cost and effects of two or more possible treatment options. The costs are incurred by the treatment and by clinical events that occur, either as an efficacy event or as a safety event, while sometimes the background cost of the severity of the disease is also required. The starting point is the pivotal clinical trial that records the relative rates of different efficacy and safety events or reports improvements in disease severity due to the new intervention.

To create a cost-effectiveness analysis from a clinical trial, two options exist. First, the trial can include case report forms that capture all resource utilization that occurred during the trial. The resource utilization can be verified against the clinical case report form, such as every heart attack should have an emergency room visit in the resource utilization form and a heart attack in the clinical case report form.

Although this is an excellent way to verify events and resources required, this imposes a bit more upfront work. First, the case report forms must be designed to capture the major types of cost that are expected during the trial. Second, the patient is required to be assessed at least every 3–6 months, for a retrospective review of resource(s) used in the time period since the last assessment. Recall has proven to be very high at 3–6 months for major events, since most people can recall being in the hospital and the number of days spent there. Less major events such as doctor visits and number of therapy sessions can also have high accurate recall if rare. But the recording of frequent low-impact resources such as the number of daily over-the-counter medications taken is rarely accurate and is often messy data with errors and omissions. One option to improve the data quality is to request daily diaries or to simply inquire about the resources needed in the last week as an estimate of the longer time period.

The case report forms for resource utilization are necessary to capture all resource utilization, even though a patient's identification may be linked to a single-source database like an insurance plan that captures most cost categories. Most trials are not linked to a single-source resource database, and even then, gaps such as secondary insurance and out-of-pocket expenses for over-the-counter medications or devices are not captured. Furthermore, the addition of the resource utilization database can help verify any linkable data, but more important is that at the time of the assessment for resource utilization information, we can also easily capture quality of life.

If there were no resource utilization case report forms and there was no linkable cost data, a second option would be to use external data sources to provide a cost estimate for all recorded clinical events. The external data can come from a local data source for costs per events, or from national or local databases, or from published cost estimates for similar events requiring a systematic literature review to ensure comprehensiveness.

For both the first and second options, the usual steps are to estimate the resource utilization and then apply a unit cost to derive total costs per patient or event. In both cases, the unit costs should be a local cost to predict future local costs and savings if an intervention is approved locally for future funding decisions.

The methods to accurately depict the resource utilization and unit costs can be subject to review. In the accounting world, the estimation of cost follows the guidance of cost accounting governed and regulated by Generally Accepted Accounting Principles (GAAP). For cost-effectiveness analysis, there is an absence of exact standards, but books and guidelines on health economics are available that provide broader statements. Health economics introduces cost concepts similar to cost accounting while GAAP provide more precise rules for conducting and reporting cost estimates. Some examples include whether the historical price or fair market value should be used for the estimate of the cost of a capital expenditure, such as the cost of an existing CT scanner or MRI machine. Another example would be the correct method to account for depreciation, and if depreciation was used, then how it should be reported. The GAAP rules are applied for profit agencies and hopefully followed for non-profit agencies but it is unclear if they are followed for economic analysis. Instead, we suggest reviewing the ISPOR guidelines and the relevant important textbooks, which are written for masters and PhD students and researchers.

Measurement of Resource Utilization

An important step in estimating resource utilization is to exclude resources used by the patient in the trial that are not considered to be disease or event related. Sometimes, it is easy to exclude the costs of the treatment for an event that is not clearly disease related, such as excluding the cost of treating abdominal pain for a patient enrolled in a trial to prevent heart attacks.

The issue may at first seem straightforward, but if many patients developed abdominal pain during the trial, or if abdominal pain is an expected adverse event based on the Phase I safety study, then the cost of treating the abdominal pain must be estimated and included. A full-cost approach or a clinically relevant approach should produce similar results, and any events removed must be determined by clinical opinion. If a cost-effectiveness analysis is based on a systematic literature review, NHS guidelines mandate including all the resource utilization of all events, whether statistically different between groups or not.

Attribution and Adjustment for Comorbidities

An important issue for isolating cause or no cause of a clinical event or resource use is to account for the effects of other comorbidities. Quite often patients will have multiple comorbidities such as diabetes, obesity, heart problems and joint pain. When a clinical event occurs, the cause of the event will be complicated. We will highlight three different methods to quantify the rate of events and how to attribute the events to one disease: (1) adjust for known risk factors, (2) use attribution percent and (3) use excess rates of events by comparing to a control group.

For some diseases or events, there are defined risk criteria that have been established to stratify the level of risk of the event. At different levels of risk based on the presence of factors, clinicians have reached consensus on how to increase the therapy for higher-risk patients. For example, the risk of stroke from cardiac arrhythmia is stratified by the CHADS2 score, where points are accumulated by the presence of Congestive heart failure, Hypertension, Age 75 or older, Diabetes and two points for one of prior stroke, TIA or thromboembolism. The tool is used to predict the future risk of having a stroke. Patients with scores of 0 may require daily aspirin; patients with scores of 1 or 2 may require aspirin, warfarin or perhaps other anticoagulant and for patients with scores of 2 or greater, the risk of stroke is considered moderate to high and the patient is recommended to be on warfarin or another anticoagulant, and not aspirin. The CHADS2 highlights the multi-factorial causation of a clinical event where any of the CHADS2 factors could be responsible for a stroke. When we wish to assess the attribution of one factor, such as hypertension, we can use multiple regression with stroke as the outcome and the CHADS2 factors as explanatory variables to predict the effect of each factor on the rate of stroke.

A similar problem occurs with osteoporosis where a fracture may not be fully attributable to the underlying low bone mineral density. Osteoporosis is defined as having bone mineral density that is 2 standard deviations below peak female bone density from a reference population, often cited as the NHANES non-hispanic cohort, using a Hologic densitometer. However, fractures occur at all ages in men and women who do not have low bone mineral density, quite often the result of an accident or severe fall. For patients with osteoporosis who are often but not always elderly, a low-grade fall such as stumbling on a sidewalk or from a fall off one or two steps on a staircase can cause a hip fracture. For osteoporosis, the attribution of a hip fracture has been addressed by consensus, and by review of a population such as in the province of Quebec, where women who are at a higher risk for hip fracture than men, if they had a hip fracture they were later asked to have a bone mineral density assessment. Based on these two methods, the attribution of hip fractures to osteoporosis was over 90% for women, rising with age. Meanwhile, the other types of fracture that are common in osteoporosis such as wrist fractures had as low as 50% attribution to osteoporosis, depending on the age.

The third option is to use a matched case-control study and assess the excess risk of events for the cases, the group with the known risk factor, versus controls, the group without the risk factor. This has been done, as an example, for diabetes which is a disease that is difficult to separate diabetes from its casual factors such as obesity. In the province of Ontario with a population of 13 million in 2004, we identified newly diagnosed type 1 and 2 diabetes cases aged 35 and over from the validated Ontario Diabetes Database and matched 1:2 using propensity scores with controls (non-diabetes cases) (Goeree et al. 2009). Matching was conducted based on age groups, sex and residence by postal code since residence has been proven to be an efficient proxy for socioeconomic status (wealthy neighbourhood or not), which is correlated with education levels, income and overall health status. Using linked administrative databases in the province, data on death and the following complications expected with diabetes were recorded: myocardial infarction, stroke, angina, heart failure, blindness, amputation, nephropathy and cataract. We estimate(d) the excess risk of events for the diabetes patients less than the matched controls with Kaplan–Meier curves for up to 10 years of follow-up. Based on the 0.6 million cases and 1.2 million controls, the risk of all events was statistically higher than for controls. This includes a 42% higher risk of death, where the life expectancy for a diabetes case starting at an average age of 62 years, the typical age for onset of type II diabetes, is just over 10 years versus 20 years for the controls. In other words, diabetes can account for a loss of longevity of almost 10 years, relative to the non-diabetic population.

Strategies to Isolate the Cost of an Event

A statistical problem similar to identifying if an event is disease or treatment related is to isolate the cost of an event. There are three common options to isolating a cost: (1) use a matched case-control study, (2) use within patient pre–post analysis or (3) use regression adjustment (Table 7.1).

Similar to matching to identify the risk of an event, matching cases with controls will allow the estimation of an event that is disease related.

Table 7.1   Alternate Methods for Attribution of Cost for a Clinical Event

Method	Description
Selecting Events to Include	
Full costing	Include all medical expenses all full value for an individual.
Selective attribution of events	Ignore events that are not clinically related to disease or event. For example, ignore cosmetic hair transplant for a patient with diabetes.
Attribution percentage	For cost of illness studies, only an established percentage of events can be attributed to a disease. For example, for osteoporosis, wrist fractures in 20 year olds are excluded, while wrist fractures in age 50+ are 60% attributed to osteoporosis.
Estimating Value of Events to Include	
Regression attribution	Conduct regression with cost as the outcome with the disease of interest and competing risk factors as covariates. For example, for the cost of admission to a nurse-based long-term care facility because of a hip fracture, an adjustment for dementia should be included.
Pre–post incremental costing	For a clinical event or disease onset, the cost of care for one year after the event should be reduced by the cost of care for one year prior to the event, or disease onset. For example, for a patient with a hip fracture, the one year post-fracture minus one year pre-fracture costs.
Excess costing versus control	Cost for a patient are reduced by the cost of care for a control that was matched by age, sex and other factors such as socioeconomic status, address or other comorbidities. For example, annual cost of care for a patient with diabetes versus non-diabetes control.

This method allows for the investigation of the cost of an event that is beyond typical or average cost and represents the excess cost that the disease creates. For example, the cost of a myocardial infarction for patients with diabetes is $21,466, while for patients without diabetes $18,064, then the excess cost is $3,402 (Goeree et al. 2009). This excess is really an exploratory factor because if we were building a cost-effectiveness analysis that included a cohort of diabetes patients, the cost of the myocardial infarction in the analysis would be taken for the similar cases for the observational matching study with diabetes cases. However, the excess cost for the diabetes cases versus controls provides an estimate for analysts who are building local cost-effectiveness models that have access only to the cost for the general population and would underestimate the cost of the event of the diabetes patient (Goeree et al. 2010). An excess cost or markup can be applied to provide an improved estimate of the cost of the event.

A common estimate for the cost of a clinical event is to capture the cost for care for a patient after the clinical event and subtract the cost of care for the patient before the event. Matching between patients such as to the general population provides an estimate of the excess cost related to only one factor, the marker for the disease. This method is better suited for measuring the overall burden of disease, while pre–post matching is best used for analysis of clinical events (Hopkins and Tarride 2013).

One example of the pre–post matching has been conducted with osteoporosis, where patients who have fractures often have high levels of care before their fracture due to aging. The average age for hip fractures is about 70–80 years of age and other comorbidities may be present. The one year post-fracture cost can be estimated by subtracting the cost from the year prior to the fracture, allowing for adjustment of factors such as total costs in prior year, number of comorbidities or prior nursing home use. In addition, since dementia may be contributing factor to a fall that precipitates to a fracture, it may be inappropriate to attribute the cost of a subsequent transfer to a nursing home only to the fracture, thus disregarding dementia and other comorbidities (Akobundu et al. 2006).

A limitation with using pre–post incremental costs is that the pre- and post-period for costing must be specified, such as one year. An important gap in the estimation of the cost of fractures and osteoporosis with matching methods is the exclusion of multi-year costs after a fracture, such as the need for permanent assistance in daily living (Tarride et al. 2012). Patients that have had hip fractures can experience higher costs relative to controls for up to 15 years (Hopkins et al. 2013). Similarly, including pre-fracture costs that are disease related, such as taking bisphosphonates to reduce the risk of fracture, would lead to an underestimate of the impact of osteoporosis on the cost of fractures. However, the pre–post analysis and propensity matching estimate are similar.

A related statistical problem for a fracture is that difference between the post-fracture cost minus the pre-fracture cost may be negative for some patients. The inclusion of these patients into the average cost may underestimate the typical cost, Options of censoring to the value zero or omitting the patients is possible, and an alternative solution that uses median regression has been shown to be consistent with other estimation techniques.

Regression Methods

Alternatively, a multiple regression analysis that included the competing risk factors would partially adjust the cost that can be attributable to one disease. For example, we can estimate the probability of being transferred to a long-term nursing home following a fracture after a hip fracture and adjust for contribution of dementia by adding the disease as a covariate. This relies on the assumption that our database has identified the presence of dementia. This may be problematic since some disease(s) may be under-reported in one database, such as osteoporosis which is stated as having comorbidity less than 5% of hospital admissions for hip fractures, although it is the primary causal factor. The choice of covariates is also an interesting exercise in judgement since the known risk factors must be identified, and if it is stroke, then we can use the CHADS2 score factors. Otherwise, we rely on the combination of clinical opinion and testing for univariate significance of the available factors to predict the event. Finally, we should mention that both regression adjustment and excess costing based on matching require a large number of patients in order to conduct the analysis.

Other Strategies to Estimate Costs

When large amounts of data are not available, and there are no published estimates available, there are a few novel approaches to create cost estimates. These methods include using a Delphi panel to gather clinical opinions or to conduct a time and motion study (Xie et al. 2012). The Delphi panel surveys clinical opinion on the resource utilization of the *typical case*, such as medications prescribed, rates of admissions and number of doctor therapy visits. The Delphi panel differs from a simple survey because of the second step where the responses of the blinded surveys are summarized, and members are allowed to agree to the results or provide opinions why the results are different. After the second step, which is best conducted face-to-face, a consensus is reached and the values or ranges of values are reported.

For common events with standard practice, a one-step survey or single opinion is enough. For example, for a hip fracture, there might be one emergency room visit, an X-ray before surgery, an X-ray after surgery, at least one follow-up doctor visit, a drug prescription for pain and prescribed physiotherapy sessions. In reality, there are at least 25 items to include in the cost of a hip fracture (Table 7.2).

Table 7.2 Perspective and Examples of Costs for a Hip Fracture

Perspective	*Cost*
Hospital	Emergency room visit
	X-ray and diagnostics
	Surgical procedures
	Hospital stay
	Step-down hospital stay
	Rehabilitation hospital
Health care or HMO	Home care
	Long-term residential care
	Devices
	Drugs (in hospital)
	Drugs (prescribed)
	Further doctor visits
	Physiotherapy sessions
Government	Ambulance service
	Transportation of disabled person
	Subsidized housing allowance for disability
	Home modifications for disability

(Continued)

Table 7.2 (*Continued*)   Perspective and Examples of Costs for a Hip Fracture

Perspective	Cost
Societal	Drugs (out-of-pocket)
	Caregiver wage loss
	Caregiver loss of leisure
	Patient wage loss
	Patient loss of leisure
	Hospital parking
	Other out-of-pocket medical expenses
Other intangible costs	Research and development

Note: Many costs include direct medical costs (fees, salaries, equipment disposables) and indirect medical costs (employment benefits, facility activity-based usage, facility overhead charges).

A rarely conducted time and motion study is needed when there are procedures that have not had case costing applied or when therapies can vary (Xie et al. 2014). This would include intravenous (IV) drug administration in a cancer clinic, which is often reported in administrative databases as being an average cost. However, some drugs are administered in 15 minutes and other drugs require slow infusion over two hours, but the databases suggest they have the identical average cost. A time and motion study that included a trained observer who recorded the staff's time and activities for each patient could be used to estimate a true cost for each patient and summarized by treatment procedure. After all of the resources, such as staff time and materials, have been quantified, the unit prices are applied to estimate total cost.

Unit Costs Valuation for Resources

The value assigned to most health care resource items should be based on current local market prices. This may not be the case when hospital charges are not detailed enough, as is the case in many countries. Using the average daily hospital cost may be the only option. Also, it is recommended that the quantities of resources used (i.e. numbers of units) should be reported separately from the valued resources, in order to allow total cost estimates to be updated easily should better cost estimates become available. Drummond, Manca and Sculpher (2005) have suggested reporting physical quantities separately from until it costs to facilitate generalization of study results to other settings'.

It may happen that utilization data for various types of health services and related cost data are not available for the same year. In such a case, the different reference periods should be stated explicitly, and costs should be expressed with reference to a common base year (constant value), that is, taking into account inflation over the years. Inflating cost is obtained by using the consumer price index, or when available, the more relevant health component of the consumer price index. Also, costs should be expressed in the current local currency as well as in a benchmark foreign currency, such as US dollars or Euros.

The main issue with finding a local unit cost estimate is that different local prices and practice patterns may exist for clinical events. For example, for a trial conducted in a university-affiliated institution, the diagnostic tests that are used to assess a potential clinical event may not be the same resource used in the broader community or in a less-developed country.

Perspective and Types of Costs

It is usual to divide costs into three main categories: direct, indirect and intangible costs. Intangible costs are non-monetary costs due to the pain, suffering and reduced quality of life of patients who experience the disease. As the name indicates, intangible costs refer to costs that are difficult to quantify and value. This may explain why, in practice, they are not typically included in cost estimates. Another reason for not including these costs is double counting (i.e. pain would lead to reduced quality of life, and increased drug costs).

Direct costs are easily identified costs that directly apply to a medical service, such as a fee for a service, the cost of a drug or emergency room visit. Indirect costs are costs that must be indirectly attributed to a single event, such as employment benefits must be applied to a wage for the time it takes to do a procedure for a technologist, annual depreciation and upkeep for expensive medical equipment must be applied for every procedure performed, or the overall cost of running a hospital must be averaged and attributed to a single procedure.

The classification of cost that is more important and must be stated upfront is the perspective of the cost study, and the perspective depends on the end-user of the HTA. The main types of perspectives are hospital, health care sector, government and societal (Garrison et al. 2010). The hospital perspective includes all costs that occur within a hospital that are supplied by the hospital, and this would exclude follow-up costs for a fracture where the follow-up events included a non-hospital six-month clinic visit. The hospital level of analysis is important for private for-profit hospitals that wish to estimate all of their resources that were required for a single admission to estimate a bill for their service.

At the next level of being more broad, which is more typical for HMO (Mullins et al. 2010) or for comprehensive public health care plans, is the health care perspective. The health care perspective would include the cost of health care that are provided outside a single institution, such as a visit to a doctor's office, prescribed medicines obtained from a pharmacy, physiotherapy and other rehabilitations services, ambulance charges or medical devices such as canes or walkers.

A further more comprehensive category would be a government perspective, which would include the costs for services that are provided by a public government that are not from the Ministry or Department of Health. These additional costs would include assisted living such as meals on wheels, subsidized transportation for disabled patients, sometimes mobility devices such as expensive wheelchairs, or employment compensation for disability.

The most inclusive perspective is a societal perspective, which further includes the costs are that incurred by members including the patient and their caregivers. The costs would include wage loss (Goeree et al. 1999), out-of-pocket expenses such as copayments or deductibles, and non-reimbursed services such as hospital parking. The costs incurred for a caregiver such as wage loss are also included, and the value of loss of leisure can be valued as zero, minimum wage, average industrial wage or pre-disease wage (Hopkins, Goeree, and Longo 2010).

A cost that is sometimes added, but is debatable for inclusion depending on the decision-making body, is the estimate for the time loss for leisure. This would include the four-hour session for dialysis therapy, where the patient must forfeit the four hours of being actively mobile. These costs can sometimes be included for a cost study, but the further costs may not be acceptable for decision-making bodies for reimbursement. One example would be foetal alcohol syndrome, where a foetus has been exposed to high levels of alcohol in the first trimester. The syndrome has been reported to be the most common association for high school dropouts and for incarceration. The associated costs would include the reduction or loss of lifetime wages for incomplete education compared to the population average, and the cost of jail time for a typical case (Hopkins et al. 2008).

A separate possible inclusion could be the monetary value of quality of life impairment or disability, but because we capture this impairment with quality-of-life assessments, the impairment can be included in a burden of illness study but not a comparative cost-effectiveness analysis that includes quality of life. Another cost that is stated for a burden of illness study is the cost of research for the disease, but similarly this is excluded in comparative cost-effectiveness analysis. The perspective that is allowed for a reimbursement decision is always well established and publicly available, such as the societal perspective is required in the province of Quebec.

A caution for readers of cost or burden studies is the interchangeability of the terms indirect costs and societal costs. Both terms have been used to refer to cost such as wage loss or loss of time for leisure, while indirect costs is a term that comes in cost accounting and economics for a cost that is not directly attributed to each event and must be indirectly applied. The hospital overhead for maintenance or the cost of heating or security would be a medical indirect cost. But if a family member takes time off from work to provide caregiver services, an estimate of their loss of employment benefits based on the hourly wage rate would be both a non-medical indirect cost and a societal indirect cost.

To avoid confusion, we prefer to see a clear statement in the methods section of the perspective that was taken and a list of all cost items included, and be aware that individual reviewers of journal submissions may have their own preferences for definitions. More detail for categories and perspective can be found at Drummond and Mason (2007); Drummond, Tarricone and Torbica (2013); Garrison et al. (2010); Hao and Thomas (2013); Mullins et al. (2010); Mycka et al. (2010) and Shi et al. (2010).

Burden of Illness Study

Often we are asked to provide a cost-effectiveness analysis for a trial that did not capture resource utilization as part of the trail data. We typically recommend a burden (or cost) of illness study. There are many reasons to conduct the burden of illness study, other than the direct application of the data from the burden of illness study can be used for the current and future cost-effectiveness analysis. The published burden of illness study provides to the reviewers of the economic submission assurances that the cost estimates are high quality because they have been peer reviewed.

There is a very high acceptance rate for burden of illness studies in disease-specific journals, because the study can provide a great deal of information that is collected in order to estimate overall burden. The obvious estimates are the current rates of prevalence and incidence, the types of resources required to treat the disease, the total economic burden per case or per year and the percentage of the overall health care budget. Future epidemiology and economic impact can be estimated if trends are available and applied. For the research community, the study will identify where data are lacking, or conversely, if data are sufficient, the underserviced or other important target populations such as high cost or patients with poor outcomes can be identified (Sedrine, Radican, and Reginster 2001).

The two main types of burden of illness studies are the incident-based analysis, which estimates the average lifetime cost for a patient with the disease, and the prevalence-based approach, which estimates the annual cost of treating all patients with the disease in a setting such as a country. The incident-based analysis considers only new cases and can capture costs from onset until cure or death. The prevalent-based approach considers both new and old cases within one year and identifies all costs of disease within the time period regardless of time of onset of disease. Common examples include the lifetime cost per patient with diabetes, exposure to foetal alcohol, or cost of obesity. Examples of the annual burden of disease include osteoporosis, diabetes and obesity. Even more helpful is when the average costs can be provided by age/sex strata.

Prevalence-based studies rely on more readily accessible current data, and directly informs government of the cost attributable to disease. However, the types of cost can vary between diseases which make comparisons limited, and judgement is required for assigning comorbidity costs such as side effects of drugs.

Incident-based studies are easily incorporated into economic evaluations and are the backbone of lifetime economic models. The lifetime model allows the assessment of the effect of changing policy or epidemiology such as the declining population rates of smoking or hip fractures. The lifetime models require more data and the estimates of disease progression for long periods with costs, such as probability of future rates of events and probability of survival affected by the disease, which requires assumptions on consistency of care and rates of outcomes.

The data required to estimate burden of illness are a mixture of macro-economic (top-down) and micro-economic (bottom-up) methods and are often retrospective and rarely prospective, unless created by a new registry cohort that is followed for a long period, and published many years later. Top-down costing is desirable when the costs are unique to a disease and the number of cases is known. For an example of top-down costing, we know how much is spent annually on the single-purpose drugs for osteo-porosis, and we may know from drug databases the number of patients with prescriptions. Thus, we can easily estimate the annual cost for drugs for osteoporosis. We cannot, however, estimate the number of cases who should be on an osteoporosis drug. For an example of bottom-up costing, we know from a community database that for every patient diagnosed with osteoporosis, there is on average six visits to the doctor every year.

In reality, it is favourable to derive the estimates from different data sources to verify estimates. We can provide some validity to the estimate if the estimate that is derived from different data sources is in agreement, especially for cost categories that have multiple uses. For example, the number of doctor visits in the year after a hip fracture was estimated from a physician survey, which was in agreement from a community database, which was in agreement with two provincial cohort estimates.

Budget Impact Analysis

A budget impact analysis is a stand-alone analysis, but it is also required with every cost-effectiveness analysis for drug formulary reimbursement (Mauskopf et al. 2007). The budget impact analysis provides an aggregate total dollar value change in health budget if new or alternate interventions are introduced, or when the level of use of the interventions is increased. In addition, the specific types of resources that will be required or saved should also be provided. For example the new intervention will require a specific cost, but the new intervention will save an average 1.4 hospital admissions per year per case.

The budget impact analysis also provides information for policy impact analysis, where the types of resources that are required to implement the new intervention are specified, and future changes in resources are predicted (Marshall et al. 2008). For example, if a portable X-ray machine was being introduced into outpatient clinics, then the effect on hospital-based X-ray use including staff requirements can be predicted.

A budget impact analysis is different than a static incident-based burden of illness analysis because it involves incremental costs with new interventions. In addition, a budget impact analysis is different than a cost-effectiveness analysis because of the bottom lines reported. The cost-effectiveness analysis reports the incremental average per patient cost to improve quality of life. Budget impact analysis reports the total dollar change in resources if the new strategy is implemented, in other words, provides an assessment of whether the new intervention is affordable. When the cost-effectiveness analysis and budget impact analysis are created, they rely on many of the same costing methods, while budget impact analysis ignores quality of life (Sullivan et al. 2014). It is ethically interesting that there is not an aggregate assessment on the impact on quality of life. There will be examples of approved interventions where the budget impact is very small and the cost-effectiveness is marginally favourable, and examples of rejected interventions where the cost-effectiveness analysis is favourable but the budget impact is too large to be implemented. Often, we see examples of selective approval to restrict use and limit budget impact (Table 7.1).

The recently revised ISPOR guidelines for budget impact analysis encourages the incorporation of advanced methods used in cost-effectiveness analysis, increased coordination of the accompanying cost-effectiveness analysis, how or whether to include quality of life and increased transparency for the decision-maker (Mauskopf et al. 2007).

Statistical Issues with Cost Data

There are two main issues with cost data, missing data and statistical distributions. Data can be a missing unit cost for a given resource utilization, an intermittent missed visit for resource utilization questionnaire, loss to

Table 7.3   Metaphorical Story (or Is It an Allegory) on Full Costing

> On our recent holiday, we went into a nice restaurant and ordered the chicken dinners off the menu, which was listed as $24.99 per dinner. The server asked if we wished roasted, steamed or raw vegetables. We picked the steamed vegetables. Our server asked if we wished tap water or bottled water, and we picked the bottle water. Our server asked if we wished to start with some freshly baked bread, and we agreed. The food was good and the bill was not.
>
> Our $24.99 turned into $94.99 per person after the additional cost of vegetables, premium water, fresh bread, tourist tax and state required gratuity.

follow-up or absence of resource utilization data. These issues are addressed in Chapter 9 on missing data.

Statistical distributions can present some problems for the analyst. Up front, there is general agreement that there is a skewed distribution for the cost of health care. About 10%–20% of patients account for more than 50%–90% of the total health care budget. In any given year, a large percentage will have no health care use at all. As we age, there is an increase in the average use of health care each year, but still some patients go decades without requiring any medical service.

The problem with skewed cost data is increased because of sampling uncertainty, where the functional form of the cost distribution, the degree of skewness, will randomly change based on the patients chosen for the study or analysis. In any group of patient, there will be a few high levels of users of resources and more low levels of users of resources. We are then often left to test for skewness and make an adjustment for the level of skewness for that sample. In this sense, the adjustment is arbitrary and random because the sampling is arbitrary and random. It then makes more sense to adjust for sampling bias first, by using bootstrapping. Lucky for us, bootstrapping also reduces skewness and even with a small sample, the residual skewness is not important. The simplest solution is to bootstrap the cost data and test between distributions with simple *t*-tests.

Summary

A common problem with many estimates of cost is the exclusion of items for which the data were not available through linkage of databases. The best source of cost is patient-level linkable data that include all cost silos, for example including the 25 items that make up the cost of a hip fracture. Where an important cost estimate is not available, a literature review to identify previous estimates of the cost is invaluable to compile the list of cost items to include. Instead of a literature review, a new cost of illness study that uses the best available evidence will provide the current costs for an event or a disease. Another consideration for cost estimates is to exclude items that are not event or disease related, or to reduce the cost that is attributed to the specific disease with regression adjustment, incremental or excess cost analysis. Finally, the reporting of cost should follow the many available guidelines for cost-effectiveness analysis (Caro et al. 2012; Drummond et al. 2003; Mauskopf et al. 2007). We conclude this chapter with a metaphorical story that highlights the problem of under-reporting costs (Table 7.3).

References

Akobundu E., Ju J., Blatt L., and Mullins C.D. 2006. Cost-of-illness studies: A review of current methods. *PharmacoEconomics* 24 (9): 869–890.

Caro J.J., Briggs A.H., Siebert U., and Kuntz K.M. 2012. Modeling good research practices – Overview: A report of the ISPOR-SMDM modeling good research practices task force – 1. *Value in Health: The Journal of the International Society for Pharmacoeconomics and Outcomes Research* 15 (6): 796–803.

Drummond M., Brown R., Fendrick A.M., Fullerton P., Neumann P., Taylor R., and Barbieri M. 2003. Use of pharmacoeconomics information – Report of the ISPOR task force on use of pharmacoeconomic/health economic information in health-care decision making. *Value in Health: The Journal of the International Society for Pharmacoeconomics and Outcomes Research* 6 (4): 407–416.

Drummond M., Manca A., and Sculpher M. 2005. Increasing the generalizability of economic evaluations: Recommendations for the design, analysis, and reporting of studies. *International Journal of Technology Assessment in Health Care* 21 (2): 165–171.

Drummond M., Tarricone R., and Torbica A. 2013. Assessing the added value of health technologies: Reconciling different perspectives. *Value in Health: The Journal of the International Society for Pharmacoeconomics and Outcomes Research* 16 (1 Suppl): S7–S13.

Drummond M.F., and Mason A.R. 2007. European perspective on the costs and cost-effectiveness of cancer therapies. *Journal of Clinical Oncology* 25 (2): 191–195.

Garrison L.P., Jr., Mansley E.C., Abbott T.A., III, Bresnahan B.W., Hay J.W., and Smeeding J. 2010. Good research practices for measuring drug costs in cost-effectiveness analyses: A societal perspective: the ISPOR drug cost task force report – Part II. *Value in Health: The Journal of the International Society for Pharmacoeconomics and Outcomes Research* 13 (1): 8–13.

Goeree R., O'Brien B.J., Blackhouse G., Agro K., and Goering P. 1999. The valuation of productivity costs due to premature mortality: A comparison of the human-capital and friction-cost methods for schizophrenia. *Canadian Journal of Psychiatry* 44 (5): 455–463.

Goeree R., O'Reilly D., Hopkins R., Blackhouse G., Tarride J.E., Xie F., and Lim M. 2010. General population versus disease-specific event rate and cost estimates: Potential bias for economic appraisals. *Expert Review of Pharmacoeconomics and Outcomes Research* 10 (4): 379–384.

Goeree R., O'Reilly D., Hux J., Lim M., Hopkins R., Tarride J., Blackhouse G., and Xie F. 2009. Total and excess costs of diabetes and related complications in Ontario. *Canadian Journal of Diabetes* 33 (1): 35–45.

Hao Y., and Thomas A. 2013. Health technology assessment and comparative effectiveness research: A pharmaceutical industry perspective. *Expert Review of Pharmacoeconomics and Outcomes Research* 13 (4): 447–454.

Hopkins R.B., Goeree R., and Longo C.J. 2010. Estimating the national wage loss from cancer in Canada. *Current Oncology* 17 (2): 40–49.

Hopkins R.B., Paradis J., Roshankar T., Bowen J., Tarride J.E., Blackhouse G., Lim M., O'Reilly D., Goeree R., and Longo C.J. 2008. Universal or targeted screening for fetal alcohol exposure: A cost-effectiveness analysis. *Journal of Studies on Alcohol and Drugs* 69 (4): 510–519.

Hopkins R.B., Tarride J.E., Leslie W.D., Metge C., Lix L.M., Morin S., Finlayson G., Azimaee M., Pullenayegum E., Goeree R., Adachi J.D., Papaioannou A., and Thabane L. 2013. Estimating the excess costs for patients with incident fractures, prevalent fractures, and nonfracture osteoporosis. *Osteoporosis International* 24 (2): 581–593.

Marshall D.A., Douglas P.R., Drummond M.F., Torrance G.W., MacLeod S., Manti O., Cheruvu L., and Corvari R. 2008. Guidelines for conducting pharmaceutical budget impact analyses for submission to public drug plans in Canada. *PharmacoEconomics* 26 (6): 477–495.

Mauskopf J.A., Sullivan S.D., Annemans L., Caro J., Mullins C.D., Nuijten M., Orlewska E., Watkins J., and Trueman P. 2007. Principles of good practice for budget impact analysis: Report of the ISPOR task force on good research practices – Budget impact analysis. *Value in Health: The Journal of the International Society for Pharmacoeconomics and Outcomes Research* 10 (5): 336–347.

Mullins C.D., Seal B., Seoane-Vazquez E., Sankaranarayanan J., Asche C.V., Jayadevappa R., Lee W.C., Romanus D.K., Wang J., Hay J.W., and Smeeding J. 2010. Good research practices for measuring drug costs in cost-effectiveness analyses: Medicare, medicaid and other US government payers perspectives: The ISPOR drug cost task force report – Part IV. *Value in Health: The Journal of the International Society for Pharmacoeconomics and Outcomes Research* 13 (1): 18–24.

Mycka J.M., Dellamano R., Kolassa E.M., Wonder M., Ghosh S., Hay J.W., and Smeeding J. 2010. Good research practices for measuring drug costs in cost effectiveness analyses: An industry perspective: The ISPOR drug cost task force report – Part V. *Value in Health: The Journal of the International Society for Pharmacoeconomics and Outcomes Research* 13 (1): 25–27.

Sedrine W.B., Radican L., and Reginster J.Y. 2001. On conducting burden-of-osteoporosis studies: A review of the core concepts and practical issues. A study carried out under the auspices of a WHO Collaborating Center. *Rheumatology (Oxford)* 40 (1): 7–14.

Shi L., Hodges M., Drummond M., Ahn J., Li S.C., Hu S., Augustovski F., Hay J.W., and Smeeding J. 2010. Good research practices for measuring drug costs in cost-effectiveness analyses: An international perspective: The ISPOR drug cost task force report – Part VI. *Value in Health: The Journal of the International Society for Pharmacoeconomics and Outcomes Research* 13 (1): 28–33.

Sullivan S.D., Mauskopf J.A., Augustovski F., Jaime C.J., Lee K.M., Minchin M., Orlewska E., Penna P., Rodriguez Barrios J.M., and Shau W.Y. 2014. Budget impact analysis-principles of good practice: Report of the ISPOR 2012 budget impact analysis good practice II task force. *Value in Health: The Journal of the International Society for Pharmacoeconomics and Outcomes Research* 17 (1): 5–14.

Tarride J.E., Hopkins R.B., Leslie W.D., Morin S., Adachi J.D., Papaioannou A., Bessette L., Brown J.P., and Goeree R. 2012. The burden of illness of osteoporosis in Canada. *Osteoporosis International* 23 (11): 2591–2600.

Xie F., Hopkins R.B., Burke N., Habib M., Angelis C.D., Pasetka M., Giotis A., and Goeree R. 2014. Time and labor costs associated with administration of intravenous bisphosphonates for breast or prostate cancer patients with metastatic bone disease: A time and motion study. *Hospital Practice (1995)* 42 (2): 38–45.

Xie F., Hopkins R., Burke N., Tarride J.E., and Goeree R. 2012. Patient management, and time and health care resource utilization associated with the use of intravenous bisphosphonates for patients with metastatic bone disease: A Delphi study. *Hospital Practice (Minneapolis)* 40 (2): 131–137.

Chapter 8

Health-Related Quality of Life

Most jurisdictions wish to see some form of economic analysis, such as a budget impact analysis or cost-effectiveness analysis (Drummond 1987). The decision-making body either explicitly requires cost-effectiveness analysis that includes the impact of costs and quality of life (QOL) or will use this evidence if it is provided for a submission. Because of increasing health care budgets, the role of assessing value for money for providing positive health impacts will increase. Value for money is often defined as the incremental cost per incremental health benefit, such as bad events avoided or lessen of disease severity.

A common problem with some chronic diseases is that there is often an absence of hard clinical endpoints, such as death or heart attacks, and the benefit of any therapy is to reduce symptoms. As a consequence, it is difficult for decision-makers to interpret the impact of disease-specific outcomes, such as changes in mini mental state examination for Alzheimer disease; changes in health assessment questionnaire scores for rheumatoid arthritis or changes in scales for depression, functional living, sexual function or symptom checklists. While using the disease-specific scales is suggested to assess clinical change, the desire to present the results in a form that represents society reflection of QOL based on different health states is needed.

Therefore, we have two reasons to collect generic measures of health-related quality of life (HRQOL) such as EQ-5D: first, to conduct an economic analysis to estimate a cost per quality-adjusted life year (QALY), and second, to present the benefit from a disease-specific context onto a commonly interpretable scale.

The major problem with cost-effectiveness analysis is how the QOL estimates are derived. Ideally, the QOL can be captured during a trial and the overall benefit on the new therapy on QOL is straightforward (Drummond 2001). But, when the QOL is not routinely assessed, the gap to fill in the missing QOL metrics are poorly done, either they are not considered available or worse derived for estimates of events for other diseases or the general population. This may understate the detrimental impact that clinical events have on QOL. In this chapter, we highlight the many different ways to identify QOL.

Why QOL?

The estimation of a numeric value for QOL is an attempt to measure utility, which is the term that health economist use to represent *value* for an individual. In health economics, behavioural economics, micro-economics and all branches of economics and other disciplines such as psychology and sociology, the goal of all individuals is to maximize their lifelong utility, or happiness. This is further complicated by welfare economics that suggest that it is possible to measure the utility of each person and somehow optimize the total utility for society, as a revealed preference. This relies on capturing or estimating everyone's utility, which leads us to theoretical rules what can be done (positive economics) and what should be done (normative economics), to improve everyone's utility. While this was suggested long ago, we have learned that people's happiness or utility can be increased not by consumption of goods, but by other actions such as sharing with society or more closely members of your own family. In addition, we also learned that each person's action in their own interests can be improved by acting in collaboration, and their exists a role for government in the presence of market imperfections and unequal information between buyer and seller and so on. This material is usually covered in an introductory economics class.

For reimbursement decision-making, we rely on a few simple axioms (lines of reasoning). We define a given collection of symptoms or disease condition as a *health state* (Table 8.1). Individuals have preferences for different health state(s), which is when asked we might claim that a hip fracture with rehabilitation is less preferred to a mild heart attack with quick recovery. This is our revealed preference. After interviewing millions of members of the general population, because they fund health care as taxpayers, we can determine the relative ranking of many different health states (Brazier et al. 2005). We can also determine how the different health states relate to loss of life, as a time trade-off (Churchill et al. 1987).

Table 8.1   Some Definitions Relating to Quality of Life

Term	Explanation
Health state	Non-quantitative description of a disease condition, including the medical impact, the effect on mobility, ability to perform usual activities and level of pain
Quality of life	Description of the health state
Utility	Numeric value for the health state (often death = 0 and perfect health = 1)

Note: Often the term *quality-of-life score* is intended to represent utility.

We ask many members of the general population trade-off questions on health states (QOL) such as how many years of perfect health would you prefer to living 10 years with mild osteoarthritis of the hip. If, on average, we find that the subjects said they would prefer 6.9 years with perfect health versus 10 years with chronic back pain, we would estimate their utility, the numeric value of QOL, would be 6.9/10 or 0.69 (Tengs 2000). This is similar in magnitude for utility of living with angina (0.69), renal diseases at home (0.65), symptomatic hepatitis B (0.67), tuberculosis with home confinement for three months (0.68) and complete incontinence (0.61), all of which were measured with the time trade-off method. These numbers were captured in a publication in the year 2000. To provide current accurate estimates of the utility of a condition, a systematic review and meta-analysis should be conducted.

We use the term *utility* for the scale of 0–1, although technically only the methods that capture risk and time preference such as standard gamble represent true utility, according to economic theory. That is, we have built-in value judgements for the health state of how long it will last and what the probabilities of changing from that state are. It has become convention to save the term *utility* for the numeric scale and *quality of life* as the text-based description of the health state. We think this is simpler than stating 'quality of life' and 'generic scale estimate of quality of life'.

After we have been able to determine the utility of different health states, we can compare at the decision-making level, the benefit that is achieved for a given dollar expenditure.

A few important caveats exist. First, different members of society will have different values for different disease conditions. Most parents and citizens would argue that treating a child with a condition may have higher priority than adults. In addition, the decision to add to the formulary the

Table 8.2 Factors That Impact the Health Decision beyond Cost and Health-Related Quality of Life

The treatment in question is life-saving.
The illness is a result of health care provision negligence.
The intervention would prevent more harm in the future.
The patients are children.
The intervention will have a major impact on the patient's family.
The illness under consideration is extremely severe.
The intervention will encourage more scientific and technical innovation.
The illness is rare.
There are no alternative therapies available.
The intervention will have a major impact on society at large.
The patients concerned are socially disadvantaged.
The treatment is life extending.
The condition being tackled is time-limited.
The illness is a result of corporate negligence.

first treatment for a disease may not be comparable ethically using the same metric as adding a second drug for a different disease.

In the United Kingdom, the collective preferences have been revealed and include other factors besides change in QOL (Table 8.2). After reviewing this long list, as well as understanding the uncertainty, we can safely say that a patient's utility is not always the same as society's utility for the same health state. We can find more consensus when the comparison between two similar treatments for the same disease in the same population without the concerns of equity or fairness. In these cases, we are trading off one symptom for another (red pill vs. blue pill). For example, in your current disease condition, would you prefer a reduction in joint pain from a pill that made you more nausea? Our next question is how to measure preferences for pain versus nausea.

Good Properties of Scales

The construction of scales is a lengthy and costly process, and we will discuss this with referral to our example of pain versus nausea. For both symptoms of pain and nausea, there are relative magnitudes of severity. This is opposite to a hard clinical endpoint such as death, or changes in blood pressure or cholesterol level. Instead, we need to construct scales in a series of steps.

When we discuss HRQOL, we often refer to the *generic* scale, which is meant to include a measure that is suitable for all diseases, and *disease-specific* scale, which is intended for use in patients for that particular disease, while the construction of each scale is similar for both (Marra et al. 2005).

For a disease, we often perform qualitative analysis, which could include patient interviews or focus groups. We try to gather all of the important impacts that may affect overall happiness, that is, utility. From there, we develop, test and measure how different factors impact the patient's sense of pain or nausea. Alternatively, we can use a simple scale of 1–100 of how bad the pain or nausea is. The latter method tends to be less sensitive, more variable and has less consistency for detecting changes, but we do use the scale made with factors versus the comparison of the overall scale of 1–100.

There are a series of tests of validity and reliability before the scale can be used in clinical practice. We need the scale to make sense (face validity) and it needs to include all important factors supported by theory (content validity). If we pass this stage, then we further test if the test can detect improvements for different severity of pain for a patient, or between patients such as compared to a gold standard or an other acceptable measure (reliability). For example, if pain is reduced, the patient may reduce the number of pain medications, go back to work and resume usual activities. If so, we can move on to the next steps. After we check whether all items in the scale are needed, and not too similar to other items in the scale, we can check that if a patient stays at the same level of pain over time, we verify that the scale does not change in value. Once the scale is validated and considered reliable, we can use it in clinical practice.

Generic scales are favoured by decision-makers because of their familiarity and interpretability, while clinicians use disease-specific measures for evidence of clinical improvement. Generic QOL scales may not be sensitive enough to detect changes in some diseases, especially if the disease impacts QOL on different factors than those within the generic scales. For example, the EQ-5D includes mobility, self-care, usual activities, pain/discomfort and anxiety/depression. If a disease included any items not captured in this list, then the disease-specific measure would be more sensitive, for example, fertility, which is not captured in the Health Utility Index generic scale, unless change in fertility affects anxiety or ability to perform usual activities (Ades, Lu, and Madan 2013).

Guidelines for Using QOL in HTA

There are a number of guideline documents on how to assess QOL, and we condense the Canadian guidelines for Valuing Outcomes, posted by Canadian Agency for Drugs and Technologies in Health (CADTH). The guidelines attempt to increase transparency of the submission in the methods section including reporting the assumptions and methods used to estimate changes in utility, and the source of QOL information if external but preferably disease-specific. One interesting aspect is the possibility of multiplicity of effect for changes in health states. One specific example provided by CADTH is that if there was a health state that caused a loss of work, the impact of loss of work should be included in the time trade-off analysis to value the different heath states. This highlights the problems with estimating changes in utility with data that are external to the trial. If a patient has some pain and some nausea, the combined effect on QOL from having two symptoms may be worse than adding the separate effects alone. Specifically, if you have many symptoms, your level of anxiety would rise. Only with trial data can this be estimated.

Another big problem would occur if there were symptoms for a disease for which the impact of QOL was not captured in the trial, nor are there available external published estimates of generic QOL. If a disease-specific scale was used in the trial, then a published estimate of the result of mapping the disease-specific scale onto a generic scale can be used. If there was no generic scale, or non-mapped disease-specific scale, then the only plausible method of estimating the impact on QOL is to conduct a new study that includes patients with the disease using a generic scale on patients who have or do not have that symptom.

From Utility to QALY

The term we use for the value of utility to combine the gains (or losses) in length of life with QOL is a QALY. A key assumption in using QALYs is that preferences for symptoms are constant over time (Torrance and Feeny 1989). There is always a debate that maximizing QALYs may be too restrictive, not reflecting public expectations regarding fairness or equity. One important aspect is that we discount future health equivalently, for all ages, stated as being 5% in Canada. That is, we assume that a 95-year old will consider an event that will occur in his 100th year, the same as a 30-year old

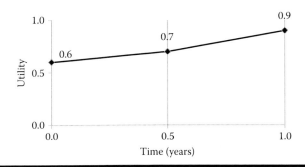

Figure 8.1 Health-related quality of life and quality-adjusted life years.

will consider the event in their 35th year. Most researchers agree that QALYs are not an ethically meaningful measure for end-of-life care, which should not be withheld because of poor economic value for money. In addition, QALYs are not good for acute illnesses or episodes, and may have different meaning for different diseases. For example, cancer guidelines in Ontario suggest taking into account the added value society puts on life-extending treatments. This produced a threshold of $50,000/QALY for most drugs to reduce symptoms and $100,000/QALY for cancer drugs that extend life.

The simple calculation to estimate QALYs from utility scores is to use the trapezoid method, which averages starting and ending values for utility for a time period, assuming a linear trend (Figure 8.1). For every individual in a study, we estimate the QALYs between assessments and then sum the QALYs allowing for discounting. The above example has this patient with utility value of 0.6 at time 0, 0.7 at 6 months and 0.9 at 12 months. Their QALYs would be the average of starting and ending point for each time frame times duration in years = (0.6 + 0.7)/2 * 0.5 years + (0.7 + 0.9)/2 * 0.5 years = 0.325 + 0.4 = 0.725 QALYs. After we have added up all the QALYs for each individual, we want to compare the two sets of patients that received the different interventions. This can get muddled, and different measures have been reported (Table 8.3).

Assessing Change in QOL Scales

Change in Level of HRQOL and Domains over Time

One way that we have been asked to assess change in QOL over time by some reviewers of article submissions is to consider the level of QOL and treat change in QOL as an endpoint. We have seen this assessment done

Table 8.3 Options for Estimating Utility from Generic Health-Related Quality of Life

Options	Tasks/requirements
Record periodic generic QOL during pivotal trial	Add case report form to clinical study
Obtain literature values for clinical events and disease severity	Conduct targeted or systematic literature review for all events and by disease severity
Conduct independent QOL cross-sectional or cohort study	Independent study design and analysis
Record periodic disease-specific QOL during pivotal trial, and map to generic scale	Statistical knowledge on how to perform regression mapping techniques

QOL, quality of life.

with post-level minus pre-levels averaged within a group and then tested between groups. This is the typical method for most clinical values such as blood pressure changes. This method however ignores the timing of any QOL benefit during the study. If one treatment provided immediate benefit and the comparator treatment had a delayed response, then the immediate benefit would not be captured.

A better method for assessing differences in QALYs is to sum the QALYs for each patient, and then compare the differences between groups with an unpaired *t*-test, which creates a few new problems. First, the scales are upfront acknowledged to be skewed, many people are healthier than others, and few may have severe symptoms. We can adjust for the skewness in the data by using a general linear model such as with a gamma distribution. In STATA, this is straightforward and the one line command would be:

```
glm QALYs treatment, family(gamma)
```

One problem with this test is highlighted by an important property of QOL measures that is not taken into consideration, the between patient variability in preferences for the same health state. There is higher variability in the values that different patients will place on identical health states, which in turn suggests that the gains in utility for changing health states will also be variable. Thus, we need to incorporate baseline QOL as a covariate in the glm regression.

```
glm QALYs treatment baseQOL, family(gamma)
```

The statistical *p*-value for the treatment variable will determine if there is a difference in QALYs between groups, adjusting for skewness and preferences for health states.

The change in QOL is a frequentist concept and is based on interpretation that is typical for a trial. In reality, the change in QALYs is not always reported and the change in QALYs is reported as part of the cost-effectiveness results. When there is the desire to be consistent with the economic evidence, an alternate measure is reported (Stalmeier et al. 2001). The measure is the confidence interval for the bootstrapped cost-effectiveness results (see the University of Pennsylvania website for STATA code for bootstrapping and other cost-effectiveness analysis codes). From the final bootstrap results, we can assess the percentage of replicates that are above or below the value zero for the difference between groups. If the distribution between 2.5% and 97.5% values for the bootstrap replicates for differences in QALYs does not include zero, then there is a statistical difference in QALYs. This analysis relies on the assumption that a difference between patients for the same health state is the result of sampling bias, which is reduced with bootstrapping, and uncertainty. In addition, bootstrapping removes even high levels of skewness. The added computational burden is that when we are bootstrapping to estimate the ICER, we also need to record the results for QOL alone and in summary. In reality, differences between the glm with baseline QOL and bootstrapping rarely produces different *p*-values. Since glm is easier and more easily explained, we prefer that estimation method for statistical reporting of the *p*-value for differences in QALYs between treatment groups in a trial.

Minimal Clinically Important Difference for HRQOL

A minimal clinically important difference (MCID) is an important assessment to see if a change is large enough to be important to the patient, or will lead to a change in therapy. For every disease, there may be a different MCID for each scale (Walters and Brazier 2005). This difference in MCID may be due to a level effect, where different diseases have different baseline QOL scores. A difference in QOL of 0.05 may not be important if baseline QOL is already high at 0.90 when compared to 1.0 for perfect health, while a difference in QOL of 0.05 for patients with a severe disease whose baseline

QOL is only 0.20 may be important (Gerhards et al. 2011). In general, an MCID has been reported in the 0.05–0.10 range (Lam 2010). Hence, a change in QOL score of less than 0.05 may not be important, and a change in QOL score of greater than 0.10 would be quite noteworthy.

There may be an issue with relying strictly on achieving the ICER threshold, beyond assessing if other non-economic factors are important. Since the ICER is made of two estimates, incremental cost and incremental QALYs, it is worth commenting if either the change in cost or QOL is clinically or economically meaningful.

Consider the five situations with identical values of ICERs, all having 25,000£/QALYs that using traditional decision making rules would not be considered good value for money in the United Kingdom and be rejected. Situation A is very expensive with an incremental cost of 25,000£, and a budget impact analysis after considering the number of possible cases that can be treated would be large. If there are few cases, then the budget impact is small, but the QALYs are huge providing 1.0 QALYs over two years. This change in QALYs would be equivalent to eliminating severe angina symptoms or stopping daily multiple epileptic seizures (Table 8.4).

The stand-alone impact of the incremental QALYs might be considered, although a price negotiation would lead to a favourable ICER. At the other extreme, situation E is a treatment that has essentially zero incremental costs but also of no benefit for incremental QALYs and is easily rejected. Situations C and D are also not favourable since both would not produce a meaningful change in QALYs, with neither exceeding the MCID, meanwhile both having a small effect on incremental costs. Situation B is at the margin, with meaningful incremental QALYs that would achieve the

Table 8.4 Five Situations with Identical Estimates of ICER

	A	B	C	D	E
Incremental cost (£)	25,000	2,500	250	25	2.5
Incremental QALYs	1.0 QALYs	0.1 QALYs	0.01 QALYs	0.001 QALYs	0.0001 QALYs
ICER	25,000£/ QALY	25,000£/ QALY	25,000£/ QALY	25,000£/ QALY	25,000£/ QALY

Notes: QALYs estimated over a two-year period.

ICER, incremental cost effectiveness ratio (Δcosts/ΔQALYs); QALY, quality-adjusted life year.

MCID, but the small annual cost would be 250£ per year, if discounting was not applied.

This creates an unintentional dictum: If the incremental QALYs were large enough to exceed the MCID, then the incremental cost that would create a favourable ICER could also be an impactful cost. Occasionally, we may reject treatments that have large QOL benefit and small increases in costs, if we strictly relied on a single threshold. The corollary is that if the incremental QALYs were small and did not exceed the MCID, then the incremental cost that would create a favourable ICER could also be very small and not impactful. In a sense, one observer could suppose that a review of the ICER alone without the independent assessment of meaningful incremental QALYs could potentially add treatments that are not impactful on costs nor QALYs.

Obtaining QOL Estimates from Trials and Literature

If we are lucky enough to have added a case report form to the study design, we can easily capture the impact of QOL for events and disease severity. The QOL would be estimated as a regression with QOL as the dependent variable (y) and the right-hand side independent variables would include variables for treatment, a measure for disease severity and a variable for every clinical event. This *event-based analysis* provides all of the information that we need for a trial-based economic analysis. If we added age and sex to the variables, we can use the age factor or an outside literature value that provides the effect on age or duration of disease on disease severity to extrapolate for a lifetime economic model.

If we haven't mentioned it before, including the case report form for generic QOL is the easiest to obtain and the strongest piece of evidence. The three most common scales, EQ-5D, SF-36 and HUI-3 (Konerding, Moock, and Kohlmann 2009) are relatively inexpensive, all with reasonably low fees and special rates or free use if the trials are small. The detailed scoring algorithms allow each measure to be easily scored.

If no quality of data was collected, then a systematic literature review is required to show that the researchers have obtained and synthesized all available QOL estimates. This is a bit of a messy literature review because QOL estimates can be from a cross-sectional or cohort QOL study, or from other clinical trials, or have been reported in previous cost-effectiveness analysis. A skilled medical information specialist will help to develop a search for the appropriate disease condition, but the study design can be diverse. In addition, the QOL scales may be a secondary outcome of a study and may not be reported in the title or abstract. A full-text review should be conducted if the QOL is mentioned in any of the title, abstract, keyword or MeSH headings. After the articles and QOL values have been abstracted from the articles, a meta-analysis must be conducted. This meta-analysis (single value) is a bit different than the meta-analysis of trials (comparative outcomes) and the use of meta-regression should be included to adjust for differences in studies and population.

Independent QOL Study

A lengthier process to obtain generic QOL estimates is to conduct an independent cross-sectional survey or to conduct a cohort study, although the latter is rare for only QOL analysis. The study should be large enough to capture patients with the disease who have all of the clinical events that occurred in the trial. This may not be feasible because of the rareness of some events, and a targeted literature search may be sufficient to fill in the missing values. To estimate a sample size for an observational study, we rely on the simple rule of thumb that 20 observations are necessary for every covariate that is included in the regression. This is an arbitrary rule, and sometimes the rule has been stated as needed 15 or even 10 observations for every variable. Since QOL scales tend to have high variation due to individual variation in identical health states, we suggest that 20 observations per variable should be stated as the sample size (Briggs and Gray 1998; Whitley and Ball 2002).

For example, if you are estimating the QOL based on age, sex, disease severity (e.g. blood pressure or pain level) and four clinical events, then $20 * 12 = 240$ cases would be needed. However, you need to capture cases that will include all of the clinical events and how these cases are recruited will be subject to the long list of potential biases. The study then is susceptible to criticisms of validity because of the selection of the sample, from recruiting from the doctor's office versus community or hospital, a healthy volunteer bias and so on. In reality, it may be preferable to attempt to study all of the patients in one setting, such as all patients for doctor's roster and all patients' that require certain services.

For most diseases, and especially new or rare diseases, a separate QOL study is incredibly valuable and often well cited in the medical literature since the results will be used many times in the future for any economic evaluation for that disease. In addition, the cross-sectional study provides a measure of impact of that disease that can be compared to other well-studied diseases. If researchers are concerned about their disease, a cross-sectional study that will include both generic and disease-specific QOL is also valuable. And this leads to our next topic, mapping between scales (Grootendorst et al. 2007).

Mapping between QOL Scales

Consider the instance that only a disease-specific scale was included as part of clinical trial. This often occurs for diseases where the primary endpoints are scales or captured as a secondary outcome. However, you forgot to include the generic QOL scales, but a very useful publication for clinical studies that captured both generic and disease-specific QOL scales may exist that will demonstrate how a change in the disease-specific scale translates into the changes in generic QOL scale.

There are a few statistical techniques that are included in the analysis. First, the generic QOL is often skewed and more important bounded (censored) by the value of one, and the techniques censored least absolute deviations or Tobit models have been suggested, although these techniques may introduce bias. As a result, ordinary least squares with multiple regression appears to be more reliable (Chan et al. 2014; Pullenayegum et al. 2011).

Second, how precise the predicted generic QOL is assessed with different methods, such as mean absolute error or an adjusted *R*-squared. If alternate models are proposed, then measures such as log likelihood (the probability that the model fits the data, log transformed) or Akaike information criterion (penalizes for adding more variables) can be used to pick the better model.

A common statistical technique to estimate reliability is the split-half method. In this method, half of the sample is randomly drawn, and a regression equation is made one half of the data to predict generic QOL based on disease-specific QOL, often adjusting for age and sex, disease severity or disease duration. The predicted formula is created, and then applied to the second half of the data, and the actual generic QOL is compared to the predicted generic QOL. However, there is a great deal of arbitrariness in splitting the data into two split halves. At the extremes, the two samples will be near identical and the other extreme is that the two samples are near opposites. If the samples are similar, then the split-half technique will likely have a better fit than if the two samples are not similar. To remedy this, we can conduct a sampling exercise such by taking different draws from the data to create the spit half and then provide an estimate of variation of the split-half fit results.

One concern with the use of split-half technique is that the results of fit will change if a different study group has been sampled. Because of this, simply reporting the overall regression fit results has been suggested for mapping.

The mapping between scales, and in particular mapping between disease-specific and generic scales, have become widespread, with most disease-specific scales having some mapping studies. The use of mapping to estimate generic QOL has been incorporated in many successful cost-effectiveness analyses in the United Kingdom. One concern noted is that the variance for a regression-fitted mapping exercise will have smaller confidence intervals than from random sampling, which is favourable for decision-makers to have less uncertainty but the variance estimates might be less valid (Barton et al. 2008).

Summary

Adding HRQOL to a clinical study may be unwelcomed for many clinical researchers, who have the mantra that the improvement in efficacy should be the only focus. We absolutely agree, and in fact, if a new treatment improved efficacy without affecting safety, then this would be a worthwhile addition to a formulary if not overpriced. The addition of quality of life attempts to place different efficacy outcomes onto a common scale, that is, is a hip fracture worse than developing type II diabetes. If there were a separate health care budget for osteoporosis and diabetes, then the analysis would simply be to select the most efficacious drugs for each disease. Unfortunately, there is a combined budget so that the selection from a set of new drugs must be made based on a common framework. The importance of using QOL scores in a common framework rises with the complexity of the disease, where trade-off across multiple symptoms or events can occur. In this chapter, we hope we have provided guidance on the statistical issues for QOL and left some final thoughts (Table 8.5).

Table 8.5 Reviewers' Notes for Reporting of QOL Analysis

1. For trial-based analysis, there will be high sampling variability for common health states with many different patients having slightly different perception of their QOL for the same health state. To account for the between-subject variability, bootstrapping is beneficial, and furthermore, bootstrapping also reduces skewness in the data.
2. Discounting for multi-year assessments should be applied on an annual basis according to the acceptable discount factor (5% Canada, 3% the United Kingdom).
3. The incremental QALYs between two treatment options that are adjusted for baseline imbalance are the current standard for assessing differences in the impact on QOL.
4. When possible, QOL estimates that are taken for a secondary data sources should be obtained from a systematic literature review, be disease-related and be from a generic scale.
5. A comment on the magnitude of the change in QALYs should be made in relationship to a minimal clinically important difference.

QALY, quality-adjusted life year; QOL, quality of life.

References

Ades A.E., Lu G., and Madan J.J. 2013. Which health-related quality-of-life outcome when planning randomized trials: Disease-specific or generic, or both? A common factor model. *Value in Health: The Journal of the International Society for Pharmacoeconomics and Outcomes Research* 16 (1): 185–194.

Barton G.R., Sach T.H., Jenkinson C., Avery A.J., Doherty M., and Muir K.R. 2008. Do estimates of cost-utility based on the EQ-5D differ from those based on the mapping of utility scores? *Health and Quality of Life Outcomes* 6: 51.

Brazier J., Akehurst R., Brennan A., Dolan P., Claxton K., McCabe C., Sculpher M., and Tsuchiya A. 2005. Should patients have a greater role in valuing health states? *Applied Health Economics and Health Policy* 4 (4): 201–208.

Briggs A.H., and Gray A.M. 1998. Power and sample size calculations for stochastic cost-effectiveness analysis. *Medical Decision Making* 18 (2 Suppl): S81–S92.

Chan K.K., Willan A.R., Gupta M., and Pullenayegum E. 2014. Underestimation of uncertainties in health utilities derived from mapping algorithms involving health-related quality-of-life measures: Statistical explanations and potential remedies. *Medical Decision Making* 34 (7): 863–872.

Churchill D.N., Torrance G.W., Taylor D.W., Barnes C.C., Ludwin D., Shimizu A., and Smith E.K. 1987. Measurement of quality of life in end-stage renal disease: The time trade-off approach. *Clinical and Investigative Medicine* 10 (1): 14–20.

Drummond M. 2001. Introducing economic and quality of life measurements into clinical studies. *Annals of Medicine* 33 (5): 344–349.

Drummond M.F. 1987. Resource allocation decisions in health care: A role for quality of life assessments? *Journal of Chronic Diseases* 40 (6): 605–619.

Gerhards S.A., Huibers M.J., Theunissen K.A., de Graaf L.E., Widdershoven G.A., and Evers S.M. 2011. The responsiveness of quality of life utilities to change in depression: A comparison of instruments (SF-6D, EQ-5D, and DFD). *Value in Health: The Journal of the International Society for Pharmacoeconomics and Outcomes Research* 14 (5): 732–739.

Grootendorst P., Marshall D., Pericak D., Bellamy N., Feeny D., and Torrance G.W. 2007. A model to estimate health utilities index mark 3 utility scores from WOMAC index scores in patients with osteoarthritis of the knee. *Journal of Rheumatology* 34 (3): 534–542.

Konerding U., Moock J., and Kohlmann T. 2009. The classification systems of the EQ-5D, the HUI II and the SF-6D: What do they have in common? *Quality of Life Research* 18 (9): 1249–1261.

Lam C.L.K. 2010. Subjective quality of life measures: General principles and concepts. In *Handbook of Disease Burdens and Quality of Life Measures*. eds. V.R. Preedy and R.R. Watson, Chapter 21, 381–399. New York: Springer.

Marra C.A., Woolcott J.C., Kopec J.A., Shojania K., Offer R., Brazier J.E., Esdaile J.M., and Anis A.H. 2005. A comparison of generic, indirect utility measures (the HUI2, HUI3, SF-6D, and the EQ-5D) and disease-specific instruments (the RAQoL and the HAQ) in rheumatoid arthritis. *Social Science and Medicine* 60 (7): 1571–1582.

Pullenayegum E.M., Tarride J.E., Xie F., and O'Reilly D. 2011. Calculating utility decrements associated with an adverse event: Marginal Tobit and CLAD coefficients should be used with caution. *Medical Decision Making* 31 (6): 790–799.

Stalmeier P.F., Goldstein M.K., Holmes A.M., Lenert L., Miyamoto J., Stiggelbout A.M., Torrance G.W., and Tsevat J. 2001. What should be reported in a methods section on utility assessment? *Medical Decision Making* 21 (3): 200–207.

Tengs T.O., and Wallace A. 2000. One thousand health-related quality-of-life estimates. *Medical Care* 38 (6): 583–637.

Walters S.J., and Brazier J.E. 2005. Comparison of the minimally important difference for two health state utility measures: EQ-5D and SF-6D. *Quality of Life Research* 14 (6): 1523–1532.

Whitley E., and Ball J. 2002. Statistics review 4: Sample size calculations. *Critical Care* 6 (4): 335–341.

Chapter 9

Missing Data Methods

It is rare to have a trial that has 100% complete data, and how the biostatistician deals with the missing data varies widely (Altman and Bland 2007). Given the many possibilities for dealing with missing data, there are many possibilities of cost-effectiveness results from the analysis of a pivotal trial or literature-based cost-effectiveness model. It is then left to the experienced reviewer who relies on his own judgement on whether the extent of missing data has the potential to impact the cost-effectiveness conclusion.

We will make a few points on the importance of handling missing data. First, if we exclude data that are incomplete, then the overall variance of the cost-effectiveness results may be larger due to the smaller sample sizes. One of the most common problems in meta-analysis is that the parameters that are required to estimate a common estimate such as relative risk for a meta-analysis are not presented in the primary publication. Even the simple results on the number of patients and the number of events are left out, with only hazard rates or regression coefficients presented. If we then leave out that problematic study, the uncertainty of the estimate of relative risk may increase, and this will increase the variance of the estimate of cost-effectiveness.

Second, the true value of the estimate of the cost-effectiveness results may be biased in one direction or another. If important data that were favourable for a new treatment were excluded from a trial of an influential study, or if missing data were left out of a meta-analysis, then the final cost-effectiveness results may be biased against the new treatment.

Third, and similar to the previous point, we may not able to identify a subgroup or subset of the patients who will have higher benefit for the new treatment. Subgroup analysis from the meta-analysis or from the trial data set relies on having enough subjects to be adequately powered to determine a potential benefit in that selected subgroup. One of the most problematic areas for reviewers of reimbursement decision-making bodies is whether a subgroup shows potential benefit more than the patient with average values of characteristics. Also note, please never use the expression *average patient*. Subgroup analysis is an essential step in the analysis, and as reviewers we often state, 'please do subgroup analysis, if you don't, we will'.

A final consideration for missing data is when there is only one appropriate study that has data which might lead to an estimate of a parameter. If, for example, we are missing the risk of a safety event, then without a single estimate, we would need to rely on clinical opinion alone. This can be very important because clinical uncertainty is one of the highest predictive factors for failing reimbursement decisions. From this, we believe that we can all agree that more data are better than some data, and some data are better than no data.

Common Trial Gaps

We first begin with a discussion of handling data within a single trial. In the second half of this chapter, we will discuss handling missing data for the purpose of conducting a meta-analysis. In a trial, there are many different types of data that can be missing, which are as follows:

1. Patients who have intermittently missed or skipped visits
2. Patients who are loss to follow-up, including because of death
3. Some centres may have not omitted variables
4. Data were randomly incorrect and unusable (e.g. age 763)

When there is missing data for a trial, there are four sets of numbers that should be reported to improve transparency and believability of the overall study findings. We should report (1) the number of missing patient visits or equivalently the percentage of incomplete data points, (2) the rates of missing data for each treatment group, (3) an assessment whether the patients for which the data are missing are different from the remaining patients for both treatment groups and (4) whether the remaining patients are still similar between the two treatment groups. Overall, these numbers provide an assessment of whether the amount of missing data is substantial and whether the reasons for missing data are different enough between the groups such that the patients remaining have different prognostic factors. This in turn indicates whether the difference in the rates of outcomes between the treatment groups can be explained by treatment effect alone.

There is a subjective assessment made about the percentage of missing data that is acceptable for a given trial duration. Based on our experience, if we see 5%–10% missing patient visits for a one-year trial, we are not too worried, only if the rates of dropouts are similar between treatments and the characteristics of the patients that droppedout are not different from the remaining patients or between groups for the remaining patients. When we have long-term clinical trials, which are themselves not frequent such as five years, a dropout rate of less than 10% each year is manageable, all else equal. However, if there are more than 10% per year, then you may have more than half of the patients with missed visits by the end of the study period. In this case, it is very unlikely that the patients that missed the visits had the same characteristics as the compliant remaining patients. One way of dealing with lots of missing visits is to impute the missing data using different methods and assessing if there are clinically meaningful differences in the results for the different methods. This of course leads to the next question, what are the options for handling missing data?, and this depends on the reason for missing data.

Missed Visits and Loss to Follow-Up

There are two types of missed visits: those occurring intermittently or those occurring at the end of the study, which are put in the catch-all phrase 'loss to follow-up'. For the intermittent missing data, the problem is even further complicated (or simplified) by case report forms that capture resource utilization and quality of life. Most resource utilization case report forms ask the question, 'Since your last visit, have you been admitted to the hospital?' If there was an admission to the hospital during the missed visit, the cost that is derived for that visit can be averaged over the current and missed period.

For quality of life, there is high variability over time for every person (low test–retest reliability), and the case report forms ask for the level of the quality at the time of the visit. For a cardiac study, the patient's quality of life may vary between visits because of having temporary inflictions such as having a cold, lack of sleep, a sore back or stress at work. In a trial, we assume these factors balance out between groups. In the case of intermittent missing responses, the values of missed intermittent quality of life assessments should be estimated. If there are small amounts of missing data, then straight line interpolation between available points does not alter the results appreciably versus when other advanced methods are used. When the missed visits are at the end of the study, this is problematic because we do not know whether a patient had a favourable endpoint, such as survival, or an unfavourable endpoint, such as death. When there is a major endpoint that is binary (yes or no), survival analysis such as a Kaplan–Meier estimate will adjust for the missing data at the end of the study (right censoring). Otherwise, if the data are continuous, the missing values can be substituted with the mean value from other similar patients for that visit (a hot deck procedure), imputed (predicted from regression) based on available data or the cases can be omitted (per-protocol basis).

When the primary outcome is a continuous measure such as blood pressure, we could use the simple option of last value carry forward. However, the European Medicines Agency (EMEA) has pointed out that this method would not account for any trend that may have begun prior to the missed visits. This underestimates the treatment effect of promising interventions and overestimates the treatment effect of harmful interventions. Instead, we again need to rely on techniques such as multiple imputation.

Explainable or Unexplainable Patterns of Missing Data

Multiple imputation relies on the assumption that we can predict the missing values from data that have been captured. In the statistical world, there is some jargon that is used in missing data for a study. Data can be considered as *missing completely at random, missing at random* and *missing not at random* (Altman and Bland 2007). For a very brief period, we will work through these definitions to highlight the potential bias of missing data. *Missing completely at random* assumes that the missingness (pattern of missing data) does not depend on the values of any variables in the data set, whether observable or not observable, and the data that are missing are unrelated to actual values of the missing data. *Missing at random* assumes that the value of a missing observation can be predicted from existing data in the data set. When the data are *missing not at random*, then the reason for the missingness may not be identifiable from the existing data.

Analysis that is based on data where there is missing data will be unbiased if the data are *missing completely at random* or *missing at random*. A bias is created if the reason that there are missing data is beyond the data captured. The key assumption to estimate the missing data is that data are

Table 9.1 Type of Missing Data, for Depression Study

Missingness Patterns	Definition	Example
Missing completely at random	Not explainable/ predictable by available data	Incorrectly completed case report form (infrequent and random).
Missing at random	Explainable/predictable by available data	Non-English patients have trouble filling out case report forms (unrelated to level of depression but can be predicted).
Missing not at random	Cannot be explained by data captured in study	Random depression episode may produce a missed visit.

missing at random or *missing completely at random* and not *missing completely at random*. In the case provided (Table 9.1), if we predicted the missing depression score with available data when there were data *missing not at random*, we would likely provide an under-prediction of the level of depression. We should try to impute missing data where the reason for missing is explainable, and this would create unbiased estimates. But since we cannot truly measure whether data are *missing not at random*, then we must assume that the data are either *missing at random* or *missing completely at random*.

In summary, we always assume that the reason for missing data is explainable by the available data, and we can impute the missing data using information that is available. If the data are truly *missing not at random*, and only explainable by information outside the study, we will never know if a bias has been created. But this gets back to our previous point, if the patients that have missing data are different than compliant responders, we should make adjustments.

Intention-to-Treat or Per-Protocol Analysis

When a trial is completed, there may be different subsets of patients:

1. Patients who were randomized and never received treatment
2. Patients who were randomized, received some treatment but discontinued early in the study because of success
3. Patients who were randomized, received some treatment but discontinued early in the study because of treatment failure, or had a serious adverse event

4. Patients who were randomized, received the treatment, completed the study, but have missing data that are intermittent or from the result of loss to follow-up for some clinical measures, but the primary outcome is complete
5. Patients who were randomized, received treatment, completed the study, and have complete data (complete cases)

If most of the patients in the study are *complete cases* with full follow-up, then you will be very lucky. Rarely, if ever, trials can obtain 100% complete data, especially the long large multicentre trials of chronic diseases. There are many tricks that can be employed to increase the level of completeness (see Sackett 1976). How we estimate the treatment effect will depend on how we include or exclude each of the subset of patients listed above.

The FDA, EMEA and Health Canada have harmonized their guidelines on how to analyze trial data in the presence of missing data. The International Conference on Harmonisation of Technical Requirements for Registration of Pharmaceuticals for Human Use (ICH) guideline E9 Statistical Principles for Clinical Trials includes the statement on intention-to-treat as a guiding principle. 'The principle that asserts that the effect of a treatment policy can be best assessed by evaluating on the basis of the intention to treat a subject (i.e. the planned treatment regimen) rather than the actual treatment given' (Section 5.2, page 28) (ICH 2014).

This principle is based on the assumption that the point of randomization is the point where bias is minimized (not eliminated), and any movement away from the original randomized allocation will increase bias.

This leads to the identification of the full analysis set (FAS), usually and improperly is called the intention-to-treat set, which includes as close as possible to the intention-to-treat ideal of including all randomized patients. Once we move away from the FAS by excluding patients, we may introduce bias. The most common exclusions would be patients who were later discovered to violate eligibility criteria and their data are removed, failure to receive treatment or missed all visits and evaluations. The potential bias would be small if there were similar reasons for exclusion in both treatment groups, if the patients that were excluded were similar to remaining patient(s) in each treatment group and if the remaining patients were still balanced between treatment groups based on prognostic factors.

Another subset of patients is referred to as *per-protocol* set of subjects, sometimes described as the *valid cases*, the *efficacy sample* or the *evaluable subjects sample*, which includes the subset of subjects from the FAS who completed their assigned treatment and evaluation, as per the protocol. However, a huge bias may be introduced if study completion can be predicted by the treatment and the final outcome. Examples leading to bias if reported as unadjusted results would include if one treatment was less pleasant, if there were barriers to receive one of the treatments or if only patients with high levels of health completed the study. Overall, we suggest that for the primary outcome, a survival analysis that allows for dropouts is descriptive. For other outcomes such as cost and quality of life and secondary clinical outcomes, imputation techniques are the current standard.

Multiple Imputation for Trial Data

There are three steps to multiple imputation analysis (Schafer 1999):

1. *Imputation:* A data set is created after imputing the missing values, with typically 5 or 10 new data sets created.
2. *Estimation:* For each data sets, which is now made of complete cases, the final analysis such as cost-effectiveness is conducted.
3. *Pooling:* The results obtained from each of the complete-case analyses are combined into an overall result, with the between-data set variation added into the overall variance.

While this seems like an onerous task, all steps are automated in most software packages. However, it is never that simple. Along the way, there are a few options that need to be specified. Is the data monotone, that is, can we impute all the baseline data first, and each subsequent time period as steps? This option can be tested and implemented in the imputation analysis. For most cases, we have cost estimates that are missing at different time points in the trial and are not monotone.

A second decision is whether the missing data should be replaced by randomly selecting other patient's values (Monte Carlo), or built with a regression model (regression), or if the missing data should be replaced with similar patient's data (propensity score method).

In addition, we need to specify the number of data sets that need to be imputed. While there could be a large number of possible choices for conducting the multiple imputation, we have seen that creating 5–10 new data sets is enough, and the type of model is not less important. This often creates a relative efficiency over 90%, where 90% is a prediction of what is achieved with the defined number of data sets relative to that which would be created with an infinite number of imputations. However, the more data sets that are imputed, the more stable the *p*-value and standard errors become. Some even suggest setting the number of imputations to be similar to the percentage of cases that are incomplete. For example, if you have 20% missing data, then you need 20 data sets to produce a stable *p*-value and standard errors (Table 9.2).

Another decision is the choice of variables to be selected in the model. Variables in the imputation model should include variables that predict the reason for missing variables using logistic regression and variables that are correlated with the missing variables. Alternatively, all available data can be used. One limitation does exist, in that the number of observations should be 10–20 times more than the number of variables that are being selected. Because of this rank condition, we have seen with a small trial that it was difficult to impute all the missing cost items. When the study is very small, the uncertainty that is added from imputing individual resource utilization or cost items should be assessed versus imputing the missed visit total cost.

To simplify matters a great deal, we can conduct the cost-effectiveness analysis at the same time as the imputation, when conducting a probabilistic cost-effectiveness analysis. If we impute the data with a single regression step, then draw one bootstrap and perform the estimation, and repeat 1000 times, we will generate the bootstrapped imputed results. This satisfies the sufficient numbers of imputations, and in addition, this also satisfies the combining of the data sets. This is very easily conducted in WinBUGS, with any missing data point being entered as 'NA'.

Table 9.2   Options for Dealing with Missing Trial Data

Missing Pattern	*Options*
Intermittent missing	Interpolate between points
	Predict with regression between points
	Multiple imputation along with other missing data
Loss to follow-up	Per-protocol analysis
	Survival analysis (for major endpoints)
	Last value carry forward
	Substitute mean visit values
	Regression prediction
	Multiple imputation (regression, propensity scoring or Monte Carlo)

Note: Different options should be assessed to see if the results are meaningfully different.

A simple but elegant solution can be created in Microsoft Excel models that are used for budget impact analysis or cost-effectiveness analysis. (Similar work has been conducted in STATA.) Within an Excel worksheet, we often incorporate the Visual Basics editor to conduct bootstrapping and simulation to estimate the cost-effectiveness plane and cost-effectiveness acceptability curve. It is very easy to add another level to the bootstrap that conducts a univariate imputation either based on regression or Monte Carlo draws, to fill in the missing data at each step before the bootstrap is drawn.

Beautiful Bootstrap

The bootstrap is designed to reduce the sampling bias by creating an unbiased sampling distribution after taking random draws of the data with replacement. The basic steps for a bootstrap, which is available in every statistical software package, are to draw a data point, record and put the data back, then repeat this process (draw with replacement), until a sample is created (usually the same number of patients as the clinical trial size), obtain the summary statistics (usually the mean), save the mean, discard the data and repeat many times such as 1000. *This seems like a lot of work, and it is a good time to pull up your boots by their straps.* This will create a new sampling distribution to simulate as if 1000 studies were conducted. The process should be repeated, and if the new bootstrap procedures produce a different bootstrap final value, then the number of replicates should be increased from 1,000 to say 5,000 or even 10,000 to produce reproducible stable estimates. This is often seen in small trials, where more than 10,000 replicates are needed to produce reproducible results, with stable p-values and standard errors. Bootstrapping is preferred to other methods for generating confidence intervals such as jackknifing (draw without replacement) where all data are not random which does not create an independent sampling distribution, or less defined techniques, such as kernel density estimation, which are similar to a trimmed and reweighted distribution.

Meta-Analysis Gaps

Missing data for a meta-analysis are in many ways easier to deal with than missing data for a trial. For each missing estimate, we focus on deriving the one missing data parameter (mean or standard deviation [SD]) for that trial using available data. Thus, we are conducting a univariate imputation technique, instead of worrying about multiple imputation. However, the immediate impact is more severe increasing the possibility of creating an erroneous result for a summary of a body of evidence if the imputation is conducted improperly (Higgins and Green 2011).

There are numerous reviews and simulation studies on different methods for deriving the missing mean or SD parameters for a study that has provided some guidance.

Listed below are different methods that have been reviewed in the literature. The bottom line on the different techniques is that different methods will create results that may be meaningfully different. To be sure that the main findings do not vary by the choice of different methods, it is suggested that you try more than one method and verify the results are consistent.

Missing Measures of Central Tendency

The estimation of missing measure of central tendency can be straight-forward, requiring only a simple manipulation of available data. A key problem is that the types of data that are available often vary in each new analysis. Sometimes, a trial will provide median and minimum and maximum values, or other values for variance. Other times, there will be only the median or geometric mean. When the data that are published cannot be manipulated to produce the missing mean value, and request from the original author is not successful, then we need to rely on assumptions such as that the distribution of the data is distributed normally. If the data were normally distributed, then the mean would equal the median, and both the median and mean would be midway between the upper and lower limits of the 95% confidence interval. If the data have some skewness, then Hozo, Djulbegovic and Hozo (2005) have demonstrated that we approximate the mean if we are given the median, minimum and maximum values (Tables 9.3 and 9.4).

Missing Measures of Variance

To impute the missing SD for meta-analyses of the weighted mean difference, which we currently referred to as mean difference, we can use data manipulation, approximate the value from similar studies or make statistical assumptions about the distributions.

Table 9.3 Options for Estimating Missing Mean Values

Available Data	Solution
Median, min, max	Mean = [minimum + (2 * median) + maximum]/4 Mean = median if $n > 70$
Median, and Q1 and Q3	Mean = [Q1 + (2 * median) + Q3]/4
Median only	Use with caution as the mean, assess if this study contributes to heterogeneity
Geometric mean only	Use with caution as the mean, assess if this study contributes to heterogeneity

Table 9.4 Options for Estimating Missing Standard Deviations

Available Data	Solution
Data Manipulation	
Standard error	SD = standard error * square root (n)
95% Confidence interval only	SD = (upper limit − lower limit)/3.92
p-value	In excel: SD = mean/{ = NORMINV[(p-value/2),0,1]}
t or Z score	SD = mean/[t(or Z) score]
Q1, Q3 only	SD = (Q3 − Q1)/1.35
Minimum, maximum	SD = (maximum − minimum)/4
From Other Studies	
No data for one study	Use largest SD of other studies
No SD data for more than one study, available data for others	Bucks regression: Estimate mean/SD ratio for available data and apply ratio to derive missing SD given a mean[a]
Assumption of Distribution	
Mean	Assume the data follow a Poisson distribution similar to count data Poisson: variance = SD^2 = mean
Mean	SD = mean * square root (n)

[a] Some argue that we should take the natural logs of available means and standard deviations, estimate the ratio, apply the ratio and then rescale.

SD, standard deviation.

Data manipulation is the most common method for filling in missing SDs and should be tried first after requesting the publication's data from the authors for more details. For data manipulation, we are simply relying on the statistical formula that was used to estimate the link between SD, confidence intervals, t statistics and p-values. If none of these are available, we often assume the data are normal and use the quartiles $Q1$ and $Q3$ if available. Similar to ±1.96 SDs that will capture 95% of the data if normally distributed, ±0.675 will capture 50% of the data if normally distributed. This creates the rule that the SD will be $(Q3 - Q1)/1.35$. When we are left with only the minimum and maximum value of a variable, it is a stretch to estimate the SD $=$ (maximum $-$ minimum)/4, because an outlier data point in the original distribution will cause the estimated SD to be overestimated. But please note, that the estimated SD will be larger than the true SD. This provides a conservative estimate.

The easiest method to estimate SD is to rely on data from other studies, such as selecting the largest SD that is available from other studies. The impact of the study that will come from the largest SD will be that the study will have the smallest relative weight and contribute least to the overall effect. While this is the most conservative assumption with the least impact, using the mean of the available SDs would be a neutral assumption where the true value could be larger or smaller. To offset the impact of the magnitude of effect, where some studies have larger treatment responses Buck's regression, which suggest that the mean/SD as a ratio, can be assumed. That is, we create a ratio of the mean/SD for each study, average and then use the ratio to fill in the missing SD given a mean. An extension of this method is to take the natural logs of the available means and SD to create the ratio. However, taking the natural logs of data such as cost data has recently fallen out of favour, because the regression creates an extra amount of statistical error that is un-judicially *smeared* back onto the regression estimates to make a poor fit. Statistically speaking, a regression of log(A) with covariate log(B) is not an efficient way to estimate the relationship of A (SD) versus B (arithmetic mean).

A separate issue is how to deal with data when there is a single study that provided a mean effect and no measure of variance is available or easily derived. One option is to assume that the data have a typical distribution with a defined mean–variance relationship. A common distribution would be Poisson, for exponential processes such as for count data, where the mean equals the variance. We have also seen a simple claim that the standard error equals the mean, although we are not sure of the assumption behind this.

Another option occurs if the data that we have are skewed, and we wish to correct for this skewness, we can assume that the data follow a gamma distribution. With a gamma distribution, the mean is defined by $\alpha\beta$, and the variance is defined by $\alpha\beta^2$. Rearranging the equations, we create the expressions $\alpha = (\text{mean}/SD)^2$, and $\beta = SD^2/\text{mean}$. We can substitute in the mean and SD to estimate α and β, which we then substitute back to get the mean and SD for a gamma distribution.

Imputation for missing variance for a proportion is straightforward based on the Wald estimation, or sometimes referred to as the *binomial approximation to the normal*. The formula is variance $= p * (1 - p)/n$. The square root is the SD, which, only in this case, is also the standard error because it is a population estimate.

In summary, there are many different ways to estimate the missing mean or SD in order to conduct a meta-analysis. Quite often the methods used to fill in the missing values are not reported in the manuscript for a meta-analysis, although the choice of the different methods may be influential. Since it is possible that a meta-analysis will be published and the data that were imputed was later found by the original author, the methods for how the missing data were estimated should be available to justify the numbers, or else the data might be considered estimated in error. In addition, we always suggest trying different methods to see if the results are consistent, and if that study with the imputed data was an important contributor to heterogeneity.

Missing Data for Diagnostic Accuracy Studies

To conduct a meta-analysis for diagnostic accuracy, STATA software requires the values of four counts of true positive (TP), true negative (TN), false positive (FP) and false negative (FN). Unfortunately, most publications provide the statistics of sensitivity, specificity and perhaps predictive values and likelihood ratios (see Chapter 2). In order to pool the data, we can usually derive the four required counts, if there is a statistic that involves positive cases and a statistic that involves negative cases.

If we know the total number of positive cases (TP and FN) or equivalently the prevalence, then with a measure of sensitivity, we can derive the numbers that satisfy sensitivity $= TP/(TP + FN)$.

Often, we are given the sensitivity with a confidence interval and specificity with a confidence interval. In this case, there is only one set of the four required counts that will create the estimates and their confidence intervals.

Finding the unique counts can be done by trial and error or simulated within Excel. The only caution is that the confidence intervals are usually derived with a binomial distribution (Wald method) so that the confidence intervals will never cross the value of 1.0 (Simel, Samsa, and Matchar 1991).

For sensitivity, the confidence intervals are $p \pm Z * \sqrt{[p*(1-p)]/(\text{TP}+\text{FN})}$, where p is the sensitivity. For specificity, the confidence intervals are $p \pm Z * \sqrt{[p*(1-p)]/(\text{TN}+\text{FP})}$, where p is the specificity.

Deriving the missing four counts gets trickier when we are given other measures such as predictive values without sensitivity or specificity. However, the same general methods apply that there will only be one set of unique counts that will generate the confidence intervals.

Unknown Lifetime Variances for Costs

For estimating long-term costs, we usually report the first-year costs as *event costs* and second and subsequent years as *state costs*. It is often assumed in an economic model that the mean and SD of *state costs* are constant for the remainder of the life for the cohort of patients. If the mean or SD of the cost had a trend over time, a considerable bias may be created. In addition, the long-term costs of a chronic disease and the follow-up costs of a systemic complication may create systematic bias if the trend in mean or variance in costs that is observed empirically is not included. For lifetime cost-effectiveness analysis, there may be considerable bias such as overestimating costs and the size of confidence intervals of projected costs, and perhaps quality of life.

To investigate the possible trend in long-term costs, we conducted a study that followed diabetes patients in the province of Ontario for 11 years, 1994–2004. With a cohort of 610,852 cases, we identified major complications (amputation, angina, blindness, heart failure, myocardial infarction, nephropathy and stroke). We then estimated the annual total cost which was the sum of hospitalization, outpatient services, public drug coverage, emergency room visits and home care services for up to 11 years of follow-up. We compared the true cost estimate to the assumption of constant mean and variance of cost over time to provide an estimate of bias. The amount of systematic bias by not including the empirical time trends in mean and variance was estimated by comparing the present value of projected lifetime costs using trended and non-trended data. Further possible reduction in bias when the cost distributions are assumed log normal and Itö calculus was investigated (Figure 9.1; Table 9.5).

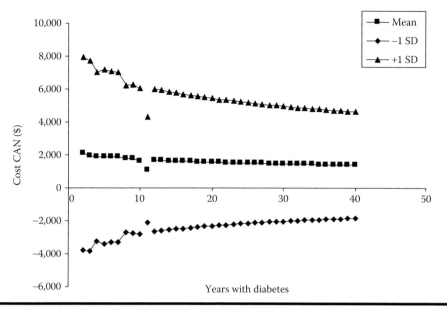

Figure 9.1   Drift in variance of annual cost per patient with diabetes.

Table 9.5   Itö Trend in Mean and Variance for Log Normal Stochastic Processes

Variable	Trend
Variance	$\sigma^2 t$
Mean	$[\mu - (1/2)\sigma^2]t$

We discovered that for the overall diabetes cohort, the mean of the *state costs* for an incident diabetic patient falls 1.17% per year. Failing to include this trend overestimated the discounted projected lifetime costs by 12%. The SD of costs also fell 2.07% per year and excluding this trend represented an increase in 52% in the size of the confidence intervals around the projected lifetime costs. The long-term costs of all complications fell on average by 5.25% per year, and the SD fell on average by 4.19% per year, which translates into an overstatement of mean follow-up costs by 39% and confidence interval width by 86% (Hopkins 2008).

The addition of a drift term can be easily estimated with Itö's formula for the drift of stochastic (random) processes, if we want to assume the costs are log normal. Further research on whether the observed trend in mean and variance for *state costs* for similar cases or for other diseases would be helpful.

Summary

1. Any imputation technique must be clearly specified and a reference provided.
2. The assumptions for each imputation technique should also be specified.
3. The main method of imputation should be provided, as well as a statement that a different method as sensitivity analysis provided consistent results.
4. If space allows, the raw data that were imputed for the meta-analysis should be provided. Any mean or SD imputed should be marked with an asterisk, or other note, for clarity.

References

Altman D.G., and Bland J.M. 2007. Missing data. *British Medical Journal* 334 (7590): 424.

Higgins J., and Green S. (eds.) 2011. General principles for dealing with missing data. Chapter 16.1.2. In *Cochrane Handbook for Systematic Reviews of Interventions*, The Cochrane Collaboration. http://handbook.cochrane.org/. Accessed on December 2, 2014.

Hopkins R., O'Reilly D., and Goeree R. 2008. Systematic bias in the projection of lifetime costs of chronic diseases and costs of systemic complications: Demonstration using a population based diabetes and matched non-diabetes cohort from the province of Ontario. *Medical Decision Making* 28 (1): 150–155.

Hozo S.P., Djulbegovic B., and Hozo I. 2005. Estimating the mean and variance from the median, range, and the size of a sample. *BMC Medical Research Methodology* 5: 13.

International Conference on Harmonisation of Technical Requirements for Registration of Pharmaceuticals for Human Use (ICH). 2014. 'Statistical principles for clinical trials'. Available from http://www.ich.org/. Accessed on December 2, 2014.

Sackett D.L., and Haynes R.B. 1976. A critical review of the determinants of patient compliance with therapeutic regimens. In *Compliance with Therapeutic Regimens*, eds. Sackett D.L., and Haynes R.B., Baltimore, MD, The Johns Hopkins University Press, pp. 26–39.

Schafer J.L. 1999. Multiple imputation: A primer. *Statistical Methods in Medical Research* 8 (1): 3–15.

Simel D.L., Samsa G.P., and Matchar D.B. 1991. Likelihood ratios with confidence: Sample size estimation for diagnostic test studies. *Journal of Clinical Epidemiology* 44 (8): 763–770.

Chapter 10

Concluding Remarks

Concluding Remarks

In this book, we have introduced some of the biostatistics that are required to conduct cost-effectiveness analysis with a focus on how to reduce uncertainty. In this chapter, we will also provide an emphasis on the quality of reporting of biostatistics, including how to write different sections of a statistical section of an academic paper, a report, a grant application or a statistical analysis plan. One of the surprises that we give to students who are completing their advanced degrees in biostatistics is that more time will be spent on writing than on conducting analysis. It seems worthwhile to mention a few tips to help the process for those of us that considered English as a second language after their first language of calculus or economics.

Second, we end with thoughts on future direction(s) where there is much work to be done for future biostatistics research, namely, the cost-effectiveness analysis for genetically engineered products, the biologics. The analysis of biologics creates an interesting problem because of the small sample sizes of clinical studies and variable budget impact. We will highlight the problem at the overarching level and provide a possible solution.

Finally, we will provide some details on the ways the submission for reimbursements decisions could have been done differently in Canada. We will build on our review of reimbursement decisions for Canada, which was published in *PharmacoEconomics* (Rocchi et al. 2012).

Academic Writing from a Biostatistician's Point of View

Writing is a benchmark for academics and researchers for promotion based on the ability to produce quality research. The more articles an assistant professor can write, the greater the chances of promotion to tenure. The more a researcher can write, the easier it is to deliver reports or analysis plans. Incredible stress is created when one must write, unless there is a framework for effective writing. To demonstrate a framework for writing, we will follow the typical steps for preparing an article for academic submission to a peer-reviewed journal. We include some points that we have learned from others in sentences and paragraphs, with the purpose of writing for brevity, clarity and continuity.

The first step is the preparation of an ugly first draft, which can be edited for improvement and continually refined until submitted. To begin the preparation of the first draft, we need an outline of the necessary content, and this is the easiest part. For every study type, there is a guideline checklist that editors from academic journals have created in the hopes that writers, like us, will follow. All of the checklists for different types of studies have been consolidated on the enhancing the quality and transparency of health research (EQUATOR) website (http://www.equator-network.org/) (EQUATOR Network 2014) (Table 10.1).

The reporting standards are excellent sources for ensuring completeness of reporting, and this is important because a study that is published may be reviewed for systematic reviews and rated for quality of evidence based on these checklists. A study that was performed perfectly would be rated low if the journal article that described the study missed a few items. It was also be important to think of how the study would be viewed by GRADE criteria (Brozek et al. 2009) and the risk of bias tool (Armijo-Olivo et al. 2012). For example, if there was a randomized controlled trial and the journal article only stated that the patients were randomized electronically, then the risk of bias would be considered high if (1) the sequence generation for a randomized controlled trial was not explained, (2) the allocation concealment was not described or (3) the details of how blinding occurred for participants, personnel and outcome assessors were not provided.

Beyond the methods and results sections, the reporting guidelines provide a bit of guidance for the introduction and discussion sections. Typically for a 3500-word article that has been rated high, we see that the text of the methods section can have between 1000 and 1500 words, whereas the text of the results section can have between 500 and 1000 words.

Table 10.1 Common Reporting Guidelines

CONSORT	The CONSORT 2010 statement: updated guidelines for reporting parallel group randomized trials
STROBE	The STROBE statement: guidelines for reporting observational studies
PRISMA	The PRISMA statement: preferred reporting items for systematic reviews and meta-analyses
STARD	The STARD initiative: towards complete and accurate reporting of studies of diagnostic accuracy
CHEERS	Consolidates and updates previous guidelines for reporting and reviewing health economic evaluation submissions
Drummond checklist	Increasing the generalizability of economic evaluations: recommendations for the design, analysis and reporting of studies

Source: Data from EQUATOR Network website (http://www.equator-network.org/).

CHEERS, consolidated health economic evaluation reporting standards; CONSORT; PRISMA, preferred reporting items for systematic reviews and meta-analyses; STARD, standards for reporting of diagnostic accuracy; STROBE, strengthening the reporting of observational studies in epidemiology.

Introduction

The introduction section is limited in word count, as little as 1 page or 250 words, in some journals. When we review an article, we look for a few things in the introduction section, mostly to see if the research question is well stated. For general or economic journals, a description of the disease, including recent estimates of prevalence or incidence, as well as an estimate of economic burden are needed. For disease-specific journals, a definition of the disease would not be necessary, such as defining osteoporosis in an osteoporosis journal.

After this introductory statement, we look to see if the following six specific questions have been answered:

1. What is the problem?
2. Why is it a problem?
3. What do we know about the problem?
4. What are the gaps in the knowledge about the problem?
5. How will this study fill in the stated gaps in knowledge?
6. What are the primary and secondary objectives of this study?

In order to increase clarity, it may be better to work through a specific example and imagine that the questions had been answered by a biostatistician. In our example, the purpose of the study was to estimate the relative cost-effectiveness between three drugs, including one new drug.

What is the problem? There are three drugs that can be used to treat the disease, and each has different rates of clinical benefit, efficacy and safety, impacts on quality of life and cost.

Why is it a problem? This is rarely mentioned, but only implied. Yet, answering this question sets up the entire discussion section and provides a reason for the clinician or decision maker to continue to read. We suggest a statement similar to this: 'In order for decision-makers to consider optimizing health care resources, it would be helpful to provide an assessment of the value for money that each drug provides'.

What do we know about the problem? Here, we can briefly mention if earlier evidence was created, such as previous cost-effectiveness analysis.

What are the gaps in the knowledge about the problem? This is the space that we would like to see a few comments about how to improve the quality of evidence that previously existed. Were all three comparators previously analyzed, is there any local jurisdiction evidence, was there a gap in the analysis and is there any new evidence that can update previous results?

How will this study fill in the stated gaps in knowledge? An overarching statement or two will provide a continuation of the argument that the previous gaps will be addressed. Here we need to see a mention of a new source of data or a new analysis that was not previously conducted that can now be conducted.

What are the primary and secondary objectives of this study? Finally, we need the primary and secondary objectives of the study. The primary objective is to assess the relative cost-effectiveness of the different treatment options, and the secondary objective is usually to assess the uncertainty in the analysis with probabilistic sensitivity analysis or to assess the relative cost-effectiveness for different patients with subgroup analysis. Most of the questions can be addressed with their own paragraph, or sometimes the paragraphs can be combined into four or five paragraphs at the least.

Discussion and Conclusion

The discussion and conclusion should answer some basic questions:

1. What is the main finding of the study?
2. Is the finding different from other studies, or did the study provide a different recommendation, such as choice of drug, than previous studies? If so, a description of the other studies should be provided with an explanation of the different findings.

3. What were the study's strengths and limitations? An acknowledgement that no study is perfect should be implied.
4. From the previous point, a mention of the ideal study should be made, as well as suggestions for future research.

Each of these questions can have multiple paragraphs and should be evenly balanced. Other questions that should be addressed depend on the type of study, with additional questions for cost-effectiveness analysis following our suggested sections for a health technology assessment (HTA) report, including budget and health systems impact analysis, and an assessment of social, ethical and legal considerations.

Sentences and Paragraphs

For most academic writing, a good sentence should be about 15–40 words long, with most sentences being about 25 words like this one. Short sentences are choppy. They are hard to read. They seem grade school level. Please avoid them. However, a sentence that is longer may increase readability by being closer to the attention span of a typical reader, providing that the sentence continues the logical flow of the study design and results (37 words).

At the larger scale, a paragraph is required to provide the collective information of one thought. For all paragraphs in academic writing, the first sentence is the topic sentence and other sentences provide support to the topic. This is the opposite of storytelling, where a paragraph builds up the main point. As an example, remember the story

> Jack and Jill went up the hill to fetch a pail of water.
> Jack fell down and broke his crown and Jill came tumbling after.
>
> **Anonymous**

For academic writing, every paragraph should start off with the main fact or premise.

> An eight-year old boy and his seven-year old sister were seen in the emergency room resulting from a fall on a hill. The city was notified of the safety hazard, and the boy and girl were discharged home after negative x-rays.

In addition, the number of sentences can vary, but we find the most common range as three to five sentences, with occasionally longer paragraphs with a maximum of seven or eight sentences mixed in. For most of the methods and results, the material is factual and very dense such that shorter paragraphs may be more readable, whereas longer paragraphs are more common in the discussion section.

Time Management for Writing

There are a few rough estimates for the time it takes to write a draft of a manuscript for publication, or word count for an HTA report. For-profit medical writers often quote five days to write a 3500-word manuscript, with one day being spent each on the methods, results including tables and figures, discussion, introduction and abstract, and references with final editing. Similarly, based on estimates from various web pages, the time to write a draft of technical material can be about 6–12 hours per 1000 words. This is often the ugly first draft and a few stages of editing are necessary. A round of major editing for rearranging the order to improve flow in a logical sequence, rewriting, checking content against external references and adding information that was omitted takes about 2.5–4 hours per 1000 words. The next stage is editing that includes major editing and rewriting awkward sentences and paragraphs, which would take about 1–2.5 hours per 1000 words. Another stage is copy editing, that is, correcting spelling and grammar, which can take about 35–60 minutes per 1000 words. Finally, there is copy editing for last-minute mistakes, which takes on average 17 minutes per 1000 words to proofread twice. Overall, including the ugly first draft, the total time to write and edit 1000 words would be 10–19 hours and the time to prepare a 3500-word manuscript would be 35–70 hours or one to two weeks. The time to write an HTA report with 10,000 words, which includes all of the stages of editing, should take 100–190 hours or three to five weeks. Start writing now!

Future Research

For most cost-effectiveness analyses, we are working on the methods that take us away from ideal situations where everything is simple. There are a number of statistical issues that are being introduced, where consensus is being reached on proper methodology and reporting, and many of with these issues being addressed by the special working groups at the ISPOR (http://www.ispor.org/sigs/sigsindex.asp): Health Technology Assessment, Medical Devices and Diagnostics, Medical Nutrition Products—Outcomes

Research, Medication Adherence and Persistence, Patient Centered, Preference-Based Methods, Personalized Medicine and Rare Diseases Special Interest Groups.

One upcoming issue that everyone knows is on the horizon and will dominate future research is the statistical and economic assessment relating to genetics. Consider the problem: The International Human Genome Sequencing Consortium in 2004 reported by the National Institutes of Health/National Human Genome Research Institute suggests that there may be 20,000–25,000 genes that make up the human genome, most of which are still not isolated and their function determined. It may be that most of the genes are the common genes that everyone has to produce two feet, two eyes, and so on.

This will still leave perhaps thousands of genes that could relate to health and the development of specific diseases. If we think of a disease that has only five genes that determine the presence and severity of a disease, and if the genes are present or absent, this creates $2^5 = 32$ unique gene combinations. In statistical terms, this would create 32 possible subgroups.

In a simple futurist world, we will have five drugs with each drug intended to replace the missing gene. However, the development of the unique drugs will likely come long after we have some trial-and-error drugs based on the available gene information, which may be worrisome. Instead, suppose we have isolated three genes that contribute to disease (G1, G2 and G3), and we have developed three drugs to treat the disease (Drug A, Drug B and Drug C), and suppose that the response depends on the genetic make-up of the patients.

We see from Table 10.2 that genotype G1 responds best to Drug A, G2 responds best to Drug B and G3 responds best to Drug C. However, on average, the cost-effectiveness analysis indicated that Drug C is the cheapest and most cost-effective drug for all genotypes. Ethically, we need to consider if G1 genotype is a unique patient population that requires its own cost-effectiveness analysis. If so, every unique genotype is its own subgroup that may require an independent cost-effectiveness analysis.

Table 10.2   Responsiveness to Three Drugs for Different Genotypes

Genotype	Drug A (%)	Drug B (%)	Drug C (%)
G1	80	10	50
G2	10	80	50
G3	10	10	50

Oh, by the way, the results are for having each gene separately, but there are eight combinations of genes that need to be investigated: G1–G2–blank, G1–blank–G3 and so on. Given that each gene has different rates of occurrences, the possibility of adequately powering a study to assess all eight unique combinations may be difficult.

One option to investigate the potential subgroups that have promising cost-effectiveness is to separate the favourable from unfavourable genotypes with mixture models. A mixture model is a non-informative separation of statistical distributions, identifying the probability that a subject will fall into one of the two available distributions. In cost-effectiveness analysis, the distributions would be group A with unfavourable cost-effectiveness and group B with favourable cost-effectiveness. The procedure involves drawing a sample from each treatment group and then estimating the mean incremental costs and QALYs. If the results are not favourable, the characteristics of the two treatments are recorded in group A, whereas if the cost-effectiveness was favourable, the characteristics of the two treatments would be recorded in group B. After many draws, the characteristics of each treatment group are compared between A and B. Any difference for either treatment group indicates a possible subgroup to evaluate the cost-effectiveness. This technique is exploratory and would precede any formal subgroup analysis that could be conducted with subsets of patients or with regression-adjusted outcomes (Figure 10.1).

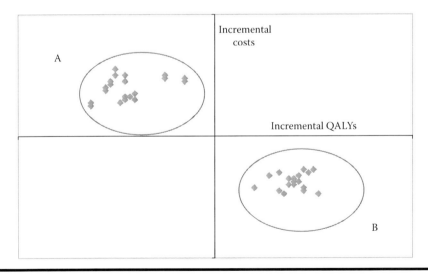

Figure 10.1   Investigation of potential subgroups (group A and group B) with mixture models. Each characteristic of the patients will have a probability of being in group A (cost ineffective) and group B (cost effective).

Improving Reimbursement Submissions

In our *PharmacoEconomics* article (Rocchi et al. 2012), we tested for the impact of many possible factors that led to low approval rates for reimbursement recommendations in Canada, which has among the lowest rates of rejection for drugs that were approved in other countries. From those data, which included all submissions from the start of the Common Drug Review process in 2009 until the end of 2012, including 148 submissions, we separated the factors into clinical and economic. The clinical and economic factors could explain about 80% of the entire attributable fraction that can be assigned to predict rejection (Table 10.3). Clinical factors could explain 65% of the probability of rejection, whereas economic factors could explain 35% of the probability of rejection.

Table 10.3 Attributable Fractions to Submission Characteristics for the Common Drug Review Canada, 2009–2012

Submission Factor	Attribution Factor for Rejection (%)
Clinical factors	65
Clinical uncertainty	26
Active comparator	10
Scale	9
Health Canada approval	8
Clinical	3
First in class	3
Not appropriate comparator	3
Qualitative statement of outcome	3
First in disease	0
Combination	0
Economic factors	35
Pricing	14
Evidence price	10
Economic	8
ICER not attractive	3

For us, this was surprising because we had thought that the major reason for rejection was poor cost-effectiveness results that led to poor value for money value propositions. The main economic reason, we thought, would be that the ICER would not be considered attractive. Instead, this factor alone explained only 5% of the probability of rejection for reimbursement. A similar factor that led to rejection was that price alone was used for the decision accounted for 10%. This factor indicated that the new product was essentially equivalent clinically to existing products and a higher price alone led to the rejection. Similarly, a higher price was indicative of rejection, but this is also based on higher price alone and did not apparently incorporate the cost-effectiveness results. Meanwhile, a lack of believability of the economic results accounted for 8% of the probability of rejection. Improvements to the estimation of cost or quality of life could have shifted the attractiveness of the ICER (see Chapters 7 and 8).

More surprising to us was the importance that clinical factors had on the high rate of rejection. Some of these clinical factors can be clearly linked to work that was incomplete, and other factors highlight that work could have done differently. Given that the application for reimbursement approval can only be submitted once, and reconsideration must be made with new clinical evidence or a change in price, it may have been disappointing for the submissions that were rejected for being incomplete. Being incomplete could have been complicated by the factors such as not having the appropriate comparator (3%) and an active comparator was not used (10%). We believe that these factors could have been overcome by meta-analysis or network meta-analysis (see Chapters 4 and 5). For example, a cost-effectiveness submission may have included one comparator, and that comparator is not the current standard of care. A submission that does not include all available comparators, including standard of care, is incomplete.

Further rejection from clinical factors was based on submissions that provided benefit from the new product for outcomes that were not the best selected outcome from the possible set. This was stated directly as having a qualitative statement of outcome (3%) or a mention of a scale (9%). These two factors may be partly related to the contributing factor first in class, which was associated with rejection (3%). First-in-class drugs may target a new outcome that has not been validated. For the qualitative statement of the variable, or mention of a scale, it is likely that the primary outcome upon which the submission was based was not validated. This may have been improved by providing evidence, or creating evidence such as risk equations or clinical consensus, that validates the outcome as being relevant for the patient (see Chapter 6).

The factor that contributed the most to rejection was a mention of clinical uncertainty, which accounted for 26% of the total attributable fraction. Clinical uncertainty can be reduced with meta-analysis, network meta-analysis, developing risk equations or published clinical consensus (see Chapters 4 through 7).

In most cases, we see that the reimbursement could have been done differently or that additional work could have conducted to support the submission. It is possible that a new product may not have a clinical improvement over current standard of care or that the price that was being proposed by the manufacturer was too high relative to the value of the clinical benefit. In these cases, the rejection of the new product for receiving reimbursement approval for the public plans is appropriate. However, from the outside we cannot separate these new products from the products that do have clinical promise, but the reimbursement submission could have been improved in quality. For the latter, there may have been a lost opportunity.

Summary

In this book, we have provided an overview of a health technology agreement (HTA), highlighted the steps to conduct a high-quality HTA or value for money analysis, given examples of the more common statistical techniques that are required, and described some of the leading-edge methods and their effects on value for money decisions. We believe that there have been many times when submissions have not captured the full value of an intervention and underestimated the treatment's value for money. The examples we covered suggest that this shortcoming could be addressed with appropriate robust comparisons to all treatments using meta-analysis and network meta-analysis, capturing the full impact on quality of life, estimating the full cost of a clinical event, and projecting any future value of quality of life benefit or cost savings.

There has always been criticisms of the selection process for which services to fund in the public sector, including using value for money. This debate probably began with creation of the United Kingdom's National Health Service in 1948, Canada's public health system in 1966, and United States' health programs such as Medicaid and Medicare in 1965 and 1996, respectively. Since 1980s, the health economic analysis has suggested using value for money as just one estimate among many to guide the recommendation for decision to fund new treatments.

Although the methodological advances have continued, the strain of the ability to fund healthcare has increased, and will continue to do so for a few major reasons. First, the number of senior citizens is expected to increase by at least 5% annually until 2023, the end of the postwar baby boom. Second, the annual inflation rate for healthcare expenditures has been historically higher than overall inflation. Third, there may be an upper limit of the size of the healthcare budget that should be relative to total public sector expenditures, and an upper limit of the size of government relative to the overall economy.

To address the increasing demand for healthcare dollars versus a limited supply, the limiting of the growth (or cutting) of healthcare expenditures has occurred by delisting services, moving some services out of the public sector into the private sector, limiting access based on financial need or high-risk status, or by declining requests to fund new services. In the future, the value for money for any change in provision of service should be provided, but not necessarily acted on, because of the balance with the crucial factors of ethics and fairness.

References

Armijo-Olivo S., Stiles C.R., Hagen N.A., Biondo P.D., and Cummings G.G. 2012. Assessment of study quality for systematic reviews: A comparison of the Cochrane collaboration risk of bias tool and the effective public health practice project quality assessment tool: Methodological research. *Journal of Evaluation in Clinical Practice* 18 (1): 12–18.

Brozek J.L., Akl E.A., Alonso-Coello P., Lang D., Jaeschke R., Williams J.W., Phillips B., Lelgemann M., Lethaby A., Bousquet J., Guyatt G.H., and Schunemann H.J. 2009. Grading quality of evidence and strength of recommendations in clinical practice guidelines. Part 1 of 3. An overview of the GRADE approach and grading quality of evidence about interventions. *Allergy* 64 (5): 669–677.

EQUATOR Network. 2014. Enhancing the quality and transparency of health research (EQUATOR) network. Available from http://www.equator-network.org/. Accessed on December 2, 2014.

Rocchi A., Miller E., Hopkins R.B., and Goeree R. 2012. Common drug review recommendations an evidence base for expectations. *PharmacoEconomics* 30 (3): 229–246.

Index

Note: Locators followed by "*f*" and "*t*" denote figures and tables in the text

A

Academic writing, Biostatistician's view, 232
  discussion and conclusion, 234–235
  overview, 233–234
  preparing for academic submission,
      steps, 232
  reporting guidelines, 233*t*
  risk of bias, 232
  sentences and paragraphs, 235–236
  time management for writing, 236
Access impact, HTA ethical values, 30
Active medical device, 11–12, 11*t*
Administrative data, 55
Akaike's Information Criterion (AIC), 158
American College of Rheumatology (ACR)
      score, 146
Antiplatelet activity, 3
Area under the curve (AUC), 93, 94*t*
Autocorrelation plot, 138

B

Bayesian inference using Gibbs sampling
      (BUGS) software, 122
Bayesian methods
  advanced models, 143–146
    combining RCTs and observational
        data, 144
    covariate adjustment, 144–145
    hierarchical outcomes, 145–146
  Bayesian theorem, 130, 130*f*

interpretation of results, 129–130
meta-analysis comment on frequentist
      and, 68–69
  combine data from sources, 69
  combine evidence, 68
  interpretation of statistical results, 69
power for trials of rare diseases, 128–129
steps for meta-analysis, 131*t*
  assess convergence, 137–142
  assign prior(s), 134–135
  conduct simulation, 135, 137
  executing Bayes model, 136*f*
  report findings, 142–143
  specify model, 131, 133–134
  suggested items for reporting, 143*t*
  WinBUGS model, 131, 132*t*–133*t*,
      135, 142
Bayesian MTC, 122
Bayesian Output Analysis (BOA), assessing
      convergence, 139*t*–141*t*
BayesWatch checklist, 142–143
Best linear unbiased estimator (BLUE), 75
Binomial approximation, 227
Biostatistician's view, academic writing, 232
  discussion and conclusion, 234–235
  overview, 233–234
  preparing for academic submission,
      steps, 232
  reporting guidelines, 233*t*
  risk of bias, 232
  sentences and paragraphs, 235–236
  time management for writing, 236

Biostatistics
  quality of reporting, 231
  research, 231
  roles in steps of HTA, 20, 21*t*
Bootstrapping, 39, 41, 223
Bottom-up costing, 193
Bucher method, 108
Budget impact analysis, 193–195
  information for policy impact analysis, 193
  statistical issues with cost data, 194–195

C

Canadian Agency for Drugs and
    Technologies in Health (CADTH),
    117, 204
Canadian Institute for Health Information, 59
Case-control study, 50
Categorical data, 70
CHADS2 score, 182, 186
Chronic diseases, problems, 199
Clinical events
  cost of, 185
  lifelong risk estimation, 174
  methods for attribution of cost for, 184*t*
  to resource utilization to costs, 180–182
    case report form verification, 180
    full-cost approach, 182
    GAAP, 181
    measurement of resource utilization,
        181–182
    over-the-counter medications, 180–181
    steps to estimate, 181
  risk criteria, 182
Clinically relevant approach, 182
Clinical opinion, drawback of, 57
Clinical trials
  cost-effectiveness analysis of, 46–47
  create cost-effectiveness from, 180
  drug-eluting stent, 53–54
  E9 statistical principles, 220
  four phases, 4–7
  impact on HRQOL, 56
  impact on QOL, 56
  pragmatic, 41
  resource utilization with, 57
  safety and efficacy, 49–50

statistical issue and difference between
    phases, 7–9, 8*t*
*The Cochrane Handbook for Systematic
    Reviews of Interventions*, 28, 67, 81
Cochran's *Q*, 77
Cohen's kappa
  score estimation, 104
  statistic, 67–68
Common Drug Review (CDR) process, 13,
    239, 239*t*
Common treatment effect, 171–172
Comorbidities, attribution and adjustment
    for, 182–189
  CHADS2 score, 182
  matched case-control study, 183
  methods to quantify, 182
  regression methods, 186
  strategies to estimate costs, 186–188
  strategies to isolate cost of event, 184–186
  unit costs valuation for resources,
      188–189
Confidence intervals (CIs), 88–89, 109, 127,
    144, 223, 227–229
  for fixed effects, 86
  funnel plot with, 90*f*
  for ICER, 40*t*, 41
  lower, 39
  odds ratio, 72–73
  statistical failure of, 41
Continuous data, 70
  outcomes for, 74–75
Convergence, Bayesian method
  assessing with BOA, 139*t*–141*t*
  autocorrelation plot, 137–138
  Gelman–Rubin test, 138
  Geweke test, 142
  Heidelberger and Welch test, 142
  MC error, 138
  Raftery and Lewis test, 138
  trace, 138
COPD analysis, 55
  goal of intervention, 57
Cost-effectiveness analysis, 37–41, 129,
    199, 210
  bootstrapping, 207
  create from clinical trial, 180
  estimation for drugs, 234

lifetime, 228
objective of, 180
potential subgroups investigation, 238, 238*f*
QOL estimation, 199–200
results estimation, 215
statistical techniques, 211
use of meta-analysis for, 91*t*
WinBUGS for, 131
Costs and cost of illness studies, 57–58
absence of, 58
benefit of, 58
budget impact analysis, 193–195
information for policy impact
analysis, 193
statistical issues with cost data, 194–195
burden of illness study, 191–193
incident-based analysis, 192
macroeconomic/microeconomic
methods, 193
prevalence-based approach, 192
from clinical events to resource
utilization to, 180–182
case report form verification, 180
full-cost approach, 182
GAAP, 181
measurement of resource utilization,
181–182
over-the-counter medications, 180–181
steps to estimate, 181
comorbidities, attribution and adjustment
for, 182–189
CHADS2 score, 182
matched case-control study, 183
methods to quantify, 182
regression methods, 186
strategies to estimate costs, 186–188
strategies to isolate cost of event,
184–186
unit costs valuation for resources,
188–189
of hip fracture, 187*t*–188*t*
introduction to resource utilization and,
44–46
perspective and types of, 189–191
direct cost, 189
government, 190
health care, 190

hospital, 190
indirect cost, 189, 191
intangible cost, 189
societal, 190
of visit, 58, 58*t*
Covariate adjustment, Bayesian model,
144–145
Cox model, 153
Cox test, 153
dips in Kaplan–Meier curve, 154
proportional hazard assumption, 154, 155*f*
Cox–Snell residual plots, 158
C-reactive protein (CRP) scale, 146
Credibility interval, 129–130
Crossover mechanism, 172–173
Cross-sectional data, life table from, 173–175
life expectancy estimation, 173–174
lifetime risk estimation, 174

D

Data
administrative, 55
categorical, 70
to conduct HTA, sources and uses of,
51*t*–52*t*
continuous, 70, 74–75
for HTA, quality of, 53
for ITC for STATA, 114*t*
life table from cross-sectional, 173–175
manipulation, 226
missing, 215–216
common trial gaps, 216
for diagnostic accuracy studies, 227–228
explainable or unexplainable patterns
of, 218–219
meta-analysis gaps, 223–228
multiple imputation for trial, 221–223
unknown lifetime variances for costs,
228–229
for outcome in meta-analysis, 70–72
requirements, secondary, 50, 52
requirements to complete HTA, 37
statistical issues with cost, 194–195
taxonomy for, 70–71
types of, 50, 52
way to classify, 70

Decision analytic model, 47–48, 48*f*
Decision-making process
 consideration of cost in drug
  reimbursement, 15
 for drugs and devices, 1
Delphi panel method, 186–187
DerSimonian and Laird approach, 76
Device
 classification of medical
  devices, 10–12, 10*t*
 class of, 10*t*
 definitions for different classes, 12
 harmonization of classification
  system, 11*t*
 leading to differential regulatory
  approval, 11*t*
 regulatory approval, 10–12
 reimbursement approval, 16–17
Diabetes modelling, 168–169
Diagnostic accuracy studies
 meta-analysis of, 90–95
  AUC of SROC, 93, 94*t*
  bivariate forest plot, 98, 99*f*
  decision impacts, 93
  and economic models, 95*t*
  example, 92*t*
  HSROC, 99
  measures, 103
  outcomes, 90, 91*t*, 96*t*
  sensitivity test, 92, 95–98
  SNout, 92
  specificity test, 92, 95–98
  SPin, 92
  SROC plot, 98, 100*f*
  STATA commands, 96, 97*t*, 100*t*
 missing data for, 227–228
 network meta-analysis of, 124–125
Dichotomous data
 DerSimonian and Laird approach, 76
 outcomes, 72
 presence of zeroes, 73
Direct costs, 189
Drugs
 approval, 2, 170
 classification of studies by phase or
  objective, 4–7
 clinical factors for rejection, 239–241

 combinations of genes, 238
 comparison between, 111
 development of unique, 237
 for different genes, 237, 237*t*
 effect size of, 123
 estimation of cost-effectiveness, 234
 first-in-class, 240
 homogeneity with, 123
 interactions, 166
 Kaplan–Meier survival estimates for, 152*f*
 long-term benefit estimation, 166
 osteoporosis, 108
 prices across countries, 16*f*
 rate of events in placebo arm for, 113*t*
 regulatory approval
  for prescription, 3
  by trial phases, 5*f*
 reimbursement approval, 13–14
  clinical evidence, 14–15
  consideration of cost, 15
  initiation of drug review, 14
  price negotiations, 15–16
 side effect, 3–4
 STATA code for comparison of, 118
 tested in humans, 3–4
 trial-and-error, 237
 trial phases for, 5*t*
 vs. placebo-controlled trials, 110, 115*f*

E

Egger test, 81
EMBASE, Medline database, 24
Equity impact, HTA ethical values, 30
Erythrocyte sedimentation rate (ESR)
  scale, 146
European Medicines Agency (EMEA), 1, 218
Euroquol 5 Dimension (EQ-5D), 43
Exponential model, 156–162
 hazard rate of mortality, 159–160, 160*f*
 lifetime extrapolation, 156–157
 post-estimation tests, 158

F

Feasibility of adoption, 20
Fieller's theorem, 39

Fixed effects model, 76–77
   confidence interval for, 86
   meta-analyses results from, 85*t*, 86
Food and Drug Administration (FDA), 1, 3
Fracture risk assessment tool (FRAX)
      model, 168
Fractures, odds ratio estimation, 131
FRAX equation, 145
Frequentist approach, 127, 144
   change in QOL, 207
   meta-analysis comment on Bayesian and,
      68–69
      combine data from sources, 69
      combine evidence, 68
      interpretation of statistical results, 69
      replication probability, 128
Full analysis set (FAS), 220
Full-cost approach, 182, 194*t*

G

Gelman–Rubin test, 138
Generally Accepted Accounting Principles
      (GAAP), 181
Geweke test, 142
Global Harmonization Task Force (GHTF), 11
Gompertz model, 156–162
   hazard rate of mortality, 159–160, 160*f*
   lifetime extrapolation, 156–157
   post-estimation tests, 158
Grades of Recommendation, Assessment,
      Development and Evaluation
      (GRADE) approach, 31–32, 31*t*, 116
   checklist, 82
   criteria, 232

H

Harbord test, 81
Head-to-head trials
   evidence, 107*t*, 123, 124
   indirect network diagram, 110*f*
   placebo-controlled trials, 105–109
   results differ from network
      meta-analysis, 109
Health Assessment Questionnaire (HAQ)
      scale, 146

Health Economic Evaluations Database
      (HEED), 24
Health-related quality of life (HRQOL)
   advantage of using, 41
   cross-sectional analysis, 56
   domains over time and change in level
      of, 205–207
   estimating utility from generic, 206*t*
   generic measures of, 199
   impact of health decision beyond cost
      and, 202*t*
   introduction to, 41–44
   minimal clinically important difference
      for, 207–209
   QALY and, 205*f*
   scales, 41, 42
      common, 209
      construction of, 203
      disease-specific, 42, 199, 204, 212
      generic, 43, 44*t*, 203, 204
      mapping between QOL, 211–212
      properties of, 202–203
      tests for clinical practice, 203
Health technology assessment (HTA), 17–20
   aggregation and appraisal of evidence,
      25–27
   biostatistics roles in, 21*t*
   data requirements to complete, 37
   economic evaluation, 29–30, 29*t*
   field evaluation, 28–29
   findings and recommendations,
      formulation and dissemination of,
      30–32
   gathering evidence, 24–25
   guidelines for using QOL in, 204
   impact of assessment reports, 32
   need for modelling, 46
      decision analytic model, 47–48, 48*f*
      Markov model, 48–49, 49*f*
   objectives of, 17
   problem specification, 22–24
   quality of data, 53
   report, 235, 236
   scope by potential users, 21*t*–22*t*
   secondary data requirements, 50
      effectiveness *vs.* efficacy, 53–54
      epidemiology, 59

Health technology assessment (HTA)
(*Continued*)
  HRQOL, 55–56
  long-term outcomes, 54–55
  rare diseases, 52–53
  resource utilization and costs, 56–58
  social, ethical and legal
    considerations, 30
  sources and uses of data to conduct,
    51*t*–52*t*
  steps in, 20*t*
  synthesize and consolidate evidence,
    27–28
  topic for assessment, 20–22
Heidelberger and Welch test, 142
Heterogeneity, 75, 123
  adjustment in meta-analysis, 78–80
  assess within common comparators,
    114, 116
  options to deal with, 79, 79*t*
  preliminary analysis with assessment of
    random or fixed effects, 76–77
    testing for heterogeneity, 77–78
    weighting of study, 75–76
Heteroskedasticity, 75
Hierarchical outcomes, Bayesian models,
  145–146
Hierarchical summary receiver operator
  curve (HSROC), 99–100
Hospital visit
  average cost, 179
  cost of return, 179
  repeated, 59
  resource utilization and costs, 57

I

Imputation technique, 221, 224
Incident-based analysis, 192
Incredible stress, 232
Incremental cost-effectiveness ratio (ICER),
  37–38, 208–209, 208*t*
  calculation of, 38*t*
  confidence intervals, 39, 40*t*, 41
  incremental cost evaluation, 39
  unit costs, 44
Indirect costs, 189, 191

Indirect meta-analysis
  conduct across comparators, 116–120
  terminology for, 106*t*
Indirect treatment comparison (ITC)
    analysis, 108
  evidence, 111*f*, 123
  STATA
    code using meta-regression, 117*t*
    data for, 114*t*
    output from, 119*t*
  steps to assess integrity of, 123
  steps to conduct, 109*t*
  Wells CADTH software, 118*f*, 119*f*
Inflating cost, 189
Intangible costs, 189
Intention-to-treat set, 220
International Conference on Harmonisation
    (ICH), 3, 220
Interval variable, 71
Invasive device, 11–12, 11*t*
Inverse probability of censoring weighting
    (IPCW) model, 171
  crossover mechanism, 172–173
  properties of trials affect, 171*t*
Inverse variance weighting, 75, 83
I^2 statistic, 77
  between-study variance effect, 78
  forest plots with, 78*f*
  heterogeneity levels defined, 77*t*, 78

K

Kaplan–Meier analysis, 150–156
  Cox test, 153
  curves for common treatment effect, 172
  estimation, 152*f*, 218
  log-rank test, 153
  proportion of patients, 150, 152*t*
  recap of possible estimates, 154, 156*t*
  STATA code, 150, 151*t*
  Wilcoxon test, 153
Knowledge transfer, 32

L

Life expectancy, estimation, 173–174
Lifelong risk of clinical event, estimation, 174

Lifetime economic model, 47, 54, 156,
    162, 192
Log-rank test, 153
Long-term cohort study, 53
Lumley method, 112

M

Mantel–Haenszel (M–H) weighting,
    75–76
Markov model, 48–49, 49*f*
Matched case-control study, 183
McMaster Health Utility Index (HUI-3), 43
Medical device classification system
    (Canada, Europe and The United
    States), 10–12, 10*t*
Medical subject headings (MeSHs), 25
Medline database, 24
Mega-analysis, 23
Meta-analysis, 27, 210
    choice of statistical software
        to conduct, 66*t*
    comment on frequentist and Bayesian
        approaches, 68–69
        combine data from sources, 69
        combine evidence, 68
        interpretation of statistical
            results, 69
    of diagnostic accuracy studies,
        90–95, 227
        AUC of SROC, 93, 94*t*
        decision impacts, 93
        and economic models, 95*t*
        example, 92*t*
        measures, 103
        outcomes, 90, 91*t*
        sensitivity test, 92
        SNout, 92
        specificity test, 92
        SPin, 92
    example, 82–83, 85–90
        data from studies, 83*t*
        for diagnostic accuracy, 95–100
        outliers, 86–87, 87*f*
        risk-adjusted or unadjusted analysis,
            87–89, 89*t*
        STATA code, 83, 84*t*–85*t*

gaps, 223
    for diagnostic accuracy studies,
        227–228
    estimate missing mean values, 225*t*
    estimate missing SDs, 225*t*
    missing measures of central
        tendency, 224
    missing measures of variance,
        224–227
initial steps before, 67–68
network
    Bayesian MTC, 122
    consistency in outcomes for linking
        arms, 112–114
    of diagnostic accuracy, 124–125
    example of, 122–124
    head-to-head and placebo-controlled
        trials, 105–109
    heterogeneity within comparators,
        114–116
    indirect meta-analysis across
        comparators, 116–120
    potential network diagram of linking
        studies, 110–112
    report results, 121, 121*t*
    software, 116–120
    subgroup and sensitivity analyses,
        120–121
    theoretical foundations of, 108
objectives for systematic review, 27–28,
    66–67
overview, 65–67
problems in, 215
steps for Bayesian methods, 131*t*
    assess convergence, 137–142
    assign prior(s), 134–135
    conduct simulation, 135, 137
    executing Bayes model, 136*f*
    report findings, 142–143
    specify model, 131, 133–134
    suggested items for reporting, 143*t*
    WinBUGS model, 131, 132*t*–133*t*
steps in, 69–82
    adjustment for heterogeneity, 78–80
    assess overall strength of evidence,
        81–82
    assess publication bias, 80–81

Meta-analysis (*Continued*)
    identify data type for outcome, 70–72
    preliminary analysis with
        heterogeneity assessment, 75–78
    select appropriate outcome measure,
        72–75, 73*t*
  subgroup analysis, 80, 89*t*, 216
  use for cost-effectiveness analysis, 91*t*
Meta-regression, 80, 124, 144–145
  risk as covariate, STATA output from,
    87–89, 89*t*
  STATA code for ITCs using, 117*t*
Minimal clinically important difference
    (MCID) assessment, 207–209
Missed visits, 217–218
Missing data
  assumption to estimate, 218–219
  considerations of, 218
  dealing with, 222*t*
  importance of handling, 215–216
  meta-analysis gaps, 223
    for diagnostic accuracy studies, 227–228
    estimate missing mean values, 225*t*
    estimate missing SDs, 225*t*
    missing measures of central
        tendency, 224
    missing measures of variance, 224–227
  subjective assessment on, 217
  trial gaps, 216
    explainable/unexplainable patterns of,
        218–219
    intention-to-treat or per-protocol
        analysis, 219–221
    missed visits and loss to follow-up,
        217–218
    multiple imputation for trial data,
        221–223
    numbers to improve transparency, 216
    subsets of patients, 219–220
  types of, 216, 219*t*
  unknown lifetime variances for costs
    drift in, 229*f*
    event, 228
    Itö trend in, 229*t*
    long-term, 228, 229
    state, 228
Mixed treatment comparisons (MTCs), 105

Mixture model, 238
Money, value for, 16, 20, 29, 199, 234
  metric used for, 37–38
Monte Carlo (MC) error, 138
Mount Hood Challenge Meetings, 169
Multiple imputation analysis
  steps to, 221
  for trial data, 221–223

N

Network meta-analysis
  Bayesian MTC, 122
  comparators
    heterogeneity within, 114–116
    indirect meta-analysis across, 116–120
  consistency in outcomes for linking
    arms, 112–114
  of diagnostic accuracy, 124–125
  example of, 122
    adjustment for difference in baseline
        characteristics, 123–124
    homogeneity and consistency of
        evidence, 123
  head-to-head and placebo-controlled
    trials, 105–109
    comparators with, 111*f*
    drugs *vs.*, 110
    effect size of, 123
    evidence, 107*t*, 123, 124
    forest plot of drug *vs.*, 115*f*
    indirect network diagram, 110*f*, 112*f*
    rate of events for drugs, 113*t*
    results differ from, 109
  potential network diagram of linking
    studies, 110–112
  report results, 121, 121*t*
  software, 116–120
  subgroup and sensitivity analyses, 120–121
  theoretical foundations of, 108
New drug application (NDA), 9
New drug submission (NDS), 9
Nominal, ordinal, interval and ratio (NOIR)
    classification, 70–71, 71*t*
Non-drug non-device
  medical program, 12
  technologies, 2, 19

O

Odds ratio, 72–73
Ontario Health Technology Advisory
    Committee (OHTAC), 17, 19
Ordered probit model, 145
Ordinal variable, 70–71
Osteoporosis, 108, 183
    attribution of hip fractures, 183
    drugs, 108
    pre–post analysis, 185
Outcomes
    Bayesian models, hierarchical, 145–146
    clinical studies, 23
    for continuous data, 74–75
    diabetes modelling, long-term, 168–169
    diagnostic accuracy, 91*t*, 96*t*
    meta-analysis
        appropriate measure, 72–75, 73*t*
        type of data for each, 70–72
    network meta-analysis
        consistency for common linking arms,
            112–114
        diagnostic, 124
    surrogate, 169–170
    type of economic evaluation studies
        by, 29*t*
Over-the-counter drugs, 2

P

pan-Canadian Pharmaceutical Alliance
    (pCPA), 16
Parametric models, 157
    survival curves for, 162*f*, 165*f*
    survival predictions for, 166*t*
Patent Medicine Price Review Board
    (PMPRB), 15
Patient Global Assessment scale, 146
Patient, indication, comparator and outcome
    (PICO) format, 22, 23*t*
    osteoporosis patients review, 24
    setting and timing factors, 24
Per-protocol set, patients, 220–221
Peto odds ratio, 74
PharmacoEconomics, 231, 239
Physician Global Assessment scale, 146

Pilot study, 6–7
Placebo-controlled trials, 133–134
    comparators with, 111*f*
    drugs *vs.*, 110
    effect size of, 123
    forest plot of drug *vs.*, 115*f*
    head-to-head and, 105–109
    indirect network diagram, 110*f*, 112*f*
    rate of events for drugs, 113*t*
Poisson regression, 174
Posterior distribution, 69, 130
Post-estimation tests, 158
Post-hoc subgroup analysis, 80
Pragmatic trial, 41
Pre–post analysis, 185–186
Prevalence-based approach, 192
Principles of Medical Devices
    Classification, 11
Prior distribution, 69, 130
    informative, 135, 144–145
    non-informative, 135
PRISMA checklist, 25, 26*t*–27*t*, 142
Proportional hazard assumption, 154, 155*f*
Psoriasis Area Severity Index (PASI)
    score, 145
Pubic health care and drug expenditures
    (Canada, 1985–2012), 14*f*
Publication bias, 80, 89–90
    Egger test, 81
    funnel plot, 81, 89, 90*f*
    Harbord test, 81
    L'Abbe plot, 81, 87*f*
    statistical test, 81
PubMed, Medline database, 24
Pure Food and Drugs Act, 1906, 3

Q

Qnorm plot, outliers, 87, 88*f*
Quality-adjusted life years (QALYs), 38, 199
    assumption in using, 204
    change in, 207
    dominance, 40–41
    HRQOL and, 205*f*
    incremental, 208–209
    method for assessing differences in, 206
    from utility to, 204–205

Quality of life (QOL), 200–202
  analysis report, 213*t*
  assessing change in scales
    change in level of HRQOL and
      domains over time, 205–207
    minimal clinically important
      difference for HRQOL, 207–209
  change in, 207, 208
  definitions relating to, 201*t*
  disease-specific, 211
  estimates from trials and literature, 209–210
  estimation for, 200, 201, 210
  evidence for, 55
  generic, 211–212
  guidelines for using in HTA, 204
  independent study, 210–211
  mapping between scales, 211–212
  population trade-off questions on, 201
  utility for, 201

R

Raftery and Lewis test, 138
Random effects model, 76–77
  DerSimonian and Laird approach, 76
  distribution, 76
  forest plot, 86, 86*f*
  meta-analyses results from, 85*t*, 86
  pooled effect, 77
  weight adjusted for, 76
Randomized controlled trials (RCTs), 9,
    50, 128
  to conduct, 52
  observational data and combining, 128
Rank preserving structural failure time
    (RPSFT) model, 170–171
  factor affecting, 172
  properties of trials affect, 171*t*
Ratio variable, 71
Receiver operator curve (ROC), 93
Reference Manager, 27, 67
Regression model, 55, 157–158, 162, 173–174,
    186, 221
Regulatory approval, 1–2
  for devices, 10–12
  of drug by trial phases, 5*f*

issues with, 9–10
  preclinical development, 3–4
  for prescription drugs, 3
  for public health and non-drug
    non-device approvals, 12–13
Regulatory authority, 2
Reimbursement approval, 1
  decision-making process, 15, 200
  for devices, 16–17
  differences across countries, 13
  for drugs, 13–14
    clinical evidence, 14–15
    consideration of cost, 15
    initiation of drug review, 14
    price negotiations, 15–16
  review for, 15
Reimbursement submissions, improving,
    239–241, 239*t*
Reporting of Bayes used in clinical
    studies (ROBUST) checklist,
    142
Resource utilization
  case report, 217
  and costs
    with clinical trials, 57
    introduction to, 44–46
  to costs, clinical events, 180–182
    case report form
      verification, 180
    full-cost approach, 182
    GAAP, 181
    measurement of resource utilization,
      181–182
    over-the-counter medications,
      180–181
    steps to estimate, 181
Reye's syndrome, 4
Risk-adjusted or unadjusted analysis,
    87–89, 89*t*
Risk equations, establishing and using,
    162–169
  confounder, 168
  diabetes modelling, 168–169
  effect modifiers, 167–168
  FRAX model, 168
R-project software, 142

S

Sample size formula, 129
Schoenfeld residuals, proportional hazard
    assumption, 154, 155*f*
Search strategy, 25
Short Form (SF-36), 43
Side effect, 3–4, 6
Simpson's Paradox, 73
Single European Act, 1987, 3
Societal costs, 191
Split-half method, 211, 212
Standard deviation (SD), 223
  of costs, 229
  options for estimating missing,
    225*t*, 226
STATA software
  code
    command for diagnostic accuracy, 96,
      97*t*, 100*t*
    comparison of drugs, 118
    to estimate survival curves, 160, 161*t*,
      163*t*–165*t*
    hazard rate of mortality,
      159*t*–160*t*
    for ITC using meta-regression, 117*t*
    Kaplan–Meier analysis in,
      150, 151*t*
    for meta-analysis, 83, 84*t*–85*t*
  data for ITC for, 114*t*
  data format to conduct survival
    analysis, 151*t*
  meta-analysis for diagnostic
    accuracy, 227
  output
    for ITC, 119*t*
    from meta-regression analysis,
      87–89, 89*t*
Statistical power, 128
Sullivan's method, 54, 173–174
Summary receiver operator curve (SROC),
    93, 94*t*, 100*f*
Surrogates, 169
  acceptability of, 169–170
  approval of drugs, 170
  outcomes, 169

  role for diseases, 169
  validation study, 170
Survival analysis, 149
  acceptability of surrogates, 169–170
  adjustment for crossover bias, 170–173
    common treatment effect, 171
    mechanism factors, 172–173
    properties of trials affect
      IPCW/RPSFT, 171*t*
  exponential, Gompertz and Weibull
    models, 156–162
    hazard rate of mortality, 159–160,
      160*f*
    lifetime extrapolation, 156–157
    post-estimation tests, 158
  Kaplan–Meier analysis, 150–156
    Cox test, 153
    estimation, 152*f*
    log-rank test, 153
    proportion of patients, 150, 152*t*
    recap of possible estimates,
      154, 156*t*
    STATA code, 150, 151*t*
    Wilcoxon test, 153
  life table from cross-sectional data,
    173–175
    life expectancy estimation,
      173–174
    lifetime risk estimation, 174
  paramertic models
    curves for, 162*f*, 165*f*
    predictions for, 166*t*
  risk equations, establishing and using,
    162–169
    confounder, 168
    diabetes modelling, 168–169
    effect modifiers, 167–168
    FRAX model, 168
  types of models, 157, 158*t*

T

Target intervention, 23
*The New England Journal
    of Medicine*, 107
Top-down costing, 193

Trapezoid method, 205
True treatment effect, 172

U

Unit costs, 47, 58, 181, 194
  in ICER calculation, 44
  valuation for resources, 188–189
U.S. Food and Drug Administration
  (USFDA), 3, 170

V

Validation study, 170
Value for money, 16, 20, 29, 199, 234
  metric used for, 37–38

W

Wald estimation, 227
Weibull model, 156–162
  hazard rate of mortality, 159–160, 160*f*
  lifetime extrapolation, 156–157
  post-estimation tests, 158
Wells CADTH software, 117, 118,
  118*f*, 119*f*
Wilcoxon test, 153
WinBUGS model, 117, 122, 131, 135,
  142, 222
  Bayesian, 132*t*–133*t*
  code, 143–144, 146
  for cost-effectiveness or
    meta-analysis, 131